Quiet Genocide

Quiet Genocide

Guatemala 1981-1983

edited by Etelle Higonnet
With a preface by Juan Méndez and
an introduction by Greg Grandin

Translations Reviewed by Marcie Mersky

Transaction Publishers
New Brunswick (U.S.A.) and London (U.K.)

Library of Congress Catalog Number: 2009009208
ISBN: 978-1-4128-0796-8
Printed in the United States of America

Library of Congress Cataloging-in-Publication Data

Higonnet, Etelle.
    Quiet genocide : Guatemala 1981-1983 / Etelle Higonnet.
        p. cm.
    Includes bibliographical references.
    ISBN 978-1-4128-0796-8 (alk. paper)
        1. Genocide--Guatemala. 2. Crimes against humanity--Guatemala.
    3. Guatemala--History. I. Title.

KGD5645.H54 2009
972.8105'2--dc22

                                                        2009009208

Contents

List of Abbreviations

AAAS	American Association for the Advancement of Science
AAAC / AAAS	Asociación Americana para el Avance de la Ciencia
AVEMILGUA	Asociación de Veteranos Militares de Guatemala
B.V.	Baja Verapaz
CEH	Comisión para el Esclarecimiento Histórico [*Commission on Historical Clarification in Guatemala*]
CEIDEC	Centro de Estudios Integrales y de Desarrollo Comunal [*Center for Integrated Studies and Community Development*]
CIA	Central Intelligence Agency, USA
CPR	Comunidades de Población en Resistencia [*Communities of Population in Resistance*]
CUC	Comité de Unidad Campesina [*Peasant Unity Committee*]
EGP	Ejército Guerrillero de los Pobres [*People's Guerilla Army*]
EAFG	Equipo Antropológico Forense de Guatemala [*Guatemalan Forensic Anthropology Team*]

FAFG	Fundacion de Antropología Forense de Guatemala
GCC	Guatemalan Constitutional Court
FAR	Fuerzas Armadas Rebeldes [*Armed Rebel Forces*]
ICTR	International Criminal Tribunal Rwanda
ICTY	International Criminal Tribunal Yugoslavia
ODHA	Oficina de Derechos Humanos del Arzobispado de Guatemala [*Human Rights Office of the Archbishopric of Guatemala*]
NSA	National Security Archive
OAS	Organization of American States
PAC	Patrullas de Auto-Defensa Civil [*Civil Defence Patrols*]
PGT	Partido Guatemalteco del Trabajo [*Guatemalan Labour Party,* a communist party]
PMA	Policía Militar Ambulante [*Mobile Military Police*]
PRODERE	Program for Displaced People, Refugees and Returnees in Central America (part of the United Nations Office for Project Services)
REMHI	Proyecto Interdiocesano, Recuperación de la Memoria Histórica [*Recovery of Historical Memory Project*]
UNHCR	United Nations High Commissioner for Refugees
UNOPS	United Nations Office for Project Services
URNG	Unidad Revolucionaria Nacional Guatemalteca [*Guatemalan National Revolutionary Unity*]

Glossary

Alcaldes auxiliares	*Auxiliary mayor.* Village level authority.
Aldea	*Village*
Campesino	*Peasant*
Comisionados militares	*Military Commissioners*
Corporación municipal	*Municipal government*
Costa Sur	*South Coast.* Refers to the broad Pacific coastal plain that stretches from the ocean some 60-80 kilometers inland, until reaching the volcanic chain that crosses the southern part of country from El Salvador to Mexico; many of Guatemala's largest plantations are concentrated in this region.
Departamento	*Department.* Administrative division that corresponds to a province or state.
Destacamento	*Outpost; military outpost; detachment*
Enfrentamiento armado interno	*Internal armed conflict.* CEH uses the term "enfrentamiento" throughout, as the Guatemalan conflict was never formally recognized as an internal armed conflict under international law; but there is no way in the translation to make the distinction.

Estado Mayor de la Defensa	*Joint Chiefs of Staff*
Finca	*Plantation*
Finqueros	*Plantation owners*
Fuerzas de Tareas	*Task force*
Fundamentos del grupo	*Foundations of the group*
Instituto Nacional de Estadística	*National Statistics Institute*
Ladino	*Ladino.* Non-indigenous population
Mando Político Militar	*Political Military Command*
Matanza	*Mass killing*
Municipio	*Municipality.* Administrative division that corresponds to a county, comprised of a main town (cabecera), or county seat, and multiple villages (aldeas).
Patrulla Civil/Patrulla de Autodefensa/PAC	*Civil Patrol.* Para-military structures organized by the Army beginning in 1981 and disbanded formally in 1996; participation was mandatory for all men over age 14.
Policía Militar Ambulante	*Mobile Military Police*
Policía Nacional	*National Police*
Polo de Desarrollo	*Development Pole.* Regional groups of militarized strategic hamlets established by the Army to concentrate and control the local population.
Principales	*Principales.* Traditional indigenous authorities
PRODERE	*Program for Displaced People, Refugees and Returnees in Central America*
Registrado	*Documented*

Editor's Note

Etelle Higonnet

The eyes of the buried will close together on the day of justice, or they will never close.
— Miguel Angel Asturias, Guatemala's Nobel Laureate for Literature

The Commission on Historical Clarification in Guatemala (*Comisión para el Esclarecimiento Histórico, CEH*) constituted a landmark achievement in global human rights scholarship and activism. Amongst other things, this institution took the courageous step of writing in its final report that genocide had taken place in Guatemala. We have assembled and translated the section of the CEH's final report devoted to genocide, in order to make that vital genocide claim available to a general English-speaking public. Our aim has been to shed light on a dark chapter of Central American Cold War history—one that has been neglected and marginalized for too long. We believe that it is important to study this genocide, and specifically crucial to revisit the genocide findings of the CEH report for three reasons.

First, this text is important to Guatemalan and even to world history because of the magnitude of human suffering it reveals. Fundamental moral imperatives oblige us to pay attention to one of the great human tragedies of our time. That is our task, as citizens of an inter-connected world and as human rights advocates generally.

Second, the CEH was a path-breaking body in its time. It created precedents in the world of transitional justice and truth commissions. Its marriage of human rights scholarship and activism on the ground informed how subsequent truth commissions have grappled with the atrocities they were designed to uncover. Its work should thus be studied by transitional justice professionals as a corpus of great import, especially given the fast-evolving state of transitional justice and the ever-growing importance of truth commissions around the world. By learning from past truth-telling entities, human rights practitioners can glean valuable insights about how to engage with the question of genocide in the future.

Third, the genocide findings of the CEH will be of great interest to Latin Americanists, scholars not only of Guatemala but of Central America and of the Cold War in the Southern Cone. The Guatemalan military's campaigns of terror and the genocide it carried out between 1981 and 1983 sent ripples throughout the entire hemisphere, shaping the sub-region militarily, politically, and culturally. Anyone interested in the "dirty wars" of Latin America will find the Guatemalan genocide and the CEH's analysis thereof to be a vital piece of the region's historical puzzle.

Preface: Genocide in Guatemala

Juan E. Méndez[1]

The Convention on the Prevention and Punishment of the Crime of Genocide, approved in 1948, was the first multilateral treaty designed to protect human rights. It was, therefore, a precursor to the broad cross-cultural agreements that characterize multiple human rights conventions signed and ratified since the end of World War II, both at the universal and at regional levels. The Genocide Convention is unique among these treaties in that, very soon after its entry into force, the International Court of Justice announced all of its provisions declaratory of pre-existing obligations and of customary international law. In addition, the Genocide Convention is one of the most widely accepted and ratified instruments in the human rights canon. Despite all of this, preventing and punishing genocide remains a rare and difficult enterprise in today's world, even sixty years after this solemn undertaking by all members of the international community.

Punishment of the crime of genocide was made difficult by the fact that the Convention did not create an organ of implementation, effectively relying on State parties to prosecute and punish genocide under their own domestic jurisdictions or to open their own courts to prosecute crimes committed elsewhere under the principle of universal jurisdiction. The Cold War years created an impasse during which both of those possibilities became illusory. In the 1990s, however, the international community created ad hoc courts to prosecute genocide, war crimes and crimes against humanity committed in the former Yugoslavia and in Rwanda. Later, "hybrid" courts (applying domestic law but with support from the international community and participation of foreign judges and prosecutors) were developed for Sierra Leone and Cambodia. By far the most promising institution to break the cycle of impunity for genocide is the International Criminal Court, a permanent judicial body created by the Rome Statute of 1998 that started operations in 2002. The Rome Statute now has 104 State parties.

Prevention of genocide, however, continues to pose a significant challenge to the international community. Powerful signatories like the United States understand the prevention of genocide norm as *allowing* but not *obligating* the State party to take action, whether unilaterally or through international organizations, to protect populations threatened with genocide. Other States understand the norm to be obligatory, but to be implemented exclusively through multilateral organs empowered by treaties to order the legitimate use of force outside of situations of self-defense. In the case of the United Nations, that organ is the Security Council, and given the veto power bestowed by the Charter on each one of the five permanent members, the decision to use force in a non-consensual manner rests ultimately in the ability to reach a consensus between the United States, the United Kingdom, France, Russia, and China. This is not necessarily an impossible standard, but as the case of Darfur beginning in 2003 and 2004 demonstrates, it is extraordinarily difficult to reach such an agreement, even in the face of ongoing atrocities. In addition, the UN and regional organizations are ill-prepared to generate the kind of actions that can stave off the threat of genocide short of multilateral armed intervention.

In the aftermath of the inability to prevent genocide in Rwanda and Srebrenica in 1994 and 1995, the United Nations conducted serious introspective studies that identified gaps in the capacities available to it to prevent genocide.[2] In 2001, the Security Council passed Resolution 1366 by which it asked the Secretary-General to bring to its attention situations that, if left unattended, posed the risk of genocide, as well as to suggest actions that could be adopted to prevent that occurrence. Citing that resolution, Kofi Annan created the position of Special Advisor to the Secretary-General on the Prevention of Genocide, to which he appointed me in July of 2004, on a part-time basis and with very limited resources. This decision to "start small" was meant as an experiment and as such subject to careful and rigorous scrutiny with a view to improving its performance. In 2006, an Advisory Committee on Prevention of Genocide also appointed by Kofi Annan produced just such an evaluation and formulated recommendations that were left to Mr. Ban Ki-moon, the new Secretary-General, to implement. The post will almost certainly become full-time, and if other recommendations are also applied, the office will become a more effective tool in the prevention of genocide.

Lack of political will is certainly the most determinant factor in our inability to prevent genocide. The relative absence of capacities in international organizations to develop effective conflict prevention strategies is also important. Still, we should not underestimate the complexity of preventing genocide in the context of an architecture of world order that is based on the principle of the sovereign equality of nations and its corollary: the principle of non-intervention in the internal affairs of a member State. The doctrine of Responsibility to Protect, most recently spelled out in the Summit Outcome document of 2005, establishes important limitations to both. Sovereignty is now understood to be a right that carries with it responsibilities, both to the international community and to the State's own citizens; and non-intervention is not an obstacle to action inspired in concern over the fundamental rights of the human person. But the line drawn is far from clear in specific cases. In addition, it has proven difficult to generate a "culture of prevention" within the United Nations, in the sense of units and departments that are equipped to gather and analyze information, to provide political organs with early warning about unfolding developments, and to act preemptively in peace-making and conflict prevention, rather than reacting in the form of peace-making or conflict resolution after the worst has happened.

Part of the problem lies in the cumbersome language of the Genocide Convention. Precisely because it is one of the earliest human rights treaties, it fails to create mechanisms of implementation; its language also lacks precision and can lead to divergent interpretation of facts, often against a background of political or ideological interests. In that sense, use of the word "genocide" has become a central problem in prevention. First, some ideologically-driven actors are too quick to use the word to disqualify the adversary while ignoring it when similar crimes are committed by friends. Inflammatory language is always an enemy of effective human rights protection. Among those with a capacity to act, the use of the word is also problematic. As recent history shows, in 1994 the Clinton Administration refused to categorize the events in Rwanda as genocide, for fear that a finding of genocide would oblige it to act. In reverse, ten years later the George W. Bush Administration was quick to qualify the events in Darfur as genocide, but added in the next breath that such a qualification did not generate any obligation to act. Indeed, Darfur exemplifies how disputes over whether the facts warrant the use of the word genocide become more important than taking action to curb mass atrocities, whatever the legal label that should ultimately be assigned to them.

The debate is made difficult because the Convention's definition adds a subjective element in the requirement of specific intent (or *mens rea*) to eliminate in whole or in part a human group designated by ethnicity, race, religion or national origin. There is no question that even a highly subjective element can be proven through objective evidence; the problem

is that such proof requires an analysis of tragic episodes *after the fact.*
As international criminal courts of recent vintage have shown, that is
possible through rigorous judicial action in the context of punishment.[3]
It comes too late, however, to be of any use in the obligation to prevent.
For that reason, the terms of reference of the Office of the Special Advisor on the Prevention of Genocide specifically state that the SAPG will
not qualify conflicts or make determinations as to whether the facts on
the ground are sufficient to satisfy the Convention's definition of genocide. The preventive character of the function of the OSAPG makes it
necessary to act to demand protection of populations at risk *before* all
the facts on the ground meet the definition, and even if they ultimately
do not meet them. After all, the international community has a moral and
legal obligation to act in the face of war crimes, crimes against humanity
and genocide, and not only in the latter case.[4]

Although it is easy to understand why there is a pragmatic need not to
define certain events as genocide before the international community can
act to stop them, the UN is nonetheless handicapped in its moral authority
to exercise preventive action, by the fact that it does not officially recognize certain events of the past as amounting to genocide. For example,
the UN has never officially recognized the massacres of Armenians by
the Ottoman Empire between 1915 and 1923 as constituting genocide.
The 1999 Report of the UN Group of Experts on the killing of hundreds
of thousands of Cambodians in the late 1970s by the Pol Pot regime
found grounds to prosecute its leaders for committing genocide against
religious groups and ethnic minorities, but in the case of many other
victims the motivation was based on class and ideology.[5] Such crimes
against humanity may well constitute *politicide*, as some scholars claim,
but they do not neatly fit the definition of genocide in the 1948 Convention. In my thirty months as SAPG I had multiple awkward occasions
to face questions about past episodes and was challenged repeatedly for
my refusal to violate my terms of reference or go beyond what the UN
was prepared to say. Some critics felt there was something hypocritical
in stating that I was trying to prevent genocide in the present and in the
future but refusing to recognize genocide in the past. On the other hand,
if my mandate did not authorize me to qualify events of the present from
the perspective of the definition of genocide, it could hardly empower me
to adjudicate contested claims about events in the past, much less when
the resources available to me did not include any capacity to conduct
thorough and rigorous investigation or research.

In practice, I decided to use the word genocide when I could make reference to an authoritative adjudicatory body that had settled the question. In that sense, the UN is clearly on record calling the Holocaust by its name of genocide. In the same vein, the massacre of almost one million Rwandans in only a few weeks in 1994 has also been adjudicated as genocide by the International Criminal Tribunal for Rwanda (ICTR), and the ad hoc court for the former Yugoslavia (ICTY) has ruled in the same way at least with regard to the killing of 8,000 Bosnians in Srebrenica in 1995.[6] The matter has more than a historical interest, and it goes beyond the question of choice of terminology, important as this is in the public discourse of international affairs. It also has bearing on the issue of "indicators" or warning signs that the SAPG must analyze in order to exercise the function of early warning. In the literature of genocide prevention there is unanimity in listing previous incidents of genocide or genocide-like situations as a risk factor in identifying country situations that merit attention. In the same vein, denial of previous facts of this sort, or of responsibility for them in the face of overwhelming evidence, is considered an even greater risk factor.[7]

In this light, the contribution made by the Commission on Historical Clarification in Guatemala (*Comisión para el Esclarecimiento Histórico—CEH*) acquires great significance in the struggle to build blocks to enable us to prevent genocide in the future. The CEH is the result of a peace agreement brokered by the United Nations, and it conducted its investigations with financial and human resources contributed by the UN. It was also chaired by an eminent jurist of world renown, Professor Christian Tomuschat of Germany, and its two other members, both Guatemalan citizens, had impeccable reputations and enjoyed the respect of the whole Guatemalan society, including its indigenous majority. More significantly, however, the CEH report is important for future preventive strategies because it is a powerful, persuasive document, arrived at after a rigorous and exhaustive methodological approach and a painstaking effort conducted in the whole territory of the country and during a prolonged period of study.

The whole UN experience in Guatemala starting in the 1990s stands as a great success story for the organization, from the early facilitation of peace talks to its more active role in mediating them. The UN also succeeded in including key human rights and democratization principles in the agreements, and then accompanied the early stages of implementation by deploying a strong cadre of professional staff and by securing important resources from the international community. The research conducted by the CEH and its powerful final product are the crowning jewel in that successful experience. It must be said that Guatemalans were by no means passive beneficiaries of an inspired and generous international community. The CEH methodology and its report might not have been as good without the project launched only a few months before by the Catholic Church, called *Recuperación de la Memoria Histórica—REMHI.*[8] And neither REMHI nor CEH would have succeeded but for the courage of Guatemalan human rights monitors, local community leaders and surviving victims. They kept the memory of the conflict of the early 80s alive even after the most dangerous circumstances, and they never wavered in demanding justice for the atrocities. I still remember a fact-finding trip I made for Human Rights Watch (then Americas Watch) in the mid-1980s and my conversation with an Italian priest in an isolated village, who had kept a diary recording vivid descriptions of those crimes made to him by parishioners seeking solace and help. The diary was a treasure trove of documentation and eyewitness accounts gathered contemporaneously with the events themselves. It was a closely held secret at the time, but I realized instantly how useful these accounts would be when the hour of reckoning came—and how their very existence kept alive the promise of reckoning even during the darkest hours.[9]

The CEH is an exercise in truth-seeking and truth-telling. In that sense, it is one of the mechanisms created in the last quarter century by which societies deal with legacies of mass atrocity as they make transitions from dictatorship to democracy or from conflict to peace. These social and political experiments have been attempted in very diverse societies, ranging from the Southern Cone of Latin America, to Eastern Europe, to South Africa and to multiple current attempts to provide victims with a voice. In addition to truth-telling, they include criminal prosecutions against the perpetrators, reparations offered to the victims, the reform of institutions and the disqualification of known abusers from serving in them, and reconciliation-aimed inter-communal talks where necessary. Taken together, these practices amount to a new horizon of human rights protection called "transitional justice." The adjective is not meant to qualify the nature of the justice that is pursued, but to recognize the complexity of pursuing it in a context of transition.

Recovering the past and setting the record straight by way of truth commissions has become an instrument of choice, especially in those countries—like Guatemala—where massive human rights violations are attended by equally massive denial. One almost expects denial and refusal to accept responsibility by the perpetrators and by the institutions they still control, as in the present-day armed forces of Guatemala. But what is especially harmful to the success of the democratization drive is the attitude towards these events by those who consider themselves "ordinary citizens" and "innocent bystanders." It is not a question of forcing people who had no control over the events to share the blame; it is, however, crucial that they confront the past and recognize the special plight of their fellow citizens who have been victimized on racial or ethnic grounds. That recognition is an inescapable first step towards building a more humane, inclusive society. Sad to say, Guatemala today does not offer assurances that that recognition will be achieved. Nevertheless, the CEH report goes a long way towards laying the necessary groundwork for a new Guatemala.

The problem, however, is not exclusive to Guatemalans. As convincingly argued in the following pages, the tragic abuses in Guatemala had external actors who also refuse to live up to their responsibility to acknowledge the past in order to move forward. The denial by Latin American generals that these tragedies even took place, or that they were part and parcel of a deliberate "dirty war" strategy, is only a more grotesque version of the *plausible deniability* devised by the Central Intelligence Agency of the United States to disguise and justify covert operations. Dirty wars, with their result in forced disappearances, attacks on civilian population, extreme torture and "extraordinary renditions" across borders, are only covert operations writ large. In addition—and this is especially the case in Guatemala—they were at the time denied by American officials and diplomats who knew better, and at best were tolerated—at worst actively encouraged and supported—by American foreign policy.

Transitional justice mechanisms are necessary to heal the open wounds of the recent past and to prevent their repetition in the future. We do not claim that by themselves these practices will prevent recurrence. We really cannot know what will happen in the future or how relevant actors will react to the disclosure of the truth and to attempts at redress. If prevention were our only justification, we would need to recognize that the opposing claim (that letting bygones be bygones is a better way to avoid repetition) could be equally plausible in certain circumstances. That is why we insist on truth and justice for their own sake, not as instruments of prevention. At the same time, we firmly believe and hope that facing history squarely will indeed guide us in avoiding the fate announced by Santayana in his famous dictum about those who refuse to acknowledge the past. This hope may not be empirically demonstrable, but it is nonetheless the implied promise and guiding principle of the Genocide Convention of 1948 and its operating assumption. It is also the explicit justification of the Rome Statute for an International Criminal Court and of all the international efforts to create institutions of justice in the 1990s. It is, no doubt, the impetus for the UN exemplary investment in Guatemala that led to the CEH.

In order for these efforts to have a preventive effect it is not enough to accompany and assist societal and national practices, as was done in Guatemala. It is crucial that the results of the efforts are broadly discussed, critiqued, debated, and absorbed by the national culture. Not enough of this is happening in Guatemala today to offer any certainty about the long-term legacy of the CEH. And certainly not enough is done internationally either, considering the very few instances in which, as in Guatemala, an internationally supported body has reached an authoritative, definitive conclusion about the genocidal nature of the campaign against a country's indigenous population. That is why I consider it a privilege to be asked to offer a few words as preface to this important publication. More importantly, it is an honor to be asked to contribute to a book whose authors realize the need to fill that crucial vacuum, but in addition they do so by putting in the hands of the reader a work of enormous depth, quality, and scientific rigor.

May 2007

Notes

1. Former Special Advisor to the Secretary-General (United Nations) on the Prevention of Genocide, 2004-2007. President, International Center for Transitional Justice (2004 to present).

2. United Nations, *Report of the Independent Inquiry into UN actions during the 1994 Rwanda Genocide* ("Carlsson report"), 15 December 1999, www.un.org/News/ossg/rwanda_report.

3. ICTY, *Prosecutor v Radislav Krstic* (IT-98-33), Appellate judgment of 19 April 2004; ICTR, *Prosecutor v Jean-Paul Akayesu* (ICTR-96-4-T), judgment of 2 September 1998.

4. United Nations, *Report to the Secretary-General of the International Commission of Inquiry on Darfur*, February 2005, www.un.org/News/DH/Sudan/com_inq_darfur.

5. The 1999 UN Report, the latter is accessible online at: http://www1.umn.edu/humanrts/cambodia-1999.html

6. United Nations, *Report to the Secretary-General of the International Commission of Inquiry on Darfur*, February 2005, www.un.org/News/DH/Sudan/com_inq_darfur.

7. Gregory Stanton, *The Eight Stages of Genocide* (Washington: Genocide Watch, 1998).

8. It is impossible to mention REMHI without offering a heart-felt tribute to its inspirer and director, Mons. Juan Gerardi, murdered on 26 April 1998, only two days after presenting the final REMHI report to an expectant and grateful Guatemalan society.

9. There is at least one very moving account of these atrocities based on testimonies and records gathered in similar fashion: Ricardo Falla, SJ, *Massacres in the Jungle: Ixcan, Guatemala, 1975-1982*, Boulder: Westview, 1994.

Politics by Other Means:
Guatemala's Quiet Genocide

Greg Grandin

Between 1981 and 1983, the Guatemalan anti-communist army and its right-wing paramilitary allies executed over one hundred thousand Mayan peasants so unlucky as to live in a region identified as the seedbed of a Leftist insurgency. The killing was savage, markedly more brutal than similar repressive campaigns conducted elsewhere in Latin America during the same period.

In some towns, troops murdered children by beating them on rocks or throwing them into rivers as their parents watched. "Adiós, niño"—goodbye, child—said one soldier, before pitching an infant to drown. They gutted living victims, amputated genitalia, arms, and legs, committed mass rapes, and burned victims alive. According to a surviving witness of one massacre, soldiers "grabbed pregnant women, cut open their stomachs and pulled the fetus out."[1]

But for the international community, Guatemala's was, and remains, a quiet genocide. It went largely unobserved by the U.S. press as it was happening; today it is mostly ignored by pundits and scholars who over the last decade have made genocide a category fundamental for understanding and responding to political violence.[2]

In the aftermath of the Guatemalan "dirty" war, which both predated the genocide and continued for over a decade after that period of heightened killing, no perpetrator has ever been tried for war crimes or crimes against humanity in Guatemala. However, while judicial accountability remains practically non-existent, the peace accords that finally ended the war in 1996 mandated a truth commission, the Commission for Historical Clarification (*Comisión para el Esclarecimiento Histórico*, CEH).

1

Historical Background to the Historical Clarification Commission's Findings

Before presenting a translation of the CEH's genocide findings, it is crucial to situate the CEH's work against a historical background. The CEH named three mutually-dependent "structural" or "historical" causes of state violence which led to genocide: economic exploitation, principally associated with Guatemala's plantation economy, racism directed at the country's majority Mayan population, and political authoritarianism, that is, profoundly undemocratic and unrepresentative political institutions.

Colonial Exploitation and State Violence

The transition to coffee cultivation at the end of the nineteenth century intensified colonial exploitation, racism, and authoritarianism. Guatemala's plantation elites absorbed vast amounts of land and came to rely on the state—described by the CEH as "racist in theory and practice"—to ensure the cheap supply of labor, mostly Mayans from highland communities. A series of forced labor laws combined with land loss to "increase the economic subordination" of Mayans and poor Ladinos. This model of coercive development in turn militarized the state, which focused its energies on enforcing legislation, particularly the acquisition of labor through debt and vagrancy laws, beneficial to the coffee oligarchy.[3]

The violence of the Guatemalan State had been "fundamentally aimed against the excluded, the poor, and the Maya, as well as those who struggled in favor of just and more equitable society…. Thus a vicious circle was created in which social injustice led to protest and subsequently to political instability, to which there were always only two responses: repression or military coups." Actions taken either in response to social exploitation or in defense of entrenched interests, the commission argued, served as the mainspring of social conflict: Confronted with demands for reform, the "state increasingly resorted to violence and terror in order to maintain social control. Political violence was thus a direct expression of structural violence."[4]

One aspect of the left's challenge to this status quo was the promise of state-administered justice. The emergence of liberal nationalism in nineteenth-century Guatemala created an unsustainable contradiction between the promise of justice and the reality of systemic abuse. On the one hand state institutions, an expanding government bureaucracy harnessed all of its local expressions—department prefects, police, military, jails, telephones, telegraphs, roads, judges, and mayors—to the task of ensuring cheap, abundant, and quiescent Indian labor for coffee planters. Taxes, military conscription, obligations to provide free or under-compensated labor on public works, and vagrancy laws forced peasants off their own small plots of land and onto plantations. Once there, they found themselves utterly dependent on the will and disposition of planters. Plantations had their own jails, stockades, and whipping posts, and planters fought any attempt by the state to intervene in their labor relations, or to use their workers on public projects. Most intimately and physically, planter control over the bodies of workers was an elemental part of plantation life. Along with the ability to exact labor came the near complete impunity to incarcerate, whip, and rape. In areas outside the plantation zone, ladino power was less encompassing, but Ladinos still exerted control over municipal governments and established an array of exploitative practices.

The Reform Decade

On the other hand this extension of government power, which gradually closed off methods of evasive resistance such as flight and migration, forced a more direct engagement by marginalized groups with the state. Since the beginning of the twentieth century, rural activists called on the government to temper planter authority, using the language of liberal nationalism to do so. For ten years between 1944 and 1954 it did, or at least its promise to do so was more tangible.

The dynamic of structural violence eased and even reversed for a ten-year period when, following a democratic revolution in 1944, two reformist administrations, headed respectively by Juan José Arévalo and Jacobo Arbenz, curtailed many of the prerogatives and privileges of the coffee oligarchy. Guatemala's democratic decade, writes the CEH, "awoke the energies and hopes" of those who had "yearned to overcome the past." An awakening took place in a larger global context in which "the world was entering a new political period with the defeat of fascism and the promised offered by capitalist economic development." The new governments ratified a social democratic constitution, curtailed forced labor, legalized unions, enacted a labor code, expanded the vote, and passed a far-reaching land reform. Such measures "increased ideological polarization and domestic conflict," which in turn were "fueled by the tensions of the east-west struggle."[5] An "archaic judicial structure" that could not deal with the conflicts generated by the rapid expansion of new rights granted by the land and labor reforms aggravated social tensions and deepened polarization.

While the "defenders of the established order" quickly mobilized against the state, opposition came from other sectors as well. Rural peasant and indigenous mobilization along with the legalization and growing influence of the Communist Party reinforced an anticommunism that had deep roots among the middle-class, Catholic Church, and military. In turn, resistance to reform both radicalized and divided revolutionary parties.

The 1954 Coup, Ensuing Political Violence, and Cold War Anticommunism.

The reform period came to an abrupt end with the CIA's 1954 overthrow of Arbenz, which the commission describes as a national "trauma" that had a "collective political effect" on a generation of young, reform-minded Guatemalans: "so drastic was the closing of channels of participation and so extensive was the recourse to violence that it is considered one of the factors that led to the guerilla insurgency of 1960."[6] Expectations raised and struggles fought during this period reverberated throughout Guatemala's subsequent civil war. In the countryside, many land conflicts that fueled peasant participation in political movements and in the insurgency date back to the 1953 land reform.

U.S. intervention jump-started the "exclusivist dynamic" that had defined Guatemalan history until 1944. After the 1954 coup, the Guatemalan state once again put "itself at the bidding of a minority at the expense of the majority."[7] Two consequences of the coup helped propel post-1954 political violence.

First, Cold War anticommunism revitalized nationalist racism against Maya Indians and reinvigorated old forms and justifications of domination. A racially divided and economically stratified Guatemala was a tinderbox; anticommunism was the match. "What happened during the period of armed conflict," writes the CEH, "can be summed up as a process by which the radius of exclusion and the notion of an internal enemy" extended through the whole of society.[8] Second, the Cold War fundamentally transformed the possibilities of political alliances. In the past, the state responded to demands made by political movements not only with repression, but with concessions and negotiations as well. The triumph of the 1944 revolution was the highpoint of this pattern. Following 1954 and intensifying after the 1959 Cuban Revolution, Guatemalan elites increasingly turned to the United States for technical support in order to crush domestic threats to their power. The balance tipped in the state's favor and repression gave way to full-scale terror.

Guatemala's post-1954 history was a struggle to define expanding state power, between two competing models of state formation: one represented by the social democratic principles of the October Revolution; and the other by the imperatives of national security after 1954. Since its inauguration with the 1954 U.S.-backed coup, Guatemala's anti-Communist state had to adopt the challenge it sought to contain. In response to the October Revolution's rural organizing, the military, the state, and private counterrevolutionaries in the decades after 1954 built their own institutional base of peasant support. In the 1960s and 1970s, through military commissioners, planters, and paramilitary groups, the primary vanguard of the counterrevolution, namely the *Movimiento de Liberación Nacional*, created a network of rural power in the highlands on the southern coast, providing land to supporters and tapping into community divisions and hostility toward political liberalization.

After 1954, peasant and working-class movements became the primary carriers not only of democratization—a project Guatemalan Liberals had long since abandoned— but also of social democratization. Reformers demanded that the state use its power to rein in the abuses of capital, to fulfill the promise of the October Revolution. The state was both unable and unwilling to do so.

State Intervention Turns into Terror

The alchemy of postwar counterinsurgent repression throughout the 1960s and 1970s was that it transfigured the promise of state intervention into terror. Lacking not only a monopoly of legitimate violence but the capacity for illegitimate physical repression to counter seemingly inextinguishable mass mobilization that gained force throughout the 1960s and 1970s, the militarized state imported from the United States new repressive technologies to nationalize violence.[9] In this sense, government repression was both a backlash against the ongoing legacy of the October Revolution *and* the revolution's perverse realization, the hope of a postwar social democratic state (1944-1954) mutated into the nightmare of a post-coup counterinsurgent terror state.

In Guatemala, the ensuing nationalized terror entailed incorporating quasi-independent death squads directly into military structures. The United States was instrumental in this process. In the early 1960s, after the high cost of the Korean War and following the threat of the Cuban Revolution, the United States, through its USAID Public Safety Program, focused on strengthening the domestic security forces of nations like Guatemala it deemed vulnerable to Communism. For despite the easy overthrow of Arbenz, Guatemala in the 1960s stood on the brink of chaos. The regime the United States had put in place in 1954 was corrupt and repressive, pushing many reformers to support a Cuban-inspired armed insurgency. Bombings, bank robberies, sabotage, murders and kidnappings, carried out by both the right and the left, plagued the capital. In December 1965, U.S. security advisor John Longan arrived in Guatemala City to create a small "action unit to mastermind a campaign against terrorists which would have access to all information from law enforcement agencies."[10] Longan dubbed the campaign "Operación Limpieza"—Operation Cleansing—and placed Guatemala's brutal military colonel Rafael Arriaga Bosque in charge of its operations.

Hoping to professionalize Guatemala's intelligence system, Longan and other American advisors centralized the operations of the police and military, training them to gather, analyze and act on intelligence in a coordinated and rapid manner.[11] Equipped with state of the art telecommunications and surveillance equipment and operating out of military headquarters, Arriaga began to carry out widespread raids.

By January 1966, the American embassy was pleased with the results. "Arriaga appears to be doing relatively good job," said one report, noting that the military and police were cooperating with each other "both in collection, analysis of intelligence and in actual operations.... Security forces under Arriaga are conducting large-scale joint 'sweeps' of suspect urban areas."[12] By the end of February, eighty operations and a number of extrajudicial executions had taken place. Then between March 3 and March 5, Operación Limpieza netted its largest catch: over thirty leftists captured, interrogated, tortured, and executed—their bodies placed in sacks and dropped into the Pacific from U.S.-supplied helicopters. Some of their remains washed back to shore. Despite pleas from Guatemala's archbishop and over 500 petitions of habeas corpus filed by relatives, the government and the American Embassy remained silent about the fate of the executed.

Among those eliminated in this first collective Latin American Cold War disappearance were former Arbenz advisors who advocated a negotiated settlement to the still embryonic civil war and a return of the left to the electoral arena. After their executions, a young, Cuba-influenced generation of revolutionaries dismissed such a position as not only naïve but suicidal. Even the CIA admitted that an "intolerable status quo" combined with the "efficiency" of the U.S.-created security forces drove "usually moderate groups to violence."

Operación Limpieza was a decisive step forward in the radicalization of not just Guatemala's civil war but the broader Latin American Cold War, foreshadowing the application of similar tactics of "disappearances" throughout the continent in the 1970s and 1980s. In Guatemala, it strengthened an intelligence system with central command over death squads that through the course of the civil war would be responsible for tens of thousands of disappearances and executions and countless tortures. It invested awesome power in Arriaga Bosque (one of Guatemala's "most effective and enlightened leaders," according to the American Embassy), who a few months after these executions would lead Guatemala's first scorched-earth campaign (1966-1967) that killed 8,000 civilians, mostly in the eastern lowland part of the country, in order to uproot a few hundred guerrillas.[13]

The nationalization and centralization of terror also relied upon an increasingly visible performance of what previously had been private acts such as rape, torture, and murder. As repression escalated throughout the 1970s, rape, mutilation, torture, and murder morphed from everyday acts of planter control and increasingly became the trademark of government-linked death squads, both the representation and essence of public state power.

Despite this escalating violence, by the late 1970s, more than twenty years after the overthrow of Jacobo Arbenz, the Guatemalan government stood on the point of collapse. Government repression, carried out by the military and allied death squads against reformist politicians, a radicalized Catholic Church, indigenous activists, and a revived labor and peasant movement swelled the ranks of a left-wing insurgency that by the end of the decade was operating in eighteen of Guatemala's twenty-two departments. Between 1978 and 1980, security forces carried out a number of spectacular acts of violence. Some of the most notable atrocities included the collective disappearance in two instances of over forty labor leaders and the firebombing of the Spanish embassy after a group of peasants and students occupied it to protest growing repression in the Mayan highlands. Such acts isolated the Guatemalan government from the international community and further alienated it from its own population.

There was logic to this violence: it was directed primarily at perceived threats to either planters, industrialists, or the state. Yet it was nonetheless revanchist, scattershot, and reactive, not linked to a larger plan of stabilization or rule.

Planning the Genocide

In response to this crisis, a cohort of young modernizing officers emerged within the military that increasingly identified the kind of chaos that plagued Guatemala as an obstacle to national security. A coup in March 1982 brought General Efraín Ríos Montt to power and gave these military reformers a chance to put their ideas into practice.[14] Héctor Gramajo (1994), one of the leaders of the young officers, writes that "for a period of three months following the coup, there developed in the heart of the military a serious analysis of the national situation and an honest self-criticism...." The strength of the insurgency, the officers concluded, could not simply be blamed on communism but rather on "problems that have very long and deep roots in the social system."[15] Military strategists began to understand "terrorism as primarily caused by underdevelopment, by misery, by poverty" and to define the pursuit of national security as a total war comprised of multiple fronts: "military, political, and, above all, social and economic. The hearts and minds of the people were the objective."[16]

While Latin American militaries long acknowledged the link between national security and development, this new doctrine—codified in a National Plan of Security and Development and executed through sequential campaign policy papers—represented a breakthrough for an army that had long served as the corrupt private gendarme of the oligarchy. Each step of the plan outlined specific tasks and built on the previous accomplishments. The final objective was the defeat of the guerrilla through the fortification of the state. Short-term goals included the temporary suspension of indiscriminate urban death squad violence, improvement in the administrative functions of the government, and an anti-corruption campaign—all designed to increase the legitimacy of the state. Long-term targets entailed convening a constituent assembly, adopting a new constitution, elections, political liberalization, "de-militarization" of state agencies, and normalizing relations with other countries. The power of the military, however, especially its intelligence apparatus, would remain intact, its authority enshrined in a new constitution obscured behind the lacquer of democratic rule.

Yet before the military could implement such a vision, the rural insurgency had to be destroyed. In the months prior to the March 1982 coup, army detachments moved into the western highlands and initiated a campaign of massacres and executions in Mayan communities, identified as the support base of the rebels. The massacres continued until early 1983, but already their execution was placed under a more precise command structure following the 1982 coup. Military analysts marked communities and regions according to colors: *White* spared those thought to have no rebel influence; *pink* identified areas in which the insurgency had limited presence, where suspected guerrillas and their supporters were to be killed but the communities left standing; *red* gave no quarter—all were to be executed and villages destroyed. "One of the first things we did," says Gramajo, "was draw up a document for the campaign with annexes and appendices. It was a complete job with planning down to the last detail."[17] The truth commission documented 626 massacres taking place throughout the course of Guatemala's nearly four decade long civil war. The vast majority of these collective killings, close to 600, occurred between late 1981 and early 1993 and often entailed the razing of entire villages. In some departments, as much as eighty percent of the population was driven from their homes for some period, with entire villages at times left abandoned. The campaign broke the agricultural cycle, leading to hunger and widespread deprivation.

In arguing that this operation included acts of genocide, the CEH documented the racial assumptions strategists used in its design. As part of a larger plan of achieving stability through state fortification, defense intellectuals believed indigenous peasant communities needed to be integrated into government institutions. Analysts focused on what they identified as the "closed," caste-like isolation of Mayans as the reason for their supposed collective susceptibility to communism: "the existence of diverse ethnic groups, with different languages and dialects demonstrates the partial nature of national integration due to a lack of a common identity."[18] The most important problems the army faced in the rebellious Quiche region, wrote one strategist, were "of a social and economic nature, owing principally to the characteristics of the Ixil [A Mayan ethnic group considered by military strategists to be particularly unruly] which because of its special sociological traits have also been distrustful of all that is related to Ladinos."[19] Mayans, said a 1982 military campaign plan, "have joined the guerrillas due to a lack of communication with the state."[20] The National Plan of Security and Development called for nationalism to be "disseminated in the countryside," particularly through a literacy campaign that would make Indians more "susceptible" to "new ideas." Another 1982 military action plan called for the establishment of a "spirit of nationalism and the creation of channels of participation and integration for the different ethnic groups that make up our nationality." To these strategic considerations officers added racist fears, amplified by Guatemala's apartheid-like social system, that Mayans were easily manipulated by outsiders, for example, or that their participation in the insurgency was driven by desire for racial vengeance.

The army's scorched earth campaign was designed to respond to the race problem identified by military strategists. It brutally cut off communities from the insurgency and broke down the communal structures, which military analysts identified as seedbeds of guerrilla support. This explains the singularly savage nature of the Guatemalan counterinsurgency, which, while comprising the most centralized and rationalized phase of the war, was executed on the ground with a racist frenzy aimed not just at eliminating the guerrillas and their real and potential supporters but colonizing the spaces, symbols, and social relations analysts believed to be outside of state control.

The Genocide

Terror was made spectacle: Soldiers, commissioners and civil patrolmen raped women in front of husbands and children. In September 1982, in Sechaj, a village in the department of Alta Verapaz, civil patrolmen captured, beat, and tortured PGT activist Francisco Xi then turned him over to soldiers. Before executing him, soldiers amputated his tongue and testicles and put them on public display, a none-too-subtle rendering impotent of voice and virility.[21] In another nearby village, security forces publicly tortured and killed groups of men in village chapels, disposing of their bodies in sacred caves. They turned churches into torture chambers and singled out traditionalists, particularly in PGT communities, for murder.[22] "They say that the soldiers scorched earth," said Manuel Caal, who fled his home in Salac, "but it was heaven that they burned."[23]

In the majority of massacres, the CEH found "evidence of multiple ferocious acts preceding, accompanying, and following the killing of the victims. The assassination of children, often by beating them against the wall or by throwing them alive into graves to be later crushed by the bodies of dead adults; amputation of limbs; impaling victims; pouring gasoline on people and burning them alive; extraction of organs; removal of fetuses from pregnant women."[24]

Moreover, in those villages that remained united in opposition to the military and government, the army forced intra-communal violence and undermined the foundations of community. "The military destroyed ceremonial sites, sacred places, and cultural symbols. Indigenous language and dress were repressed.... Legitimate authority of the communities was destroyed."[25] It was a common tactic to make members of a community commit violence against their neighbors.[26] In 1982 in Salac, another Alta Verapaz village, soldiers and military commissioners captured 18 members of the community and took them to a military camp where they separated the victims into two groups—the strong and healthy and the weak and infirm—forcing the former to beat the latter.[27] In the same village the previous year, one survivor says that the military made residents execute by machete seventeen refugee families who had recently fled repression in their home community of Senahú. Often the army encouraged their civilian allies to avail themselves of their victims' property and surviving wives and daughters.[28] One military commissioner was forced to murder his parents, who were members of the Communist Party, thus severing the kind of generational political ties that gave the insurgency its strength.[29] Such terror not only broke local solidarity, but, following the primary objective of the pacification campaign, bound the perpetrators in an impious blood ritual to a larger impersonal state collective as represented by the military. "We brought government to the village," boasted Gramajo.[30]

Post-Massacre Militarization and Control of Rural Populations

In the wake of the killings, once soldiers had violently severed the relationship between the guerrillas and their social base, the military took charge of reconstruction so as to integrate the rural population into state structures. Survivors of the massacres, including the tens of thousands of Mayans who fled into the mountains or jungle lowlands, were offered amnesty and food in exchange for their submission to military authority.

Returning either to their home communities or newly established "model villages," often after passing a period of time in military bases for ideological "purging," they found daily life to be completely militarized. All adult men were required to serve in civil patrols, responsible for local anti-subversive policing. The infamous Patrullas de Auto-Defensa Civil (Civil Defense Patrols or PACs) were in some ways a continuation of this tradition, albeit one more directly linked to the military. The military established the PACs, or civil patrols, in the early 1980s, obliging all adult men to serve as armed sentries and placing the onus of keeping a community free of guerrilla influence on the community itself. As did the organizing associated with the Left, the civil patrols provided an effective venue for particular interests and factions to speak in the name of the community. In this case, it allowed local leaders hostile to the guerrillas an opportunity to reestablish a power base within their villages, to impose order, and to make claims on the government. In many towns, for examples, the PACs, at the same time they allowed the army to consolidate its rural authority, empowered indigenous leaders to loosen local Ladino control of politics and the economy. Although repression carried out by PACs have received a good deal of attention from human rights advocates, few scholars have connected them to Guatemala's long history of popular participation in local militias, allowing for something of a popular Jacobin citizenship asserted through armed defense of the state. As the war wound down in the late 1980s and early 1990s, civil patrols in many communities continued to dominate local life and to serve as the primary transmission belt through which the military controlled local life.

The army used food, mostly supplied by U.S.-AID and the United Nation's World Food Programme, but also by conservative U.S. evangelical organizations, to compensate refugees for work on roads and other rebuilding projects.[31] The army controlled all reconstruction efforts, coordinating the activities of new state agencies and non-governmental organizations charged with providing water, health care, and technical assistance to restart agricultural production. At the same time that the army was militarizing the countryside, it was carrying out its national-level strategy of returning Guatemala to constitutional democratic rule (accomplished in 1986), normalizing international relations, and bringing the war to an end in 1996.

The Guatemalan Genocide and Genocide Scholarship

The Guatemalan genocide was not a simple expression of irrational racial hatreds, although racism fueled its ferocity. Nor was it carried out in the name of an ideology, although anticommunism was a crucial accelerant.

Rather, the genocide was a structured response to a mounting threat, a culmination of anticommunist counterinsurgent state formation. Héctor Gramajo, a principal architect of the army's 1982 turnaround, was fond of inverting Clausewitz's observation, saying that "politics is a continuation of war by other means" to describe Guatemala's transition to democracy.[32] In this case, genocide also became a continuation of politics.

Throughout most of the second half of the twentieth century, genocide was generally associated with a centralizing, mobilizing state—Turkey, Nazi Germany, and Khmer Rouge Cambodia being paradigmatic examples.

Over the last decade however, with the emergence of the United States as the world's lone superpower, scholars have reoriented the concept, linking it less to a state on the march than a state in decay, to a breakdown in the governing order and a collapse of legal and political institutions designed to protect individual rights and provide venues to channel and resolve grievances. The concept of a "failed state" is now commonly thought of as a national-security concern, replacing the revolutionary state of the Cold War years as the primary potential threat to the international system. It follows then that such state failure, as has been described as taking place in the Balkans and Rwanda, serves to affirm the validity of Western political institutions and, at times, to justify intercession.[33] In Samantha Power's influential *A Problem from Hell: America and the Age of Genocide*, the problem is not what the United States does—support for regimes in, say, Indonesia during its massive anti-Communist executions of the 1960s and its violent occupation of East Timor in the 1970s—but what it doesn't do: act to stop genocide.

In the Guatemalan case however, genocide was not a result of state decomposition but rather state consolidation, the first step in the military's plan of national stability and return to constitutional rule.[34] And it certainly was not the result of Washington's negligence but rather a direct consequence of its intervention.

As genocide scholarship has shifted from a focus on terror organized by a consolidating state to a model centered on the international community's failure to intervene in a failed state, it shifts away from an analysis in line with the realities of Guatemala. While the new vision is neither right nor wrong in the abstract, and may be the best lens through which to engage with a Rwanda paradigm, it does not help explain relatively recent genocides. It is vital for us to critically engage with the Guatemalan genocide in analytically appropriate ways that help us understand the past and grapple with the notion of possible future justice.

Notes

1.   Comisión para el Esclarecimiento Histórico, *Memoria del silencio*, VI; 76. Hereafter cited as CEH.
2.   A recent issue of *Dissent* magazine dedicated to twentieth-century genocides ignores Guatemala, as does Eric Weitz's *A Century of Genocide: Utopias of Race and Nation*. Samantha Power's well-received, award-winning '*A Problem from Hell:'America and the Age of Genocide*, which examines the United States' response to a number of genocides, likewise fails to mention Guatemala.
3.   McCreery, 1994.
4.   CEH V; 21-22.
5.   CEH I; 100.
6.   CEH I; 107.
7.   CEH I; 86.

8.   CEH I; 83.
9.   See the discussion in Grandin 2004; 73-104.
10.   National Security Archive (NSA), Department of State, "No Evidence State of Siege under Active Consideration," December 11, 1965.
11.   National Security Archive (NSA), Department of State, "Operation Resume of Terrorist Kidnappings and Guatemala Police Effort to Counter," December 17, 1965.
12.   See the two untitled embassy cables in the National Security Archive dated January 5, 1966 and March 1, 1966.
13.   Declassified Document Reference System (http://www.ddrs.psmedia.com/), Central Intelligence Agency Report, "The Danger of a Military Coup in Guatemala," September 28, 1966.
14.   Schirmer 1998.
15.   CEH I; 198. Gramajo 1995; 181.
16.   In Schirmer, 1998; 44.
17.   CEH III; 322.
18.   *Revista Militar*; 1982.
19.   CEH III; 322.
20.   CEH, VIII, p. 39.
21.   Fundación de Antropología Forense de Guatemala, *Informe Especial*; 94.
22.   CEH, VIII; 62.
23.   Grandin; 129.
24.   CEH V; 43.
25.   CEH V; 43.
26.   CEH, VIII, p. 120.
27.   CEH, VIII, p. 90.
28.   CEH, VIII, p. 110.
29.   CEH, VIII, p. 112.
30.   Schirmer 1998; 64.
31.   Americas Watch 1984.
32.   Gramajo 1995; 441. Clausewitz wrote, "Der Krieg ist eine bloße Fortsetzung der Politik mit anderen Mitteln."
33.   Power 2002.
34.   Schirmer 1998.

References

Americas Watch. 1984. *A Nation of Prisoners*, Washington.
Central Intelligence Agency (CIA). Declassified Document Reference System (http://www.ddrs.psmedia.com/), Central Intelligence Agency, Report, "The Danger of a Military Coup in Guatemala," September 28, 1966.
Fundación de Antropología Forense de Guatemala. 2001. *Informe Especial de la Fundación de Antropología Forense de Guatemala, 1996-1999*, Guatemala City: Fundación de Antropología Forense de Guatemala.
Gramajo Morales, Héctor Alejandro. 1994 (October). "La Tesis de la Estabilidad Nacional Doce Años Después," *Visión Nacional*, Fundación para el Desarrollo Institucional de Guatemala, #1.
Gramajo Morales, Héctor Alejandro. 1995. *De la guerra ... a la guerra: La difícil transición política en Guatemala*. Guatemala: Fondo de Cultura Editorial.
Grandin, Greg. 2004. *The Last Colonial Massacre: Latin America in the Cold War*, Chicago: University of Chicago Press.

McCreery, David. 1994. *Rural Guatemala, 1760-1940*, Stanford: Stanford University Press.

National Security Archive (NSA), Department of State, "No Evidence State of Siege under Active Consideration," December 11, 1965.

National Security Archive (NSA), Department of State, "Operation Resume of Terrorist Kidnappings and Guatemala Police Effort to Counter," December 17, 1965

Power, Samantha. 2002. '*A Problem from Hell': America and the Age of Genocide*, New York: Perennial.

Revista Militar. 1982 (Sept-Dec). "Apreciación de Asuntos Civiles (G-5) para el área ixil," pp. 36-37

Schirmer, Jennifer. 1998. *The Guatemalan Military Project: A Violence Called Democracy*, Philadelphia: University of Pennsylvania Press.

Genocide

General Considerations and Legal Definitions

3198. As stated by the International Court of Justice, the Genocide Convention's terms reflect fundamental judgments and the conscience of the international community, which have legal force independent of formal ratification. Guatemala ratified the Convention on January 13, 1950. Thus, the Convention was in force during the time of the armed conflict. The CEH adopted this international instrument as the legal reference in its investigation and analysis of the issue of genocide.

3199. Article II of the Convention defines the crime of genocide and its requirements in the following terms:

"In the present Convention, genocide means any of the following acts committed with intent to destroy, in whole or in part, a national, ethnical, racial or religious group, as such:

(a) Killing members of the group;

(b) Causing serious bodily harm or mental harm to members of the group;

(c) Deliberately inflicting on the group conditions of life calculated to bring about its physical destruction in whole or in part;

(d) Imposing measures intended to prevent births within that group;

(e) Forcibly transferring children of that group to another group."

3200. This description of acts of genocide has remained constant up until the present day. For example, the Statute of the International Criminal Court, adopted in an international conference in Rome on July 17, 1998, describes the crime of genocide in exactly the same terms.

3201. The Convention contemplates several objective elements of action described in Article II that constitute the crime of genocide, and a subjective element requiring that the action be carried out with "the intention to destroy in whole or in part."

3202. Finally, the Convention establishes that the protected groups or potential victims of genocide must be national, ethnic, racial or religious groups, as such.

3203. The subjective element or the intent to destroy the group has been interpreted through international jurisprudence: "the intentionality that is particular to the crime of genocide does not need to be expressed clearly [and] can be inferred through a number of issues, such as 'the general political doctrine' that arises from the actions contemplated in Article 4 ... the reiteration of destructive and discriminatory acts" (Interpretation of the International Criminal Tribunal for ex-Yugoslavia).

3204. It is very important to distinguish between "the intent to destroy a group in whole or in part" (that is, the positive determination to do so), and the motives behind such an intent. In order to determine genocide, it is only necessary to demonstrate that there exists an intent to destroy the group, regardless of motive. For example, if the motive to destroy an ethnic group is not pure racism but rather a military objective, the crime may nevertheless be understood to be genocide.

3205. An act falls into the category of genocide as defined by the Convention even if it forms part of a more extensive policy that was not strictly aimed at physical extermination. In this sense it is significant to distinguish between a genocidal policy and acts of genocide. A genocidal policy exists when the final objective of the actions is the extermination of a group, in whole or in part. Acts of genocide exist when the final objective is not the extermination of a group but rather alternate goals of a political, economic, military or other nature—but the means used to achieve these final goals involve the extermination of a group in whole or in part.

3206. These elements of jurisprudence, which are becoming doctrine and are also sources of law, have been helpful in the analysis that follows.

Methodology

3207. In order to determine if acts committed were indeed genocide, the CEH reviewed the legal basis of the Convention and previously cited jurisprudence, and analyzed the following:

- Analysis of the general policies of the state, particularly the Doctrine of National Security supporting the Guatemalan state's counterinsurgency strategies, that helped shape the context and the intent behind actions.
- Diachronic analysis (relating time with acts and places) as well as synchronized analysis (relating acts and places with the perpetrators and victims). This analysis was modeled on sections "a," "b," "c," "d," and "e" of Article II of the Convention. The analysis was carried out chronologically, examining links between actions and the intent underlying those actions, and the Convention. The sequence of actions and their common characteristics were then examined, with the ultimate goal of establishing that the acts of violence committed by the State or its agents occurred in a repetitive manner, and were discriminatorily directed against a specific group or groups within the population.
- Analysis of acts that violate, or that the perpetrator considers to violate, the integrity of the group, occurring simultaneously with acts of physical destruction and arising from the same operation. This last form of analysis included acts indicating an attack on the integrity of the group such as rape and sexual mutilation, torture, public executions, the exhibition of cadavers, the destruction of material elements of culture, etc.

3208. The period of analysis is between 1981 and 1983, which is when most violence was recorded. Similarly the analysis focuses on set regions and certain ethnic groups. The CEH has verified that these groups and regions were located where the majority of human rights violations were concentrated. Based upon these criteria and available analytical methods, it has been possible to conduct an investigation of what took place among four selected ethnic groups, in four regions of the country:

- Maya Q'anjob'al and Maya Chuj, located in northern Huehuetenango in Barillas, Nenton, and San Mateo Ixtatan;
- Maya Ixil located in Nebaj, Cotzal and Chajul, in the department of Quiche;
- Maya K'iche' in Zacualpa, department of Quiche;
- Maya Achi in Rabinal, Baja Verapaz

The selection criteria were the following:

- Intensity of violence (largest number of victims);
- Patterns of violence (indiscriminate violence);
- Composition of victims (identifiable groups)
- Quantity of information

3209. Of course, this investigation is limited by the circumstances in which the CEH operated. The CEH was only able to document a portion of the human rights violations that occurred during the internal armed conflict. This has made it necessary to correlate quantitative data regarding levels of destruction or extermination with other sources, such as the REMHI project and the database of the Alliance for Truth.

3210. To ensure the greatest accuracy for the sources, analysis, and statistical results, a system of control and fact-checking was created specially for these investigations. The system involved random checking of samples from the CEH database, using other databases as references to evaluate the CEH's work.

3211. For quantitative analysis, the CEH database established the percentage of the human rights violations by comparing the intensity of violence in each region to its demographic base. At the same time, there was a comparative analysis of the violence against the indigenous and non-indigenous population in each region in order to establish if discrimination existed. Thus, the CEH explored if there was a substantial difference between the quality and severity of the human rights violations suffered by members of one group or another.

3212. The CEH analyzed its sources exhaustively. For each region there was a careful examination of presented and illustrative cases, individual and collective testimony, declarations by key witnesses, including agents and ex-agents of the state, and contextual reports. Maps were produced, including those related to military operations and the presence of the guerrillas in the regions. This information was compared with other sources such as Army and guerrilla campaign plans, press reports, declassified documents from the government of the United States, and field investigations.

3213. In principle, this process allowed for the separation of causal and non-causal correlations to human rights violations, eliminating the possibility that the CEH would only analyze consequences. At the same time, this process allowed for the inclusion of independent analytical variables as controls, guaranteeing objectivity towards the data gathered. The independent variables included, among others: the command structure of the armed forces, the guerrilla's political and military interest in the regions analyzed, recognized norms of international humanitarian law, and the conditions of the non-combatant, civilian population.

Period of Analysis

3214. The analysis of human rights violations registered by the CEH made possible the determination that the most violent period of the conflict occurred between 1981 and 1983. Eighty-one percent of violations occurred during this period. Forty-eight percent of the cases were registered in 1982 alone.

3215. Those acts, which coincide with the sections "a," "b," "c," "d," and "e" of Article II of the Convention must be seen alongside other actions that do not correspond exactly to the Convention—but which were committed as part of the same plan. Such violations must be taken into consideration and can be useful in expressing the subjective element of genocide, namely the intent to destroy a group in whole or in part. Such actions include the destruction of cultural elements, forced displacement, destruction of goods, and destruction of crops.

Victim Group

3216. The Convention identifies the protected groups as ethnic, national, racial or religious groups. There are subjective and objective elements in the definition of these groups. A racial, national, religious or ethnic group is one that identifies itself as such— a subjective element of identity. At the same time a group can be perceived by the rest of society as distinct, following certain common characteristics such as history, language, physical characteristics, religious practice, location within a specific territory, or particular norms of behavior. In other words, national, racial, religious and ethnic groups possess social, cultural, and economic aspects that distinguish them from other sectors of society.

3217. Article 66 of the Political Constitution of the Republic recognizes that Guatemala is composed of diverse ethnic groups:

> Guatemala is formed by diverse ethnic groups within which figure indigenous groups of Maya descent. The State recognizes, respects and supports their lifestyle, social organization, the use of indigenous clothing among men and women, languages, and dialects.

3218. For its part, the Accord on the Identity and Rights of Indigenous Peoples establishes that Guatemala is a multi-ethnic, multi-cultural, and multi-lingual nation and recognizes the identity of the Mayan people as well as the identities of the Garifuna and Xinca peoples.

3219. Apart from their recognition within the legal domain, indigenous peoples identify themselves as such. This can be seen for example in the diverse and recent declarations of their representatives: "Over the centuries, we have been subjected to institutional violence of a State separate from our culture and forms of association, a patriarchal State that has oppressed us and discriminated against us triply: for being women, for being indigenous and for being poor."[1]

3220. Demetrio Cotji Cuxil defines the Maya people as: "The collection of ethnic communities who are members of the Maya linguistic family, a concept that includes not only Mayan residents of Guatemala but also those who have been ceded to or live under the jurisdiction of other States."[2]

3221. One basis for determining if the acts committed in Guatemala were of a genocidal nature has been the analysis of the diverse ethnic groups that compose the Mayan people. Of the various possibilities referred to in the Convention, the CEH used the notion of an ethnic group (as opposed to race or religion, for example). Among these, it was possible to investigate what occurred among four peoples: the Maya Ixil, the Maya Achi, the Maya Kaqchikel, the Maya Q'anjob'al, the Maya Chuj, and the Maya K'iche'.

3222. In some of the chosen regions, two or more ethnic groups live together. The Maya Q'anjob'al and Maya Chuj live in Huehuetenango in the northern part of the municipality of Nenton, the municipality of San Mateo Ixtatan and in Barrillas. In the areas of Nebaj, Cotzal and of Chajul, Quiche, the Ki'che', Q'anjob'al and Q'eqchi' live alongside the Ixil, who are the majority.

3223. The CEH understands the indigenous people as a group within which ethnic groups identify themselves as part of a larger entity and are perceived as such. That is to say, they understand themselves and each other to be indigenous as does the larger Guatemalan society, including state institutions that recognize this status. In those cases where two or more ethnic groups live within the same region, these are understood to be members of a single Maya group.

3224. To qualify an act as a genocide, the Convention demands that the act be committed with intent to destroy a group in whole or in part. The phrase "in part" is understood as "a reasonably significant number relative to the total of the group, such as all or a significant section of the group, such as its leaders."[3] A substantial part of the group is required. In order to determine if one is dealing with a substantial part of a group, one must recognize perpetrators' destructive capacity, as directed towards the possible extermination of a group.

3225. The destructive capacity of perpetrators was determined, in each case, by the area of control over which they engaged in acts of extermination. For example, acts of genocide committed by a military unit operating in a specific region could only be analyzed in relation to the particular ethnic group found in that region. To determine if a substantial part of the group there was affected, the CEH's analysis recognized what proportion of the ethnic group was in the area under the perpetrators' control.

General Policy

> Well they wanted to destroy the villages, but luckily we have God, and we were able to escape. They wanted to wipe out the villages. It wasn't to frighten people, it wasn't to kill one, two or three, but to finish them all off at once. When I fled and escaped I heard bursts of gunfire, and then I heard a soldier who said "Kill a lot of them, kill them all because now it is time to kill."[4]

3226. The human rights violations described below occurred within the framework of the "counterinsurgency" war, also called the "counter-subversive" war—as defined according to the Doctrine of National Security. A fundamental principle of this doctrine was to prevent the transformation of existing social, political, and economic systems. According to the doctrine, strategies were to be implemented in all areas of society, including "the political sector," the "socio-economic sector," and the "psychosocial sector."[5]

3227. In accordance with the Doctrine of National Security, the Army defined the "annihilation of the internal enemy" as a strategic objective of the counterinsurgency war. The Army understood two categories of individuals, groups, and organizations as an internal enemy:

1) Those who challenged the established order by means of illegal actions and represented "revolutionary communists," and
2) those who, while not being communists, still challenged the established order.[6]

3228. This doctrine also affirmed that the "counter-subversive" war defined the population as its "objective," because it considered the conflict to be one of "subversion." This view was predicated on the notion that the guerrillas sought to achieve their goals through the population's active participation, and that "the context in which their activities took place"[7] was the general population. Thus, according to the doctrine, it was necessary to recover or maintain that population's support and force them to participate actively in the war, in favor of the Government.

3229. Since the 1970s, when the guerrillas operated in the eastern region of the country, where the majority of the population is *ladino*, the Army began to conflate the Altiplano's Maya population and the enemy.[8] The 1972 Manual of Military Intelligence G-2 expressed this clearly: "The enemy has the same sociological characteristics as the inhabitants of our Altiplano."[9]

3230. In the 1980s, the Army came to identify indigenous people as the internal enemy. The Army considered that the guerrillas had succeeded in co-opting the *Altiplano*'s majority indigenous population's demands and their historical grievances, such as the lack of available land and poverty.

> The great indigenous masses of the Altiplano of the nation have been influenced by the subversion's proclamations about the lack of available land and immense poverty. As a result of many years of enemy consciousness-raising they view the Army as an invading enemy....[10]

> By means of reports by Intelligence and studies in the different areas, it has been established that the principal reason for which the indigenous people of the Altiplano support the guerrillas is a lack of communication between the Government and the people.[11]

3231. The Army considered that "the great indigenous masses" of the *Altiplano* constituted the social base of the guerrilla movement.[12] "Having succeeded in winning over the great masses of the population, especially indigenous people, the subversive factions were initially able to declare 'liberated zones' in the *Altiplano*...."[13]

3232. The armed forces' perception was shared by civil servants in the Government. Thus, Francisco Bianchi, secretary of the then de-facto-president Efraín Ríos Montt, identified the indigenous people with the guerrilla, and affirmed that the consequence of this identification would be elimination: "The guerrillas won over many Indian collaborators, therefore the Indians were subversives, right? And how do you fight subversion? Clearly you had to kill Indians because they were collaborating with subversion."[14]

3233. Something that facilitated the Army's conflation of indigenous people with the enemy was "the de facto discrimination, exploitation, and injustice, which the indigenous people of Guatemala suffered by virtue of their origins, culture, and language."[15] Discrimination against—or at the very least historical exclusion of—indigenous peoples in Guatemala was recognized in 1982 by the then de-facto-president, Efraín Ríos Montt, in several public declarations: "The apathy, our contempt, the ignorance of the existence [of the indigenous people] etcetera, signaled to the governor, that he had marginalized a large group of citizens."[16] "I made him see that we are rediscovering our nationality that we ignored for over 500 years."[17]

3234. Racism[18] polarized Guatemalan society, dividing it into big groups: indigenous people and *ladinos*. Racism occupied an influential place in dominant Guatemalan classes' ideas about and treatment of "the Indians."[19]

3235. As described in an empirical study by Marta Casaus Arzú (based on interviews conducted by the author), those dominant Guatemalan classes' attitudes towards indigenous peoples could be broken down into three categories. "Many of them are for maintaining socio-racial segregation and avoiding integration, reinforcing mechanisms of apartheid. Others are partisans of the improvement of the race, through techniques of artificial insemination. And some incline towards ethnic cleansing. . . . Between a fourth and 10%. . . . agree with drastic solutions and are profoundly intolerant of the indigenous population. This class occasionally advocates for the extermination of the indigenous population; for its cultural and physical disappearance."[20]

3236. Racism also existed amongst members of the armed forces: "I do know one, two, or maybe even three military men who hate the indigenous race. But you can find lots of this in other parts [of the army]. . . . Because of that, they could have committed many errors."[21]

3237. Former de-facto-president Efraín Ríos Montt made a statement which revealed how he considered the "other" as distinct, or inferior: "Naturally, if a subversive operation exists in which the Indians are involved with the guerrillas, the Indians are also going to die. However, the army's philosophy is not to kill the Indians, but to win them back, to help them."[22]

3238. Moreover, racism fueled the belief of an important number of *ladinos* that "the Indians will come off the mountains to kill the *ladinos*."[23] This fear existed because some *ladinos* considered that the indigenous people must feel historical resentment towards them because of colonial experiences.[24]

3239. In this way, racism helped create an ideological context wherein the Army conflated indigenous people, an ancestral enemy, and the insurgents. Moreover, racism exacerbated a feeling towards indigenous people as distinct, inferior, almost less than human, outside the universe of moral obligations, which made their elimination less problematic.

Analysis of the Regions

3240. The following sections analyze events in regions that the CEH investigated. All these events took place in the context of the "counter-insurgency war." During this war, the State implemented a plan, one of whose objectives was "annihilating the guerrilla and parallel organizations"[25] to achieve "the reestablishment of law and order, gaining the support of the population to become citizens."[26] An analysis of human rights violations [in this war] reveals that military operations took place in three stages.

3241. The first was characterized by selective repression. Violence was targeted at specific people or sectors. Selective repression continued in later stages, alongside other violence.[27] However, the second stage was characterized by massive repression, and included razing communities and persecuting displaced survivors. Human rights violations continued in the third stage, during which mechanisms of reorganization and population control were imposed on those who survived the previous stages. The goals of the third stage were to prevent the resurgence of preexisting social structures and to maintain all civilian activity under absolute military control.

3242. The three stages formed part of a global strategy aimed at the annihilation of the enemy. It is thus necessary to analyze them together.

The first stage helped the Army obtain information on the places where later they applied massive violence in their counter-insurgency operations.

Clearly, it was during the second phase that most acts were perpetrated that fall under the rubric of international crimes as specified by the [Geneva] Conventions. These include indiscriminate massacres, mass sexual violations, acts of public torture, bombings, killings of refugees and displaced people. Violence peaked in 1982.

Violence continued in 1983, but underwent a transformation. Acts of "annihilation" were gradually replaced by actions designed to "capture, organize, reeducate and incorporate into society people who had recognized the amnesty."[28] The third stage completed "pacification," placing survivors under military control to prevent any kind of resurgence of organized opposition.

3243. The following sections review the analysis of selected regions, taking into account the sequence described above.

Notes

1.   Propuesta de Mujeres y jóvenes indígenas, viudas y huérfanos de guerra, para la reparación histórica a los pueblos indígenas. [Proposal of indigenous women and youths, war widows and orphans, for historical reparations to indigenous peoples.]
2.   Demetrio Cojtí Cuxil, *El movimiento maya*, Guatemala, 1997, p. 15
3.   Whitaker, Ben, "Revised and updated report on the question of Prevention and punishment of the crime of genocide"; UN document E/CN.4/Sub.2/1985/6, par. 29, p.16.
4.   Collective testimony, CEH, of Pexla Grande, Nebaj, Quiché. CEH. (T.C. 335).
5.   Ejército de Guatemala, "Recommendations."*Plan Nacional de Seguridad y Desarrollo* [Armed Forces of Guatemala, National Plan for Security and Development], CEM, Guatemala, 1982, p. 2.
6.   Centro de Estudios Militares, *Manual de Guerra Contrasubversiva* [Center for Military Studies, Counter-subversive War Manual], 1982. p. 5.
7.   Ibid., p. 6.
8.   The references to the "indigenous peasants" (*campesinos indígenas*) the "population of the Altiplano," "marginalized indigenous people" (*indígenas*), denote the same group of people, that is to say the indigenous people of the Altiplano, who are characterized at the same time as peasants and as historically marginalized.
9.   Centro de Estudios Militares, *Manual de Inteligencia* [Center for Military Studies, Intelligence Manual] G-2, 1972, p. 217.
10.   Ejército de Guatemala. *Plan de Campaña "Victoria 82"* [Armed Forces of Guatemala, campaign plan Victory 82], annex F, literal A, numeral 2-c.
11.   Ejército de Guatemala. *Plan de Campaña "Victoria 82"*, appendix A. "Strong points and vulnerability of the enemy ... A. Strong points: ... 5. Its social base, rooted in the indigenous peasantry, in dialects."
12.   Ibid., annex F, *literal* A, *numeral* 4-a-4.

13.   Association of Military Veterans of Guatemala (AVEMILGUA), Guatemala, testimony about an attack, 1998, p. 77.
14.   Allan Nairn, "Guatemala Can't Take 2 roads." *The New York Times*, July 20 1982, p A23.
15.   Accord on identity and rights of indigenous peoples. The problem of the exclusion of the indigenous peoples was recognized even by the Military Junta in 1982, which established in its 14 Essential Points of Prompt Action, "Achieving the reestablishment of a nationalist spirit and fostering participation and integration of the different ethnic groups that make up our nationality." *Diario El Imparcial*, April 6, 1982.
16.   *Diario El Imparcial*, November 8, 1982, p. 1.
17.   *Diario El Imparcial*, December 6, 1982, p. 1. "I made him see physical, ethnic, and economic problems and our political limits." [then de-facto-president Ríos Montt to Ronald Reagan.]
18.   For the analysis of genocide, racism figures as an element of context that provides clues to prove the subjective element of the crime. However, it is not determinative when it comes to qualifying specific acts.
19.   Marta Casaus Arzú, *Guatemala: linaje y racismo*, San José, Costa Rica : FLACSO, 1995, p. 274.
20.   Ibid., pp. 274-277.
21.   Witness (retired soldier) CEH. (T.C. 24).
22.   Foreign Broadcast Information Service, Central America, "Ríos Montt Views on Peasant Killings, Communism," June 2, 1982.
23.   Oficina de Derechos Humanos del Arzobispado de Guatemala [Office of Human Rights of the Archbishop of Guatemala], *Nunca Más* [Never Again], Vol. II, p. 130. Compare Enrique Sam Colop, Informe del Grupo de Análisis Histórico, 1998, p. 57, and Piero Gleijeses, *Shattered* Princeton, NJ: Princeton University Press, 1991. *Hope*, 1992, p.12.
24.   As an anthropologist explains, *ladinos* believe that indigenous peoples nourish resentment for the following reasons: "First, in colonial times the indigenous people was oppressed. Over the years the resentment against the *ladino* became an atavism, the hatred became a biological assumption, and thus generation upon generation inherited resentment of the *ladino*." Interview with witness (anthropologist), CEH. (T.C. 333), who drew his conclusion from a study in the Department of Chimaltenango.
25.   Ejército de Guatemala. *Plan de Campaña "Victoria 82,"* annex H, numeral I, literal G-2.
26.   Ejército de Guatemala, "Apreciación de asuntos civiles (G-5) para el área ixil" [Assessment of civilian affairs in the Ixil area], *Revista Militar*, September - December 1982, p. 31. This document was published by the *Revista Militar*, along with "Una Solución a la Operación Ixil. Plan de AACC Operación Ixil" [A Solution to the Ixil Operation. Plan for AACC operation Ixil] pp. 25-54. A witness (Military official) CEH. (T.C. 103), certified its authenticity.
27.   Selective repression was a constant in counterinsurgency policies because it had specific proposals, for example the annihilation of the leaders and the idea of affecting the organizational capacity of communities, or of inspiring terror through exemplary punishment. See Centro de Estudios Militares, *Manual de contraguerrilla [Counter-guerrilla Manual]*.

Region I (Maya Ixil People): Municipalities of San Juan Cotzal, Santa María Nebaj, and San Gaspar Chajul, Quiché

Once, I received a personal order from the head of the Joint Chiefs of Staff, to level an entire population and I said to the Major in charge of the military post at the time—look, I was given the order to disappear San Juan Cotzal.[1]

3244. Located in the northwest of the department of Quiché, the Ixil area measures 2,413 square kilometers and is composed of three municipalities, Santa María Nebaj, San Juan Cotzal, and San Gaspar Chajul.[2] According to the 1996 census there are 67,078 inhabitants, of whom 90% are Maya Ixil—61,121 people—distributed in the following manner:

Nebaj	33,795
Chajul	19,213
San Juan Cotzal	14,070

3245. In 1981, the population of the area totaled 44,784 persons, 87% of whom belonged to the Maya Ixil Group.[3] The State considered the three municipalities to be one single Ixil population: "The Ixil, some 50,000, constitute a small group of Mayan descendents and inhabit the municipalities of Nebaj, Cotzal and Chajul … comprising 92% of the population and 8% are *ladinos*,"[4] thus distinguishing simply between two groups, indigenous and *ladino*.[5]

3246. The Army considered the Ixil people as alien or distinct from the *ladino* group. This distinction between Ixil and *ladinos* is clear throughout the military document "Appraisal of Civil Affairs for the Ixil Region,"[6] which studies regional characteristics and contains a series of affirmations expressing value judgments on the nature of the Ixil population. For example:

- Attitude of the Population: because of the Ixil population's historical and ethnic characteristics, they resist cooperation with *ladino* authorities.[7]
- Passive Resistance: generally, the Ixils do not serve in the Army, due principally to the fact that military recruitments (by quota) are done in other regions of the country where the character of the indigenous people is more inclined towards military-style discipline.[8]
- Understand that the Ixils, because of their special sociological characteristics, have always been mistrustful, particularly of anything having to do with the *ladinos*.[9]

3247. Beyond the previously mentioned differentiation between indigenous and *ladinos*, the perception of the Ixils as a population with "special ... characteristics" derives from an interpretation of the Ixil people's acts of resistance in the country's recent history. Early in this century, in 1924, the population of the village of Ilom, Chajul, rose up against Lisandro Gordillo Galán, a Mexican who tried to expropriate Ixil land. According to Ilom villagers, during that period, the population incarcerated a surveyor who had to be rescued by the Nebaj and Cunen militia.[10]

3248. In a similar vein, in the thirties an indigenous uprising in Nebaj took place to protest the Ubico Vagrancy Law, which mandated forced labor by those indigenous persons who could not demonstrate regular employment.

> A company of soldiers detained 200 people, shot eight *principales* [traditional indigenous authorities] and deported 500 Ixil leaders to the Petén jungles.[11]

3249. The movement for their rights continued in recent years. Thus, in the 1980 peasant strike on the South Coast,

> seven thousand Ixils participated.... They worked primarily on the Pantaleón plantation, but when the landowners figured out the Ixils were very combative and actively participated in peasant struggles, they no longer wanted to contract them.... All Ixils were insurgents to the plantation owners....[12]

3250. The authorities from Santa Clara-CPR [Community of Population in Resistance], Chajul, also remember how plantation owners labeled them as insurgent:

> In 1975, 1976, and 1977 the Ixil peasants who went to the South Coast began to demonstrate about the bad pay, the bad salaries, and the bad food that the plantation owners gave them; they began to organize and reclaim their rights.... And then when they saw that the Ixils organized themselves in this way and demonstrated and demanded their rights, the plantation owners began to believe that all the Ixils were insurgents and guerrillas and that's what they told the Army.[13]

3251. Finally the Ixil ethnic group was not just perceived as distinct, different from the *ladino* group, but as antagonistic to authority, to economic power, and to *ladinos* in general. The affirmation is expressed in military analyses:

> Of course, the Ixil mindset identifies owners of the most productive plantations in the region, government officials, and *ladinos*, in general, with the enemy.[14]

3252. The *"insurgents"* label extended itself to be used by the Army, which specifically considered the Ixil people to be the enemy, without establishing any distinction between the civilian population and combatants. This is how the collective testimony from the Pexla Grande community expresses it:

> Well it's because I remember that during the Lucas years ... they accused us of being guerrillas and we didn't even know who those groups were, but they blamed the community for this and then they burned all our houses, they killed all our parents, our families, our grandfathers and even kids, even pregnant women and they even killed our animals and ate them.[15]

3253. The U.S. Central Intelligence Agency, in a 1982 document that appraises the Army's perspectives and actions regarding combat in Quiché, expresses it as follows:

> The well-documented belief of the Army that the Ixil indigenous population is totally in favor of the EGP, has created a situation in which it is credible to believe that the Army will leave neither combatant nor non-combatant survivors.[16]

3254. This perception was shared by the local economic powers. This is how one plantation owner from the area puts it:

> The people were never my enemy, never, until four years ago when they started to be converted, that is, the same work that Mr. Payeras did with his command in the Ixcán jungles, the indoctrination of the Ixil Indians, who are difficult to convince, for better or for worse, very difficult because they are very square.[17]

3255. Members of the military high command during the period also made claims in the same vein:

> Because the guerrillas had totally won the Ixil Triangle, what is known as Nebaj, Chajul, and San Juan Cotzal.[18]

> The conception of the other villages was that those who were not with the guerrillas went to [the municipal seats of] Nebaj, Cotzal or Chajul. The rest were with the guerrillas.[19]

3256. The Army's analysis that the population of the Ixil area served as the guerrillas' social base, in terms of food, recruitment, and as a place of refuge for the guerrillas, was without a doubt the factor that unleashed the repression,[20] since one of the Army's strategic objectives was to deny guerrilla access to the population that constituted their support base.[21] However, such claims by the Army cannot be interpreted to mean that that the entire Maya Ixil population collaborated in an organized fashion with the guerrillas, and even less so that they were all combatants. In other words, the identification of the indigenous population as the insurgency's base can explain the reason for the killings, but in absolutely no way justifies the attacks against the civilian population.[22]

3257. After this identification, the entirety of the Ixil population was considered a subversive population. During the course of the military campaign, no distinction was made among its members. In other words, the Ixil became an objective because of their being Ixil, even though the motivations behind the killing and abuse may have been principally of a strategic-military nature.

3258. In this respect, a [1981] CIA document signals:

> During the battle it was impossible to differentiate between a member of the guerrilla and an innocent civilian, and according to ... the soldiers, they were forced to fire at anything that moved. Comment: the Guatemalan authorities admitted that many civilians were assassinated in Cocob; many of them were undoubtedly non-combatants. The repercussions of this incident will reflect negatively against the Army throughout the area. [23]

3259. This definition of the Ixil ethnic group as the enemy translated into the creation of a military operation against the Ixil population in 1981, named *Operation Ixil*. This military operation contemplated a specific strategy that took into account the socio-cultural characteristics of the Ixils and emphasized the importance of an "intense, profound, and well-studied psychological campaign that rescues the Ixil mentality until they've been made to feel themselves to be part of the Guatemalan nation."[24] This military operation proved to be part of a specific policy toward the Ixil people.

3260. The Army referred to the area as the Ixil Triangle. Thus, it used the denomination of the ethnic group to identify a combat area,[25] which military forces sealed off.

3261. In 1982, the Army also created the Gumarcaj Task Force, to operate principally within the Ixil area. They also formed a company composed exclusively of Ixil people.[26] The use of members of the group against their own people is analyzed further on as one of those actions aimed against the foundations of the group.

3262. The objective of *"annihilating the enemy"* and the identification of the Ixils as internal enemy led to the partial annihilation of the Ixil ethnic group. The local inhabitants remember how then-Minister of Defense put it during a trip he made to San Juan Cotzal:

> Yes he came here.... I knew he was the Minister of Defense. It was the 15th of July, 1981, he came to say to all the Ixils, if one soldier or two officials died, that he would demolish everything, he was preparing with 30 planes and eight helicopters, he said, so as to be done with these Indians.[27]

3263. Similar sentiments were expressed, according to an eyewitness, by a perpetrator of the Acul massacre:

> Look ... there in Acul, yesterday a bunch were killed, I mean, yesterday I killed them.... If it's necessary I'll finish off half the pueblo so that peace can come to Nebaj.[28]

3264. Finally, material expressions of Mayan identity such as traditional dress and language were converted into grounds for threats or abuse. In Guatemala, traditional dress expresses an intense identification with a specific ethnic group. Differentiated attire especially associates women with their communities of origin. In the area, Ixil women were identified and persecuted for use of their traditional attire as is demonstrated by the following testimonies:

> She and her family were able to work on the South Coast, but other people couldn't because they would be killed between Santa Cruz and Sacapulas. They would be killed when the soldiers recognized they were from Nebaj. In Patulul, Suchitepequez they would [also] kill people they identified as Ixiles by the way the women dressed. They were accused of being guerrillas. In order to survive she had to change her traditional dress to that of the K'iche.[29]

> There was a well where the women washed and left their clothes, then, when the Army saw the clothes hanging—their red color—then they began to shoot.[30]

> The witness lived in Río Azul when 60 soldiers from Cocob arrived and they destroyed the village. She went to Amachel, Chajul. Later, she went to Ixcán. She remembers that at that time she wore clothes that the people in Cobán use.[31]

3265. With regards to language, the CEH documented cases in which Ixiles traveled to neighboring communities to sell their wares and were executed upon being identified by their language.

He escaped and when he could look, he saw that the soldiers were beating the five of them—blood was coming out of the father's mouth.... They were captured because they spoke Ixil, all the Ixil were considered guerrillas.[32]

3266. In conclusion, at the beginning of the 1980s, the Army identified the Maya Ixil people with the insurgency and consequently with the internal enemy, without making a distinction among those who made up that group and their diverse personal opinions, or those who supported or opposed the guerrillas. Because of the Army's identification of them as a threat, actions were taken to partially annihilate the Maya Ixil people. The military campaign plans explained that there were three possible courses of action to follow with respect to the enemy: "elimination," "annihilation," or "extermination."[33]

Facts

3267. These three courses of action—"elimination," "annihilation" or "extermination" translated into a set of human rights violations against the Maya Ixil people. These events are described in the following section.

Killing Leaders

3268. From 1980 to 1983 the Army perpetrated acts of violence against community leaders, for example the extrajudicial killing of Felipe Itzep Tum and Máximo Alvarez Itzep, both in charge of the pro-land committee.[34] Formal authorities such as mayors and auxiliary mayors were attacked in a similar manner: one case was that of Felipe Raymundo, auxiliary mayor of the village of Xexetupil who was executed in 1980, when the Army burned the *auxiliatura* [central village office][35]

3269. Members of the Catholic Church were especially victimized. Such is the case of the disappearance of Francisco Santiago Pérez, director of the Nebaj Parish Board[36] and the extrajudicial killing of Juana Marcos, leader of the local *cofradía* [religious fraternity]. Juana Marcos was illegally detained and tortured. They found her partially buried, with signs of torture, with her breasts cut off and knife wounds on her neck and back.[37] The neighbors recall this persecution in the following way:

The Army began to assassinate religious people, to kidnap catechists. Several catechists were afraid of coming into town, even though they had military ID cards.[38]

3270. Traditional Maya authorities were also victims of the repression. The CEH documented seven cases of human rights violations against Mayan priests between 1980 and 1985.[39] One relevant case was the assassination of Sebastián Ramírez, who was burned along with his family in Chajul. There were six victims of that act, among them his children, a six-year-old girl and a five-year-old boy.[40]

3271. Such acts constitute a premeditated attack deliberately aimed at the leadership[41] and, though them, at the group itself. According to a key witness, at the inauguration of the Tzalbal development pole, an Army official told the residents:

> You have to tell me who the witch doctors are that perform their magic, because they have to be finished off; we don't want the witch doctors to perform rituals against the military.[42]

3272. One case that exemplifies the direct attack against the leadership was the Army's assassination of a Maya priest in Bajilá, Chajul in 1982. The people buried him after he was killed and then the Army disinterred the body so that dogs could eat it.[43] The actions against the leadership had an enormous effect on the community in that they materially and morally weakened traditional organizational and conflict resolution structures:

> Then the Army heard … that they coordinate among various families, that's why the Army began to control that too. That's how they cut relationships among families, that's when they destroyed traditions, the way of life … that existed among the people. Because people always knew how to defend themselves, how to provide justice for some problems; but the war started, the violence, that's where it was forgotten.[44]

3273. Without prejudice to the objective element of killings, the specific selection of community leaders as targets of repression reflects the intent to partially destroy the group, which is a subjective element of the crime of genocide.[45] As indicated, the leaders are those in charge of directing the group. When they are executed, the groups' organizational structures are destroyed. Their violent deaths effectively victimize the group, as such. This is especially true in the Ixil case, where religious authority coincides with political authority.

Massacres

3274. The CEH documented 32 massacres[46] between March 1980 and November 1982. To date, the sum of the cases documented by the CEH and other sources gives a total of 52 documented massacres. In Nebaj, Cotzal and Chajul, 88% of the population was Maya Ixil. However, 96% of the victims from the region belonged to this ethnic group.[47] This signifies that almost all of the victims from the region were Maya Ixil. One explanation for the increase in number of Maya Ixil victims with regard to the population distribution is that the violence in the region was not arbitrary. On the contrary, the Army's repressive acts were primarily directed against the Maya Ixil people. None of the massacres were directed against the *ladino* population. The persecution of *ladinos* in the Ixil area was selective.[48]

3275. Massacres are collective violations of the right to life in which elements of extreme cruelty generally take place. When publicly and repeatedly perpetrated, massacres are acts directed not only against the individuals, but against the community as a whole. In this specific case, directing the massacre exclusively against the Maya population constitutes not only a violent act, but a discriminatory one as well.

3276. The following is an analysis of the period of massacres from 1980 until 1983. In the Ixil area massacres continued until 1989, mostly against displaced populations. However, this exceeds the period set for the examination of acts of genocide.

3277. The CEH documented four massacres in 1980, two of which took place in the county seats of Nebaj and Chajul. The others were in the villages of Jua, Asich and Concab, and Río de San Juan Cotzal.

In 1981, 11 massacres were documented in three Ixil municipalities, distributed in the following manner:

Nebaj

Place	Date	Victims
1. Parramos	81	40
2. Xecax	2-81	18
3. Santa Marta	4-81	11-26
4. Aul	4-82	20
5. Cocob	4-81	70-90
6. Tuchanbuc	5-81	31
7. Xeucalbitz	9-81	35

Chajul

Place	Date	Victims
8. Chulutzé	1-81	25
9. Covadonga	3-81	16

Cotzal

Place	Date	Victims
10. Asich	5-81	12
11. San Francisco	5-81	35

3278. The greatest number of massacres documented by the CEH occurred in 1982: 15 of the total 32. These were concentrated between the months of February and May in three regions:

North of Nebaj and Chajul

Place	Date	Victims
1. Sacsihuán	2-1982	
2. Estrella Polar, Chajul	3-1982	96
3. Ilom, Chajul	3-1982	85
4. Covadonga, Chajul	3-1982	20-39
5. Chel, Chajul	3-1982	95
6. Amachel, Chajul	3-1982	9

Edge of the Three Municipalities

Place	Date	Victims
7. Pulay, Nebaj	2-1982	75-125
8. Pexla, Nebaj	2-1982	75-125
9. Xix, Chajul	2-1982	8-11
10. Xolcuay, Chajul	2-1982	89
11. La Laguna	11-1982	40

South East of San Juan Cotzal and Chajul

Place	Date	Victims
12. Parramos	81	40
13. Xecax	2-81	18
14. Santa Marta	4-81	11-26
15. Acul	4-81	20

Selective Massacres

3279. The CEH documented four massacres that took place in 1980, of which two took place in the Nebaj and Chajul county seats; and others in the villages of Jua, Asich and Concab, and Río de San Juan Cotzal. The first massacres were selective punitive actions against the population, in response to guerrilla actions.

3280. The Cotzal massacre of July 28, 1980 follows this pattern. According to testimonies, the guerrillas attacked the Cotzal military post at four in the morning. The Army "blamed the people" and at 10 in the morning, the same day, the soldiers took the men out of their houses and killed them. They executed 60 people.[49]

3281. In 1981 the security forces generally utilized a "signaler" or informant.[50] This person would indicate who should die and who would be saved. For example, one witness narrates what happened at the market one day in May of 1981, during the massacre of San Francisco Cotzal:

> The Army arrived dressed in civilian clothes and then lined up the people in the central plaza—women, men and children—and started asking for identification cards. Before that, they had accused the people of being guerrillas and a man who had his face covered appeared and began to signal. The commander gave the order to shoot anyone who tried to get away. Thirty-five people died in the massacre and the soldiers took away another 35.[51]

3282. The same thing happened in the community of Acul in April of 1982. The Army and the Nebaj civil patrol gathered all the people in the church, then selected and executed about 25 people. The process was very similar, as one witness narrates it:

> Then … the Army began to order the people one by one. They would say "is this the one?," and he would say "no," with just a nod, and he moved on pointing out the people…. Yes, he would say who was guilty, that is guilty, let's say, of being a

guerrilla. They'd call him to hell and the other to heaven; that is to say, two things had names, nothing else.... [52]

3283. This process continued during the first days of 1982, in the massacre, amongst others, of the village of Cajixaj, Cotzal, where the Army executed 22 people. In the massacre of the village of Ilom, Chajul on March 23, 1982, the Army and civil patrol gathered people in the plaza, selected 96 and killed them.

> After the 15th of January, 1982, the people had to settle in Cotzal because a message arrived from the Army saying that those who stayed here would be destroyed along with the entire village. So we had to settle all the way out near Cotzal and the Cajixaj village was abandoned. When we got to Cotzal, we went to the army post and there were other masked men there ... and they put us in line, and there they chose all the people.... What happened was that they counted everybody, one by one.... Then the masked man came and the officer tells him the signal to use and the masked man only makes a gesture, he doesn't talk; "then pass," says the officer, and another comes.... "And this one?" says the officer, "this one, yes," says the masked man. He only gestures, "please come over here," says the officer, then right there is where they formed two groups, one with those who were saved and the others who were left dead there.

3284. In the cases examined by the CEH in the Ixil area, massacres with "*signalers*" generally happened with a set sequence:

- The security forces would surround the community and gather the people in the central plaza or Church (military encirclement and concentration).
- The women, children and men would be separated (separation).
- One person with a ski mask would identify those who collaborated with the guerrillas; generally this person was from the community (selection).
- Prior to the execution biblical symbolism would be used, "Today is the day of your judgment," "We will separate those that will go to heaven from those who will go to hell."
- The people chosen would be publicly executed (killing).

3285. This sequence was repeated often. The CEH documented the same pattern in the Ixil area[53] in at least four cases. This makes it possible to affirm that it was an intentional and predetermined practice.

3286. Each of these events is evidence of the Army's decision to attack and fragment the group. The Army sought to prevent flight by separating family members, to divide the community by forcing some people to act against their neighbors, and to dissuade opposition by instilling a collective terror of a danger generally identified with something divine, like "going to heaven or to hell." These measures—kill and repress—were used to destroy community ties and fragment the group, as demonstrated by forcing the entire community to take part in barbaric acts.

3287. The identification of acts of extreme cruelty with sacred cultural elements such as religion or church[54] was designed to destroy important cultural symbols by relating them to punishment. This way, many individuals began to deny their own identity, because they began to associate elements of their identity with terror. Evidently, this provoked in many people a self-imposed denial of at least some aspects of their identity.

3288. With regard to the public executions, these had a double effect: the physical elimination of some members of the group; and the creation of collective terror, demonstrating the punishment that awaited dissidents and "demonizing" any type of collective demands.

Indiscriminate Massacres

3289. The majority of the massacres registered by the CEH occurred in 1982—15 of 32 massacres, with 952 victims total. These were concentrated during the months between February and May in three regions: Northern areas of Nebaj and Chajul, the area where the three municipalities join, and the southeast areas of Cotzal and Chajul. During this period, and especially in mid February 1982, the Guatemalan Army reinforced its presence in the Ixil area and "launched an operation to sweep the Ixil Triangle clean."[55] The Army undertook the operation with combat units that had to be mobilized from other areas in Quiché. There were two infantry battalions and an additional company of troops transported by air.[56]

3290. During these months, the most common pattern was indiscriminate massacre. Distinctions were no longer made between possible guerrilla collaborators, sympathizers, and the general population. The difference between this type of massacre and massacres with the "signaler" is that there was no process to select persons for execution. Indiscriminate massacres were directed against the entire community, rather than against individuals.

> Then what the population did was leave because the Army came killing. The Army did not ask you if you were organized [with the guerrillas]. It moved against everyone equally. He who deserved it and he who didn't, all had to suffer.[57]

3291. The massacres with "signalers" continued, but attacks against the entire community were more frequent. It is also important to clarify that prior to February 1982 indiscriminate massacres had already occurred in Cocob, April 1981, and Xeucalvitz, September 1981.[58] However, in this earlier period the process of victim selection was still prevalent.

3292. In the beginning, the sequence of indiscriminate massacres was similar to that of selective massacres. Security forces closed off the community and moved everyone to the center; they would separate the men from the women, perpetrate acts of torture, and gang rape the women. However, indiscriminate massacres culminated in an attack against anyone and everyone: men, women, children and elders.

3293. The Chel case illustrates the progressive increase in violent acts that began with selective repression, continued with displacement of the community, and culminated with general repression when the community returned. This triggered renewed displacement. The zenith of the violence was then reached, with massacres and destruction of property as part of scorched earth operations.[59]

3294. In some cases of generalized repression, all of the men found in a community were executed, as occurred in the massacre on the Estrella Polar plantation, Chajul, in March of 1982, when 96 men from the plantation and from the communities of Xaxmoxac and the Caracolio plantation were killed. The massacre at Estrella Polar is told as follows:

> On the 24th of March, 1982, a day after the massacre of the Ilom village, in the Estrella Polar plantation, members of the Army from the outpost at the La Perla plantation, members of the PAC from the same place and their commander arrived around four in the morning. They gathered the people for a meeting. The men were taken into the Catholic Church and executed. Orlando Tello sent the plantation workers from Covadonga to help remove the bodies from the church and bury them. The soldiers stayed for two days on the plantation and stole the animals and food. The soldiers went to bring people from the Caracolito plantation and Xaxmoxan village. One hundred and seventy-five men were executed. The interrogation of the men lasted about four hours. Some women and children were also killed, mostly the children. Two hundred and fifty people fled from the community. Of these, 25 died from disease and starvation. Eight days after the massacre in the Estrella Polar plantation, there was a massacre in Covadonga.[60]

3295. In other situations, the soldiers executed all the people they found in a place, as occurred in the Chel massacre in April of 1982,[61] when soldiers from the La Perla plantation outpost killed 95 people. Some were decapitated or dismembered and then decapitated by machete;

others died, shot in the chest or with a *tiro de gracia* [shot to the head]; and still others perished in bonfires lit to burn the clothes. Small children were killed, beaten against rocks or tossed alive into the river in the Chel massacre, April 1982.[62]

3296. The Army used a similar method in the village of Chisís in Cotzal,[63] where military and civil patrolmen executed around 200 people, among them 20 youth that formed part of the patrol.[64] A similar pattern emerged in the Cocob, Nebaj massacre which took place on Holy Thursday in April 1981, as the community was preparing the festivities. Members of the Army—"pure *kaibiles*" [special forces units]—executed between 70 and 90 people.[65] In this case the military authorities admitted to "having assassinated many civilians in Cocob."[66]

3297. A similar event occurred in Pexla, the village next to Cocob, when in February 1982, the Army executed 125 persons including women, elderly people, men and children.

> Hello, good-day, they would say, and then they shot all of the people in their houses, they even shot children, pregnant women, and others who were behind their houses … all of the people in Chisis…. They came here three times, because the first time they killed 16 families from a place over there before burning their houses. Sixteen families were left buried in a grave, there above the section of town called Bipulay. The second time they came looking to burn the houses and kill more families, they killed around 90 families when they burned the houses…. And the third time when we'd already been formed into patrols, they killed two of our families. They came three times.[67]

3298. In the village of Pexla, the Army didn't allow the corpses to be buried.[68] Similarly in the massacre in Chulutze, Xeputul in San Juan Cotzal, where they executed 25 people, the soldiers maintained watch over the dead and if any family member came to pick them up, they were captured.[69]

3299. In these cases it is clear that the actions were aimed against the foundations of the group. In Maya culture, as in many others, it is vital to give the dead a proper burial in order to close the cycle of life and death. Likewise, this disrespect for such profound beliefs was a form of dehumanizing the victims, since is believed that only animals can be left to die without a proper burial.

> Then the [traditional community] authority wants … to come to retrieve them, take them to the cemetery, to pray for them, because our custom is that when a family member dies … we use candles and leave them in the cemetery…. Those are our

ideas because that is our custom or our form of burying the dead, because we're not animals that can be left hidden somewhere.[70]

3300. In some villages the Army didn't succeed in exterminating the entire community because the population fled to the mountains. However, those that stayed were executed. Thus, in the village of Tuchabuc, Nebaj, members of the Army killed 31 people[71] and in the village of Xix, they killed 11 residents.[72] In the case of Tuchubuc, the killing was facilitated by air support with six helicopters bringing soldiers to attack the civilian population.[73]

3301. In other cases, after a first massacre, the surviving population fled and was persecuted until they were found and executed. One Ixil woman narrated her ordeal after the Chisís massacre, where soldiers executed around 200 people, her father among them:

My dad ... he died there. When I was in the mountains ... the next day the Army arrived, found the encampment where I was with my husband.... I had my children with me ... one of my children died there.... I left again and the soldiers arrived with the patrolmen.... Now, what do we do, I asked myself ... but my husband was already dead.[74]

3302.   The indiscriminate massacres were an aggression against entire villages. This mechanism of repression constituted an affirmation that the Ixil people, in their entirety, were in favor of the EGP. Actions were not taken against individuals, organized [with the guerrilla] or not. Attacks were against the group.

And then they told the old men that there would come a moment when we would have to come here because all of Acul is aligned with the guerrillas and that's the reason we're going to finish off everyone.[75]

3303. The collective label of *"subversive"* emerged. It did not matter what people did or did not do. They were considered the enemy for merely belonging to a particular group:

In the Cotzal Army post they spoke with the commander ... he responded that he would give them peace if they told which people were with the guerrillas, to which the community responded that they didn't know the guerrillas. The commander said that he knew who the guerrillas were in the village and brought out a person who said that all of those present were guerrillas, that in Xeputul, at birth they would change the baby's name to guerrilla.[76]

3304. The indiscriminate massacres constituted the greatest deployment of violence against a community, because everyone, boys, girls, women, men, and the elderly were classified as "subversive" and could consequently be exterminated. The senselessness of this reign of terror demonstrates that acts were directed against the group as a whole.

Scorched Earth Policies

3305. The CEH only recorded three massacres in which the locality was not burned. The rest of the villages where there were massacres were physically destroyed either during or after the massacre. Likewise, many villages where there were no massacres because the population fled, were burned to the ground or destroyed. In general, the period of indiscriminate or massive massacres (1981-1982) coincides with the physical destruction of communities. These violations of international human rights law and international humanitarian law, together formed part of the scorched earth operations.

3306. One of the aims of the scorched earth operations was to "clear" the area of its population. Those who were not killed were forcibly displaced to other regions, through terror. The guerrilla would thus be left without any chance to gather food. The campaigns plans included an express order to "destroy all collective farming endeavors held by subversives in areas where it has been absolutely proven that villages, which sympathize with subversives and are organized by them, are actively participating and cooperating with subversives."[77]

3307. However, the intent went further than the metaphorical objective expressed in the phrase "drain the water to kill the fish." Once the goal of vacating areas was achieved, the population continued to be persecuted even in their places of refuge, where they suffered renewed massacres and destruction of their crops. In other words, the acts of destruction and persecution denoted and connoted an intent to exterminate.[78]

3308. According to the data registered by the CEH, the scorched earth campaigns consisted of destroying houses, burning cornfields, killing domestic animals, and destroying farm tools, clothes and millstones. A resident of the village of Ilom, Chajul clearly explains:

> After the massacre the lieutenant said: Bury your parents because at three this afternoon we're going to burn all of your houses…. So they burned all the houses, they burned all of our blankets, our beds, our floor mats, our machetes, our axes, our hats, our millstones, our corn, our coffee, our beans….[79]

3309. The scorched earth operations were carried out both in communities of origin and in those places where people had fled. This is how residents of the Cabá I village explain it:

> There are places that are dry ... principally on the edge of Chel.... When it was the dry season, the Army burned it down, and it wasn't so much people that were burned, but principally the things they carried, clothes, millstones. They would leave their things behind due to fear of the Army, and well, they would burn everything.[80]

3310. According to information collected by the CEH, the scorched earth operations carried out by the Army between 1980 and 1983 provoked the total or partial destruction of approximately 90 villages distributed in the following manner:

Nebaj	54
Costal	10
Chajul	26
Total	*90*

3311. The CEH could not reconstruct the exact number of communities that existed prior to the violence, but considers that between 70 and 90% of the communities from the Ixil area were razed.[81]
The razed communities were:[82]

Chajul

Xix Xolcuay Batzal	Ilom Xesaí Chel	Amachel	Cajchixlá
Chacalté	Xachimoxán Estrella	Cabá Pal	Bitzich
Bitziquichum Juá	Polar Covadonga	Cimientos	Xeputul Putul
Sotzil	Xejuyeb. Santa Clara	Ti'aj'a Tzotzil	Xaxboj

Nebaj

Xebitz	Xexuxcab	Salquil Parramos	Suamal Grande	Talsumnalá
Cocob	Xexocom	Grande Parramos	Xeucalbitz	Xesumal
Pexlá	Chortiz Xecocó	Chiquito Tujolom	Trapichito	K'osonip
Pulay Río	Janlay Tzalbal	Xeo Palop Bijolom	Vilakam.	Bipecpalam
Azul	Xoloché	Vicampanavitz	Laguna	Viramux
Xencuá	Tuchanbuc	Bicamalá Sumalito	Batzchocolá	Bipaná kanakil
Jacaná	Basuquil	Batzumal	Viucalvitz	Xepeum Bitz
Bictoz	Canaquil	Marta	Ixtupil	Piucual Pajilá
Cotzol	Xeipum		Sacsihuán Santa	
Vivitz.	Acul			

San Juan Cotzal

Asich Namá Cajixaj Chisis Quisis	Villa Hortensia San Felipe Chenla Chichel Xeputul San Marcos Cunlá

3312. When communities had managed to recover, the Army would attack them again, destroying their homes and their food to keep them from surviving. In some places the Army returned up to three times to burn houses and farms, as the Xoloche community explains it:

> How many times did they burn? The first time was 1981; in 1982, they returned to burn our house, just like this wooden house with roof tiles, a good house.... In 1983 we built our house, but they burned it again, when we returned again, we made small huts, very small ones.... We heard when they would come and we hid outside. When we came back our houses were gone, they burned them and we rebuilt them again because if not where else are we going to live ... ?[83]

Forced Displacement

3313. In order to survive, the population often fled from attacks. Many communities established a surveillance system so that they could flee in case the Army came close. The population knew of massacres taking place in neighboring communities. Given the news of the encroaching Army, they would seek refuge in the mountains. At first they hid nearby and returned when the Army had left.

3314. After villages were leveled, many communities totally abandoned their places of origin because they had no place left to return to. The Army had burned their homes and all of their belongings. [They fled to refuge areas instead.] The CEH identified five areas with high numbers of refugees: Sumal Grande, Nebaj, Amachel, Chajul and Xeputul, San Juan Cotzal.

3315. A study done by AVANSCO indicates that between 1985 and 1991, there was a stream of approximately 14,501 displaced persons who returned to the municipalities of Cotzal, Nebaj and Chajul. Some were forced to return after having been captured in Army sweeps, and others came back voluntarily. On top of this, the same source cites the statement by a high placed staff member at the Ministry of Development who claimed that even in 1989 as many as 10,000 persons remained in hiding in mountains of the Ixil area. The total estimate of internally displaced persons hovers around no less then 24,000 persons [in the Ixil area alone].[84]

3316. During this period, the population did not have the option to flee or not. When the Army found empty houses they would accuse local people of being guerrillas,[85] and if they found them they would kill them.[86] Under this logic, there was no possible form of salvation for the inhabitants of the region. No matter what the non-combatant civilian population's behavior, they would still be executed. The communities of Chichel[87] and Ojo de Agua,[88] from Cotzal, and Pulay and Sumal I, from Nebaj explain it as such:

> And also when the Army passed, what they would do, if they found someone ... was burn them along with the house and that's how they would die—burnt to a crisp.... There was no leeway for things to be left tranquil. Just everything had to be destroyed. All of the houses that were found empty were also burned and that's exactly why we were afraid and we had to get out and hide and then whoever didn't make it out simply waited to die.[89]

3317. During displacement, people died from hunger, cold or illness due to the harsh conditions of the displacement: the Army had burned their homes and all sources of food. Also, the Army hunted down the populations that fled, and during that period continued to massacre not only the displaced but also those who turned themselves into the Army. For example, in Cajixaj the Army executed ten families that returned after having fled to the mountain,[90] and in Tuy Coral Cay, they killed a group of people that had turned themselves in because they were hungry.

> In the beginning the Army began to burn some houses with everything in them, and the granaries where the corn was kept.... Maybe it would be better if we went to the Army, because we can find food there and if they kill us, they kill us; what to do, but at least we won't die of hunger, the people would say ... [they turned themselves in] when the Army was pissed off.... "Oh! Good you all came in," was all the officer said; the Army took them, tortured and shot them, that's where they killed a group in Tzalbal because they gave up, they turned themselves in because they were hungry.[91]

3318. The Army hunted the populations in the mountains. The CEH documented cases of persecution during the displacement to the Guacamayas Mountains,[92] San Juan Cotzal, Xesai, Chajul and the hills in Sumal, Nebaj. For example, after the Chel massacre, April 4, 1982, survivors sought refuge in the Xesaí Mountains. On April 22, after a sweep through Cheputul, Cotzal and Caba, in Chajul, troops from the Chajul detachment, accompanied by patrolmen from this same community arrived at the place of refuge near Chesai. At around 5 in the afternoon they surrounded the place where 50 people from Chel were hidden, including children, women, men and the elderly. The soldiers opened fire against the population, killing 45 of them—a defenseless civilian population.

Two persons survived the attack and three disappeared. The following day, people who had sought refuge with the guerrillas near Chel found 45 bodies that had multiple gunshot wounds on their bodies. They buried them in the same place where the tragedy occurred.[93]

3319. In another case, in March 1983, soldiers from the provisional outpost in the Sumal Hills found some people hidden in the mountains surrounding the village. They captured eight or ten people and they burned them in a bonfire.[94]

3320. The Army also hunted people from the recently rebuilt communities. That is what happened in Cotzol Village, where members of the Tzalbal detachment passed through the villages of Vipecbalam and Xeo, and later Cotzol, assassinated ten persons and leveled the new wooden and straw structures that the inhabitants had built after the last time that the Army had burned their houses. The victims were women, men and children. One girl, a daughter of one of the victims, was able to survive by pretending to be dead and lying on top of her assassinated mother.[95]

3321. A similar event occurred in Xeuvicalvitz, Nebaj, where the Army waited until the community came back from the mountains:

> On the morning of May 29, 1984, those in charge of surveillance blew the cowhorns: that was the signal that the Army was approaching. Then, a group of 100 soldiers from the Sumalito detachment arrived in Xeuvicalvitz, a village of Nebaj, and finding no one there, set up camp.

> The Army set a trap; in the afternoon they left the encampment, but there was a group that stayed hidden behind a hill. A group of 27 people came down to the village, believing that the Army had left. Everyone sought refuge in one house, because they wanted to make some food and warm themselves. It was 6:30 in the afternoon. The soldiers arrived at the village and killed 25 people inside the house, they shot them.[96]

3322. Likewise, the hunted populations were bombed during their displacement, as happened in Biclamá,[97] Sumal I,[98] Xecotz,[99] Tzalbal,[100] Xexucap,[101] and Acul,[102] all villages in Nebaj. Similarly, in Chajul, from 1982–1983 the villages of Santa Rosa,[103] Xaxboj,[104] Xeputul,[105] Santa Clara,[106] Cabá,[107] and Xaxmoxam[108] were bombed.

3323. The Army's actions all signify their intent to persecute, as does its creation of conditions that led to the population's dying of starvation, cold, thirst, and illness. They killed populations during their displacement, forcing the survivors to distance themselves more and more each time from their homelands, increasing their vulnerability, and increasing the possibilities that they would die.[109] The displacement and systematic persecution, as a part of a military campaign against the population that fled from the attacks, and the ensuing mass killings, are further evidence of the intent to destroy the group, at least partially.

Militarized Resettlement

3324. Beginning in 1983, the Army took measures to control the surviving displaced persons. These people, whether they turned themselves in or were captured by military units, were taken to the nearest military detachments or advance posts for undetermined periods of time, generally for up to two months. During their stay in military bases, they were victims of torture and cruel treatment, and some were obliged to participate in Army dragnet operations to guide the soldiers to places of refuge and point out people who collaborated with the guerrillas, some of whom were executed.

3325. In the following testimony, an Ixil woman who surrendered to the Army along with her family in December of 1982 recounts her experience:

> The population stayed in little huts around a fire in a corner of the detachment grounds.... The women from the group had to prepare food for the soldiers. One day three women had their shift ... the soldiers called one of them ... they blindfolded her, shoved a rag in her mouth so she couldn't scream and between two or three of them, they raped her.[110]

3326. The most common method of torture was to place people in a hole in the ground about one square meter, where they would be "punished" for days, without food or water. The purpose was to obtain a confession about their possible participation in guerrilla activities or to set an example to dissuade any opposition to the military occupation.

> So [in 1983] they began to say that I was a guerrilla, the Army repeatedly accused me and the Army would call me over and over and over again, and one day they left us for three days and three nights in the hole, there were 29 of us, because I was the head of a group of patrolmen, they put us in there ... without food, without water, without anything.[111]

3327. Beyond the torture, the population was "purged" by the military authorities, who selected those who could leave and resettle in their original communities or in the model villages and those who had to be executed.

When they come again, they come to cut down the crops again, our will fades, and we go to the town, we present ourselves to them, but when we do, they punished us. Me, well, when I turned myself in, they punished me, they grabbed me, beat me, but the clarification that I gave was that that's how it was, and my life was spared. Those that didn't clarify their position were killed. I saw it when I presented myself in Salquil, three, four people hung below a roof like this one, who knows what crime they'd done, and they got them, strung them up, hung them a while, they died.[112]

3328. After spending time in military bases, some members of the population were permitted to return to their place of origin or resettled in model villages. Resettlement patterns broke traditional community structures, in which homes were widely dispersed, now forcing them to concentrate in a reduced space and in unhealthy conditions. As one survivor recalls, it was "the same as keeping animals."[113]

3329. The concentration of the population in one determined place was a mechanism designed primarily for the Maya population. As one of its designers explains, it was nothing new, the idea comes from the "the reduction of the Indians" from the period of the Spanish conquest:

According to the interviewee, the pattern of concentrated settlements is nothing new to indigenous cultures. His argument is that when he began to think about how the development centers would be constructed ... he began to read about the Mayas, about how they had been "organized." ... [Before the conquest] they lived in a dispersed manner.... "When the Spanish conquered us, you know they lived like feudal lords." What they did then was reconstruct here what they had in Spain ... asking them (the indigenous peoples) to group together was not a resolution against their culture or their interests. We were building them an organized city.[114]

3330. Upon returning to their villages, the population, under military control, continued to suffer human rights violations. In Viculxcul, in February 1983, four people were detained by the Army and tortured. After that, they were thrown in the river and two survived. The daughter of one of the victims was also detained and gang-raped by eight soldiers.[115] Similarly, Santiago Pérez and his family turned themselves in to the Army in Xoloché, Nebaj. There, they tortured and interrogated Santiago Pérez, asking about his relation to the guerrillas. After that he was executed.[116]

3331. In 1984 in the community of Tuchabuc, one person returned to live in his community; he was planting corn when 30 soldiers from Parramos, Nebaj showed up. They captured his wife and took her to a hill near the village along with two other women. The soldiers raped the wife, shot and killed her, and left her nude and partially buried.[117]

3332. In this way, during the resettlement, the population continued to suffer human rights violations, which shows a pattern of sustained action against the Maya Ixil.

Acts against the Foundations of the Group

3333. What follows is an analysis of the acts investigated that, in the opinion of the CEH, were intentionally carried against the foundations of the group. These include attacks against vulnerable people, torture, rape, and the destruction of physical and spiritual elements of the culture.

Mass Killings of Especially Vulnerable Civilian Population

3334. During indiscriminate massacres carried out in the Ixil area, the Army victimized the most vulnerable members of the community, especially children and the elderly. In at least eight massacres in 1982, children were executed. The acts against children were deliberate; there was even a special technique for attacking them:

> Children of nursing age were killed by throwing them against the floor or walls.[118]

3335. These were deliberate acts directed towards the killing of absolutely defenseless beings such as children. Such acts could not result in any military advantage. A newborn baby cannot be a combatant or guerrilla collaborator.

> Ah, lots of people died, since '82, many people, there were massacres, everything, there were women who had just given birth, they were burned, children, too, were burned. And the mother that had just given birth, how could the baby possibly be to blame; that was the hardest time, the hardest.[119]

Torture

3336. In some of these cases, the community was forced to witness and participate in executions. This is how it is explained in the collective interview with the Salquil community:

> I gathered everyone up and I went running to the village, I rang the bell and everyone gathered ... the official sat down with the three people there and said.... "What do you want with those men, why are you collaborating with the guerrillas ... Look, boys, if you want peace, you yourselves will have to hang these people" ... that's how they were hung.[120]

3337. The same pattern was followed in Chisis, where soldiers called the population to the municipal seat of Cotzal, where they selected four people and executed them.[121] In the massacre in Acul, the Army ordered the *principales* to take their children and nieces and nephews to the cemetery where they would be killed: "The men from heaven have to take the men from hell."[122]

3338. The act of forcing someone to witness the execution of another or of forcing someone to execute another constitutes egregious psychological torture. Leaving corpses with signs of torture in public view was also a form of psychological torture used in this period, such as in the massacre of Covadonga, Chajul, April 5, 1982:

> When the Army, along with members of the PAC [Civil Defense Patrol squads], locked up about 40 people inside the church and the courthouse, they tortured and killed them.... In the aisle of the church they cut off two people's testicles with machetes and cut their heads off into pieces.[123]

3339. The purpose of this exemplary punishment was to prevent any form of dissent. Beyond just individual torture, these "collective tortures" sought to break the identity of the group, morally weakening them through terror, and to disarticulate their organization.

> We were digging the hole, we didn't think that we would get out alive. We were scared, we no longer had any strength. The people remained scared, fearful.[124]

3340. Another form of collective torture consisted in forcing some members of the group to act against their neighbors. For example, in the massacre of the village of Ilóm, Chajul, after separating the men from the women and children, the soldiers:

> Grabbed three people and said to them: "Go, show the people that are with the guerrillas," they said to two people from the same community. One of them said: "I don't know, I can't tell anything because I don't know anything; I don't know who's involved with the guerrillas and who's not.... Then, the soldiers said to him: "If you're not going to point out the people, then we're going to kill you," and they killed him. The other two people said: "Fine, we'll show you, but only if you don't kill us, and that's when they started to point them out...."[125]

3341. Forcing members of the community to point out suspected guerrilla collaborators was designed to make neighbors participants in acts of horror committed against their own people.[126] In this sense, the foundations of the group were affected in two ways. On the one hand, it became impossible to trust in others, because anyone could become an accuser, and on the other, the accusers themselves became victimizers, closing off any chance of integration into their community.

3342. The Army tactic of turning members of the community against their own group was also used when the Army created a military unit comprised solely of Ixils, known as Tchakaben. The young men who belonged to the unit were used to find the populations that fled to the mountains.[127]

Sexual Violence

3343. When the Army moved into the area in 1980, rape became a common practice:

> Then, control over people tightened, right; they would not let farm animals in anymore; they began to rape women when they would go to pray in the church. There was a lot of ... control.[128]

3344. During the massacres in the Ixil area, women were also raped. During the massacre of Chel, Chajul, soldiers selected 14 adolescent girls and took them to the church, where they raped them for over an hour.[129] A similar process occurred during the massacre of Pexlá,[130] a village in Nebaj, and in Xix, Chajul.[131]

3345. When mass repression began, rape also became acts of collective violence. The practice of collective rape became yet another step in the Army's pattern of operations, prior to the mass killings. The CEH documented rape against women in at least four massacres.

3346. Rape constitutes serious bodily and mental harm to the integrity of members of the group.[132] It constitutes bodily harm to integrity because it can irreversibly damage female reproductive organs, especially in the case of girls and adolescents. Regarding mental harm, it generates the material and psychological isolation of the women who were raped, within their own communities, stigmatizing them and barring them from forming new relationships and, along with that, new families.

> When the soldiers let her go, she went to her hut and told her husband what had happened. He was angry because it had been her idea to turn themselves in to the Army. When he found out about the rape he threatened to leave her and go to the mountains.[133]

3347. Rape committed in public and on a massive scale generates terror. Beyond this, the neighboring communities perceive the degree of horror that unfolds during the massacres, which is one of the causes of their own displacement.

3348. Rapes produce a profound symbolic effect on the community given that in Maya culture women are not simply biological reproducers. As transmitters of cultural values to the new generations, they perform a fundamental function for the group's social reproduction. If the women are affected, the community as a whole is deeply shaken.

3349. Finally, when carried out in public and en masse, rape, as a form of violence directed specifically against women, is an indicator of intent to exterminate the group.

3350. One study, by George Lowell, explains a gap among the demographic projections estimated by the National Statistics Institute's 1981 census and the region's health center. Focusing on the period between 1984 and 1987, it is estimated that the difference between the projected population and the actual registered population is about 50,000 people. The author believes that one of the reasons for this gap was the effect of counterinsurgency policies on Ixil female fertility.[134]

3351. In a similar study, David Stoll explains that this gap could be as large as 30,000 people. The disproportion between one study and another is probably linked to the large number of displaced persons living in total anonymity; but in any case, both studies consider the armed conflict the principle cause of this reduction of the population.[135]

Destruction of Material and Spiritual Aspects of Culture

3352. The persecution of priests or spiritual guides was particularly important in the Ixil area where, as indicated, seven Mayan priests were victims of selective repression from 1980 to 1985. One of the explanations given by the population for this attack was that the "Maya priests were persecuted because it was thought that they intervened spiritually on behalf of the guerrillas."[136]

3353. Besides attacking Maya religious leaders, the Army destroyed their sacred sites. As in Nebaj:

> In the village of Cotzol, the soldiers dug trenches in the place where the Mayan ceremonies were held; the soldiers had orders to assassinate whoever they found.... The village was razed, they burned everything: homes, clothes, dead people and animals.[137]

3354. Similarly, the Army bombed the Juil mountains where the sacred mountain of the Ixils is located, forcing the cessation of Maya rituals.[138] The Army knew that Juil is a sacred place for the Ixils, since it appears specifically in their military analysis, "Appraisal of Civilian Affairs G-5, for the Ixil area": "The Ixil region is a mix of Christianity and ancestral Maya beliefs. They carry out their rites in the sacred mount of Juil."[139]

3355. The Army occupied Maya religious centers with military outposts, just as it had Catholic churches. One witness remembers the presence of Tzalbal military outposts in the sacred place called Bitzach.[140]

3356. During the reconstruction period, the Army built model villages, destroying Mayan ruins. For example, when they began to rebuild Salquil Grande, they built the main road over an ancient Mayan ruin. These acts destroyed physical expressions of identity and are another serious indication of the intent to affect the group, as such.

Conclusions

3357. In the judgment of the CEH, the combination of violent actions perpetrated by the State against the Maya Ixil population during the period of 1980-1983 permits the conclusion that acts of genocide were committed. These acts were inspired by a strategic analysis that also was of a genocidal nature, in that one objective of the military counterinsurgency campaign was the partial destruction of the victim group, by which means they considered that the enemy would be defeated.

3358. The State adopted this analysis based on its conclusion that the Maya Ixil population had a historic propensity to subversion and that they did or could serve as a base of support for the guerrilla movement in this region. This perception equated the identity of the entire Maya Ixil population with the guerrilla and led, during a period of the confrontation, to a campaign oriented towards the partial destruction of the Maya Ixil population in conditions of total defenselessness. The principle motivation of State strategists [in crafting such a campaign] was that the destruction of these groups would translate into the defeat of the guerrillas.

3359. The intent with which these acts of violence were perpetrated is made clear both by their repeated nature, as well as by the determination of the will to exterminate, manifest in official declarations with respect to the nature of the Maya Ixil population. By associating ethnic groups with the guerrilla enemy, in various regions and during a specific period, genocidal methods were used to combat [that enemy], methods without parallel in other Latin American countries, according to information gathered by the CEH.

3360. The sequence, repetition, and massive scale of the brutal acts perpetrated collectively against the members of this ethnic group provide evidence of a pattern of aggression characteristic of genocidal acts. In one period, the Army publicly and selectively targeted religious and community leaders, thus ripping from the hearts of these communities, the basis of their social, political, and religious organization. Later, mass killings committed against entire villages—including women, children and the elderly—were perpetrated after torture and rape, which also helped destroy the fundamental elements of social cohesion among survivors. Additional evidence of this pattern is found in the persecution, capture, killings, bombings and continued aggression against displaced populations; and in the use of executions or serious violence against those who did not flee or who turned themselves into the Army because of hunger, desperation, or to claim amnesty. The systematic persecution that characterizes this period left the Ixil population without a safe haven to save their lives.

3361. The results of this military campaign include the assassination of at least 6,986 people, among them women, the elderly and children. Almost 98% of those killed were Ixiles and 14.5% of the indigenous population[141] suffered grave violations of human rights including torture, rape and forced disappearance. Along with mass killings and other acts that caused grave damage to the physical and mental integrity of the group, the Army razed at least 70% of the communities in the Ixil area, at times accompanying these actions with the occupation or destruction of sacred Mayan sites. This violence displaced more than 60% of the population, which was subjected to conditions conducive to death by starvation, cold, or sickness.

Notes

1.   Witness (high level active-duty official from the Guatemalan Military) CEH.
2.   PRODERE-UNOPS (Program for Displaced People, Refugees and Returnees in Central America), *Executive Summary of the PRODERE Guatemala sub-program final report*, 1995.
3.   The 1981 census carried out by the National Statistics Institute put the population in the area at 44,791 inhabitants, of which 87% were Maya Ixil. However, these

figures have very low reliability because the census was done during the worst period of the internal armed conflict. For this reason, a new population estimate of 48,096 people has been calculated for the Ixil region in 1979, based on data from the 1973 and 1981 censuses. The figure increases in the estimates done by military sources in 1981, which considered the Ixil to number about 50,000 inhabitants and to constitute 92% of the regional population. Ejército de Guatemala, *Apreciación de asuntos civiles (G-5) para el área Ixil* [Appraisal of Civil Affairs (G-5) for the Ixil Region], p. 33.

4.   Ibid, p. 33.

5.   The National Statistics Institute census distinguishes only between indigenous and non-indigenous. In the Ixil area, only these two population groups are differentiated, even though other Mayan groups live in the region, such as Ki'che's, Q'eqchi's y Q'anjobales. Thus, Ki'che's reside in the villages of Chortiz, Xexocom and Chanchoc, located in the southern part of Nebaj and adjacent to Aguacatán. In the northwest of Nebaj, the villages of Xexán, Buena Vista, a part of Pilas and Santa Marta, are inhabited by Q'anjobales. K'iche's reside in Chajul, in the villages of Xolcuaj, El Carrisal, Chupoy and Membrillán I, as well as in the village of San Marcos Cumlá, Ojo de Agua, Chenlá and Quinimaquin de Cotzal. In this regard, see Narciso Cojtí Macario, *El Idioma Ixil*, collection in "Conozcamos Guatemala," *Prensa Libre,* September, 1995.

6.   Ejército de Guatemala, *Apreciación de asuntos civiles (G-5) para el área ixil,* p.34.

7.   Ibid., p.34. The characterization of the Ixil as hostile to the Armed Forces of Guatemala is also found in the CIA document that states with regard to the Ixil: "Indigenous people that have been historically hostile to the Armed Forces of Guatemala." Declassified USA document, Central Intelligence Agency, G5-41, P12.41, February 1982, p. 3. Released February 1998.

8.   Ibid., p. 36.

9.   Ibid., p. 37.

10.   CEH Witness. (T.C. 321).

11.   CEH Witness (teacher and linguistic promoter from Nebaj). (T.C. 334).

12.   CEH Witness (Catholic Priest). (T.C. 336).

13.   CEH Witness (authorities from Santa Clara-CPR, Chajul). (T.C.337).

14.   Ejército de Guatemala. "Una Solución a la Operación Ixil. Plan de AACC Operación Ixil." *Revista Militar*, September-December 1982, p. 55.

15.   CEH Collective Testimony, from Pexla Grande, Nebaj, where there was a massacre of between 75 and 125 victims. February 1982. (T.C.335).

16.   Declassified document from the USA, Central Intelligence Agency, G5-41, P12.41, 1982, p. 3. Released February 1998.

17.   CEH Witness (farm owner from Ixil area). (T.C. 16).

18.   CEH Witness (retired military). (T.C. 24).

19.   CEH Witness (retired military). (T.C. 92).

20.   The *Manual of Counter-subversive War* indicates: "you must always take into account that the fundamental objective is to isolate the guerrilla forces from the population." Centro de Estudios Militares del Ejército de Guatemala [Center for Military Studies], 1982, p.138.

21.   This is how the campaign plan *Victoria 82* expresses it: "Increase the Armed Forces of Guatemala particularly in the conflict areas, in addition to relying on support from the Civil Defense units, in order to deny the subversives access to the population that constitutes its social base...." Ejército de Guatemala. *Plan de Campaña 'Victoria 82,'* Apartado C.

22.   In a similar sense, the judgment of the International Criminal Tribunal for Rwanda in its first genocide sentence: "Either way, the fact that the genocide occurred

while the RAF was in conflict with the RPF obviously can not serve as an extenuating circumstance for genocide." Chamber I, International Criminal Tribunal for Rwanda, *Case No. ICTR-96-4-T, The Prosecutor Versus Jean-Paul Akayesu;* September 2 1998, par. 127.

23.   Declassified document from the USA, Central Intelligence Agency, G5-40, P.12.40, April, 1981, p. 2. Released February, 1998.

24.   Ejército de Guatemala. *Apreciación de asuntos civiles (G-5) para el área Ixil* [Armed Forces of Guatemala, *Appraisal of civil affairs (G-5) for the Ixil area*], p. 32 ff.

25.   Ejército de Guatemala. *Plan de Campaña "Victoria 82"* [Armed Forces of Guatemala, campaign plan *Victory 82*], annex D, VI, L.

26.   According to a high-ranking military officer, "there were companies that were composed of personnel from there. There was a company of 166 men, all of whom were Ixil." CEH Witness (retired military). (T.C. 92).

27.   Collective interview with the Community of San Marcos, San Juan Cotzal. This statement was confirmed by the CEH Witness (retired military) (T.C. 24).

28.   CEH Witness (teacher and linguistic promoter from Nebaj). (T.C. 334). CI 107. The massacre of the Acul community, April 1982.

29.   C 3161. 1987. Nebaj, Patulul, Suchitepéquez.

30.   REMHI Witness. (T.4613).

31.   C 3064. December, 1982, Chajul, Quiché.

32.   C 3649.1980. Chiantla, Huehuetenango.

33.   See the campaign plans where terms such as: "Eliminate the Permanent Military units," "Annihilate the Local Clandestine Committees," "Exterminate the enemy," "The mission is to annihilate the guerrilla and parallel organizations," are used that suggest the possibility of massive action. Guatemala Armed Forces of Guatemala, *Plan de Campaña "Victoria 82,"* Annex H, sections B and G.

34.   C 3615, February 1982, San Juan Cotzal, Quiché.

35.   C 3108. 1980. Nebaj, Quiché.

36.   C 3019. 1983. Nebaj, Quiché.

37.   C 3047. April, 1980. Nebaj, Quiché.

38.   CEH Witness (Community interview with authorities from Santa Clara, Chajul). In a similar fashion, two witnesses recall that in 1980 in Nebaj there was a strong persecution of teachers and community promoters: on April 28, 1980 Noé Cam Palacios López and Mario Enrique Herrera Cano, teachers from the Tzalbal school, were savagely tortured and assassinated. CEH Witness (teacher and linguistic promoter in Nebaj). (T.C.334).

39.   C 3751. April, 1985. Nebaj, Quiché.

40.   C 3272. September, 1980. Chajul, Quiché.

41.   The *Manual of Counter-subversive War* explains how one strategy of a countersubversive war is directed against "the leaders, who as a consequence, are key elements. Arresting them or restricting their access to the people ... can perhaps impede the development of the subversion." Centro de Estudios Militares. *Manual de guerra contrasubversiva,* [Center for Military Studies, *The Manual of Counter-subversive War*], 1982, p. 74.

42.   CEH Witness (Ixil administrator). (T.C. 338).

43.   C 3848. 1982. Nebaj, Quiché.

44.   Collective Testimony, Bicalamá, Nebaj, Quiché (T.C.287).

45.   In this sense, see the prosecutor's argument in the preparation of the trial for the Kovacevic case, *Prosecutor's Pre-Trial Brief,* 20 April 1998, Milan Kovacevic Case No. IT-97-24-PT, para. 3 and 22.

46.   CEH database

47. ibid.
48. Likewise, in some places the *ladinos* were the first to leave, for example CI 60. April, 1982. Chajul, Quiché.
49. C 3129 and C 15235. July, 1980. San Juan Cotzal, Quiché.
50. The *señalador* (signaler) was a person who collaborated with the Armed Forces of Guatemala, either voluntarily or by force, to indicate who were the guerrilla sympathizers.
51. C 3141. Mayo, 1981. San Francisco Cotzal, Quiché.
52. CEH community testimony, Nebaj, Quich'e. (T.C. 339). CI 107. Acul, Nebaj, April 1982.
53. A similar process was followed in other parts of the country, for example in Zacualpa, Quiché, in Rabinal, Baja Verapaz, and in Chimeltenango where they had lists of people.
54. There is a high degree of syncretism between the Maya and Catholic religions.
55. USA declassified document, CIA, G5-41 P 12.41, February 1982, p.3. Released February 1998.
56. Ibid.
57. CEH Collective testimony. (T.C.341).
58. CEH Collective Testimony, from the Xeucalvitz community, the massacre occurred in 1985, however other sources claim it took place in September 1981. (T.C. 342).
59. CI 60, April 1982, Chel, Chajul, Quiché.
60. C 3082 and C 3452. March, 1982. Chajul, Quiché.
61. CI 60. The Chel community massacre, Chajul, April 1982.
62. Fundación de Antropología Forense de Guatemala [Guatemala Forensic Anthropology Foundation], report for the CEH, Guatemala, 1998.
63. CI 92. The massacre of the village of Chisís, February 1982.
64. CEH Collective Testimony from the Chisís community, San Juan Cotzal, Quiché. (T.C.324).
65. According to the community's collective interview, the Armed Forces of Guatemala entered "shooting and knocked down houses that they leveled with sticks and there are women and children that were left covered in soot and couldn't be recognized; that's what they did." C 16704, Cocob massacre, April 1981. In the Nebaj civil registry there are 65 deaths: 34 were children, five adolescents, 23 adults and two elderly people. Fundación de Antropología Forense de Guatemala [Guatemala Forensic Anthropology Foundation], report for the CEH, Guatemala, 1998, p. 51.
66. USA Declassified CIA document, G5-40, P12.40, April, 1981, p. 2. Released February 1998.
67. C 3318. February 1982. Nebaj, Quiché. CEH Collective Testimony from Pexla Grande, Nebaj, Quiché. (T.C. 335) and C 3318, February 1982, Nebaj, Quiché.
68. One witness explained during the community interview: "Then we went to bury them, but hidden, and with fear, because they say that the Armed Forces of Guatemala is going to return again, because if they see someone who comes to pick up those damned people, then we're going to finish them off, they would say and so then we came fearful and quickly, we came to bury them in the cemetery and then we left." CEH Collective Testimony from Nebaj, Quiché (T.C.335).
69. The case is of a massacre of a displaced population from various villages. The dates situate it as January 1981, however having been a displaced population it could have occurred in 1982. C 3293. February 1981. Chajul, Quiché.
70. CEH Collective Testimony with authorities from Pexla Grande, Nebaj, Quiché. (T.C. 335).

71. These groups had stayed in the community because they trusted that the Armed Forces of Guatemala wouldn't harm them as one testimony explains: "those that were Evangelicals said that since we were praying to God the soldiers wouldn't kill us, they said. But when the soldiers arrived they burned them there in the church. They killed 31 people." CEH Collective Testimony from the community of Tuchabuc, Nebaj, Quiché. (T.C. 343). The massacre occurred between May 1981 and April 1982.

72. The massacre was carried out in February 1982; the majority of the community had fled to the ravine, but "some didn't want to leave because they didn't want to die of hunger ... then the soldiers went from house to house and where they found someone they would kill them." CEH Collective Testimony of community authorities in Chajul, Quiché. (T.C. 344).

73. CEH Collective Testimony from the Tuchubac community, Nebaj, Quiché. (T.C.343).

74. CEH Collective Testimony from the Chisís community, San Juan Cotzal, Quiché. (T.C.324).

75. CI 107. April 1982. Acul, Nebaj, Quiché.

76. Collective Testimony of a community in San Juan Cotzal, Quiché. The act occurred prior to 1982 in the municipal seat of Cotzal. (T.C. 345).

77. Ejército de Guatemala. *Plan de Campaña "Firmeza"* [Guatemala Army, campaign plan *Firmness*] 83-1.

78. The *Victory 82* plan shows, 'the mission is to destroy the guerrilla and parallel organizations.' Ejército de Guatemala. *Plan de Campaña "Victoria 82,"* annex H, section B and G.

79. CI 61. March 1982. Ilom, Quiché.

80. CEH Collective Testimony, from Chajul, Quiché, p. 9. (T.C. 347).

81. The reconstruction was done according to the information received from: Witness (municipal functionary from Nebaj) CEH. (T.C. 254).

82. Cursive type indicates those communities whose razing was only recorded by CITGUA, a social research NGO. CITGUA, *Counterinsurgency and environmental deterioration in Guatemala,* Mexico, 1992.

83. CEH Witness. (T.C.346).

84. One source on the number of internally displaced, the OAS, estimates in its report on Communities of Population in Resistance (CPR) that there were 50,000 displaced in the Quiché Mountains in the early 80s. Edgar Gutiérrez believes that there were 25,000. See Gutiérrez, "Un nuevo Tejido Social para Guatemala: dinámica maya en los años noventa," *Revista Polémica* 3, January-June 1995, p.14.

85. According to one witness, the reaction was such because "when a patrol arrived at the village, and it was empty, but the dogs were there, the chickens, the fires lit in the houses ... but they wouldn't find anyone, this meant they collaborated with the guerrillas and the officer in charge would make the decision to burn the entire village ... this, without taking into account that when they entered there would be traps set with spears and he would react with even greater rage...." CEH Witness (member of the Armed Forces) (T.C. 92). Also a declassified USA CIA document states: "An empty village is presumed to have been supporting the EGP [*Ejército Guerrillero de los Pobres*, guerilla army of the poor], and is destroyed. There are hundreds and perhaps thousands of refugees without a house to return to." G5-41, P12.41, February 1982.

86. C 3622. January, 1982. Nebaj, Quiché.

87. They burned the community of Chichel, as the witnesses explain: "The first thing they did was burn the houses, they burned the houses and whatever they found

there they would also burn: everything including the house." Sixty houses were burned and 14 died. CEH Collective Testimony from San Juan Cotzal, Quiché, January 23, 1982.

88. They describe it in the following way in Ojo de Agua: "then if they found the people in the house they would kill them or if not, just closed the door and set it all on fire and that was it." CEH Collective Testimony from San Juan Cotzal, Quiché. (T.C. 349).

89. CEH Collective Testimony, from Nebaj, Quiché. (T.C. 286).

90. The collective testimony recalls it this way: "In Cajixaj the Armed Forces of Guatemala burned the village, the people went to the mountains; later they asked the mayor what they should do since they didn't have houses and the mayor told them to return; 10 families returned and the Armed Forces of Guatemala killed them all, no one knows how many died." CEH Collective Testimony, from a community in Chajul Quiché. (T.C. 347).

91. CEH Collective Testimony, from a community in Nebaj, Quiché. (T.C. 350).

92. C3683. April, 1981. Uspantán, Quiché.

93. CI 60, April 1982. Chel, Nebaj, Quiché.

94. C 3746. Nebaj, Quiché.

95. C 3317. April, 1983, Nebaj, Quiché.

96. C3099. May, 1984, Nebaj, Quiché.

97. "Even helicopters come, planes come to bomb these places here, but the truth is that maybe the Armed Forces of Guatemala doesn't see well anymore, it no longer controls what they were bombing; rather now they're bombing the whole population, the poor people." CEH Collective Testimony, Nebaj Quiché. (T.C. 287).

98. "Yes, the direct bombing, that is the repression, came hard on this community in 83 when the airplanes bombed, that is the Armed Forces of Guatemala waited there while the planes dropped bombs so that the people would have to come out of the guatles [huts], and the Armed Forces of Guatemala would catch them and kill them, here in Visumal people were burned to a crisp by the Armed Forces of Guatemala." CEH Collective Testimony Nebaj, Quiché (T.C. 286).

99. C 3090. 1983. Nebaj, Quiché.

100. According to C 3097, during the first months of 1980 the Armed Forces of Guatemala sent planes to bomb the village of Tzalbal. It was the first time the Ixil people had seen warplanes. The population fled to Bicamalá and in 1983 the planes came again.

101. C 3475. 1983. Nebaj, Quiché.

102. CEH Collective Testomony, Nebaj, Quiché. (T.C. 339).

103. C 3024. 1983 Chajul, Quiché.

104. C 3415. January, 1982. Chajul, Quiché.

105. C 3415. January, 1982. Chajul, Quiché.

106. C 3708, September, 1982. Chajul, Quiché.

107. C 3148, 1983, Chajul, Quiché.

108. C 3414. 1983, Chajul, Quiché.

109. Then [1982] that's where some people died of hunger, because they weren't allowing people [who came] to gather their food in this village, some stayed to die just down by the common grounds, that's where a few people were buried who had died from untreated illnesses, from hunger too. And then they destroyed the cornfield again, in 1983, when all the fruit trees were destroyed, when they left nothing, not the avocadoes, not the apples, not the peaches.' CEH Collective Testimony Nebaj, Quiché. (T.C.351).

110. C 3776. December, 1982. Nebaj, Quiché.

111. The same process is retold in the communal interview in Salquil, Nebaj, Quiché.

112. CEH Collective Testimony, Nebaj, Quiché. (T.C. 346).
113. This is how it is expressed in the community interview *"then several decided to come back more than anything, and then they were several; they arrived to live over here, but just as they are explaining it, in very enclosed spaces, just like keeping animals, closed in, because it was very tight."* CEH Collective Testimony, Chajul, Quiché. (T.C. 341).
114. Myrna Mack Chang, "Notas del Campo." April, 1988. [field notes]
115. C917. February, 1983. Nebaj, Quiché. C 3412. May, 1982. Nebaj, Quiché. C 3809. Febr, 1983. San Juan Cotzal, Quiché.
116. C 3815, June, 1983, Nebaj, Quiché.
117. C 3068, September, 1984, Nebaj, Quiché.
118. C 3002, September, 1984, Nebaj, Quiché.
119. CEH Collective Testimony San Juan Cotzal, Quiché, referring to the scorched earth in Asich. (T.C. 341).
120. CEH Collective Testimony. Nebaj, Quiché. (T.C. 351).
121. "When we went to the village of Cotzal, the soldiers picked out four people ... then they said that those were the four men, those are bad people, those are the rotten ones, we're going to rid you of these people, then you'll be liberated. If you go back to your habits, if you are collaborating with the guerrillas on a daily basis, then this is what will happen to you as well, look what they'll do." 4. CEH Collective Testimony, San Juan Cotzal, Quiché. (T.C.32).
122. Guatemala Forensic Anthropology Foundation, *Informe para la CEH*, 1998, p. 54. CI 107. 1982. Nebaj, Quiché.
123. C 3515. April, 1982. Chajul, Quiché.
124. CI 107. 1982. Nebaj, Quiché. Recounts how during the massacre in Acul, a boy was tied to a pine tree and in front of the entire community, they simulated his execution several times, only to blow his head off finally with a gunshot. His body was left exposed in front of the entire community for hours.
125. CI 61. 1982. Nebaj, Quiché.
126. In the same sense, ODHA [REMHI], *Guatemala, Nunca Más*, Volume II: 118.
127. CEH Witness (retired military). (T.C. 92).
128. CEH Collective Testimony, San Juan Cotzal, Quiché (T.C. 341).
129. CI 60. April 1982. Chel, Chajul, Quiché.
130. C 3318, February, 1982. Nebaj, Quiché.
131. CEH Collective Testimony, Chajul. (T.C. 344). It explains how in the first massacre the women were raped, then killed: "in the first massacre, they raped the women and then they killed them."
132. The UN General Assembly, on this topic "Reaffirms that rape during an armed conflict constitutes a war crime and under certain circumstances a crime against humanity and an act of genocide as is defined in the Convention for the Prevention, and Sanction of the Crime of Genocide.... " General Assembly, December 22, 1995, resolution 50.192, par. 3.
133. C 3776. December, 1982. Nebaj, Quiché.
134. George Lovell, "Maya Survival in Ixil Country, Guatemala," *Cultural Survival Quarterly* 14.4 (1990): 11.
135. Stoll, David. "The Land No Longer Gives": Land Reform in Nebaj, Guatemala." *Cultural Survival Quarterly* 14.4 (1990): 4-9.
136. CEH Witness (Nebaj municipal functionary). (T.C. 254).
137. C 3316. January, 1983 Nebaj, Quiché.
138. "The Juil mountain, near Chajul, was mentioned by Colby and Van de Berghe as one of the most sacred places for the Ixiles. The informants say that they no longer go to the caves that are there, caves that according to informants contain altars

from ancient Maya times. The people did not appear very interested in talking about them, but finally a man told us that the Armed Forces of Guatemala had been bombing the area and especially the caves, so that no one could use them to hide." CEIDEC, *Guatemala: Polos de Desarrollo,*Mexico, D.F.: Editorial Praxis, 1990, p. 81.

139.   '*Apreciación de asuntos civiles G-5 para el área ixil,*' p. 60.
140.   CEH Witness (an Ixil person from Nebaj, Quiché). (T.C. 338).
141.   Study on Genocide undertaken for the CEH by the AAAS.

Region II (Maya Achí People):
Municipality of Rabinal, Baja Verapaz

> In those days they wanted to kill all the indigenous people. He was in charge of the country. Is that Lucas Garcia guy in prison yet? How's that thing going?[1]

3362. Rabinal is one of the eight municipalities of Baja Verapaz, a department (province) located in the center of the country. It comprises an area of 504 square kilometers, or some 16% of the province. It has a municipality seat, also called Rabinal, 14 villages and 60 hamlets. Rabinal had a population of 22,730 people in 1981, of whom 82% were Maya Achí.[2]

3363. The Maya Achí people live in the municipalities of Cubulco, Rabinal, San Miguel Chicaj, Salamá and San Jerónimo, in the province of Baja Verapaz. In 1972, there were 58,000 people in these municipalities.[3] The Commission selected the municipality of Rabinal for this investigation because of the high levels of violence documented during the internal armed conflict, according to the CEH's sources. In addition, a military outpost operated in the region, and those in charge of it were responsible for almost all the human rights violations attributable to state agents in the region. In other words, for purposes of determining whether genocide occurred, the subject of the study is the Maya Achí population that lived in Rabinal.

3364. From the time of the 1944 Revolution, the Rabinal population had organized into peasant leagues that arose around the agrarian reform [of 1953 and truncated by the counter-revolution in 1954]. These peasant leagues formed the social base for the political work of guerrilla organizations in the area.[4] Julio César Macías tells how the first incursions of the FAR [*Fuerzas Armadas Rebeldes*, Armed Rebel Forces] in Rabinal in 1963 were to "organize a group of indigenous Achís who acted on their own in name of the 13 of November Movement."[5] This guerrilla *foco* [group] had no important military repercussions, but it did have a large political effect. In fact, during the 1970s the EGP [Ejército Guerrillero de los Pobres, Guerrilla Army of the Poor] took up anew the work that had been done in the area decades earlier.[6]

3365. Rabinal was not a combat zone. Although there were several guerrilla actions, most were for propaganda purposes.[7] The region was used for passage, for obtaining supplies, recruitment of cadres, or as a rearguard.[8] Geographically, the municipality is located on the border of areas where different ethnic groups live—Achís, Ki'ches and Pocomchis—and in a corridor that provides access from Guatemala City to Alta Verapaz province and the area of Ixcán, Quiché. The Army thus considered the entire area strategic and decided that it must fall under its total control.

3366. By the end of the 1970s, most of the population was organized in the CUC (Committee of Peasant Unity).[9] Communities made demands through that organization, especially those related to evictions forced by the National Electricity Institute's (INDE) Hydroelectric Project.[10] The conflict with INDE arose because the communities of the Chixoy river basin refused to abandon their lands. Many inhabitants attribute the subsequent violence to this conflict:

> Before in the community, things were peaceful, after the dam was built the problems began.

3367. In the period between 1981 and 1983, military or paramilitary groups assassinated at least 4,411 people in Rabinal (20% of the population).[11] The level of violence in the region cannot be explained by the prevalence of combat, since, as mentioned above, there were no armed confrontations. Moreover, the victims were all civilian, noncombatants. The viciousness with which the area was attacked supports the thesis that the Army considered it as a strategic area and, at one point in the conflict, identified the region's population as an internal enemy.

3368. Some 99.8% of the victims identified by the CEH were members of the Maya Achí people. The high percentage of Maya Achí victims, much higher than the distribution within the population (82% Maya Achí and 18% *ladinos*), demonstrates that violence in the region was not random. Violence did not affect all ethnicities equally, nor according to their proportionate share of the population. Rather, violence was specifically directed against the Maya Achí population. At no time was the *ladino* [non-indigenous] population of Rabinal, identified as a whole with enemy insurgents because of being *ladino*.

Facts

3369. Below, acts are described that were carried out by the Army or paramilitary groups against the population of Rabinal. The description corresponds to the sequence in which the events took place. Thus, we deal first with the killings of leaders, then massacres and scorched earth policies, then displacement and lastly, resettlement.

Killing Leaders

3370. The main targets of selective repression were community leaders. Catechists, health promoters and auxiliary mayors were executed.[12] Detentions or executions were carried out against those accused of being organized or of being guerrilla fighters:

> The judicial police caught him, he never returned. Three days later they went to look for him in the army base in Rabinal. The answer was that they shouldn't look for him, that he would come back on his own. The family went later and they told them that he had been involved in shit.[13]

3371. When they were not executed, leaders were tortured to make them collaborate with the Army. In this regard the testimony of a civil patrolman is eloquent:

> They summoned the president of the committee and the two commanders of the patrol, they stuck the president in jail and the commanders in a hole, to get the truth out of them, to know if there were guerrillas around, from three to five days, they had them there naked. There were people who said there were dead bodies in the hole.[14]

3372. The military supplanted the authority exercised by traditional leaders and auxiliary mayors. The committees, religious leaders, and even the community authorities recognized by the State no longer carried out their duties, which were assumed by civil patrol chiefs, military commissioners or Army members, who solved any community conflicts through the use of violence:

> A boy … was playing ball and the ball hit something and caused a short circuit, the commissioners went to pick him up and they stuck him in the well, then his mother came and slept for about two nights with her son, near the well.[15]

3373. Converting the leaders of different sectors of the group into specific targets of the repression increased the group's vulnerability and threatened the continuity of the group's existence. Previously, the leaders were those who led, managed, and solved conflicts within the group.

Massacres

> That massacre happened because they accused our people of being guerrillas, but we are peasants, there was no confrontation.[16]

3374. In the Rabinal region, the CEH recorded 20 massacres[17] although, as is true throughout this Report, the massacres documented by the CEH constitute only a [small] percentage of the total. According to one witness, "there was no village where there was not a massacre."[18] The massacres were concentrated in the second half of 1982 and the first half of 1983.

3375. The population points to the massacre in the municipal seat of Rabinal as the beginning of massive violence in the region. The Army summoned the inhabitants of the surrounding villages to join in the celebration of September 15, 1981 [Independence Day]. When the population had gathered in the park, after a message from the military officer in charge of the base,[19] the Army closed off the four entrances and began shooting:

> The civil patrolmen and the Army identified certain people. They had lists in their hands. Those who were nearby also died. The plaza was full of the dead, of blood, of dogs licking everything.[20]

3376. After this massacre, members of the Army set out for the villages to continue massacring. Thus, on September 20, 1981, the Army entered the communities of Pichec,[21] Panacal,[22] and la Ceiba, all neighboring villages. They appeared with lists in the houses, and tortured and executed the men:

> In general, the civil patrolmen went ahead of the soldiers informing and pointing out members of the population as bad people. They would enter the houses with a list and if they found someone who was on it they would kill him or take him away.[23]

3377. This was the pattern for the massacres of Nimacabaj,[24] las Vegas de Santo Domingo,[25] Chipuerta,[26] Chichupac,[27] and the second massacre at Panacal.[28]

3378. In 1982, selective repression turned into indiscriminate repression.

> By 1982, when things got even worse, they began to go out into the communities to kill people.

3379. In this period, perpetrators carried out the killings targeting all the members of a community, making no distinctions among persons. This is what happened in the village of Xococ,[29] where people from other villages were also killed, as well as in Río Negro,[30] Los Encuentros,[31] Plan de Sánchez, [32] and Agua Fría.[33]

3380. In these cases, methods were deliberately used to augment the number of victims: taking advantage of a market day, as in Plan de Sánchez,[34] or surrounding and cordoning off the community, as in Río Negro. At the same time, as part of the pattern of carrying out the massacres, victims were dehumanized and demonized.[35] In the case of the Río Negro massacre, while transferring the women and children to the place where they would be killed, they were herded like cattle.[36] Dehumanizing the victims made it easier for the victimizers to attack them. It was less repulsive to act thus against a different, inferior being.

3381. In no case did massacres occur simultaneously with or as a consequence of confrontations between the Army and the guerrillas. Evidence obtained during exhumations demonstrates that the victims were civilians. The forensic anthropologists' report states:

> We can affirm with absolute certainty that the persons assassinated in the massacres carried out on January 8, 1982 in the community of Chichupac, on March 13, in that of Río Negro, and on June 18 in Plan de Sánchez, did not die in combat, but rather, according to the forensic evidence, were brutally eliminated with no opportunity to defend themselves.

3382. The indiscriminate massacres were an attack against the communities themselves more than against individuals. In these cases, what the victim had or had not done was irrelevant, since even newborn children, who in no way could constitute a threat, were executed by the Army. This provides evidence of how the repression was directed against the Maya Achí people simply because they belonged to this group. In the indiscriminate massacres as many group members as possible were eliminated as enemies.

3383. Some communities like Río Negro were victims of systematic persecution aimed at their total destruction. This community suffered two massacres, the first in Xococ on February 7, 1982, with 74 victims, and the second in Río Negro on March 13, 1982, with 177 victims. A group of survivors took refuge in the community of Los Encuentros, where the Army executed 79 persons and disappeared 15 women, on May 14, 1982. Other survivors from Río Negro went to the community of Agua Fría, in the municipality of Uspantán, Quiché. On September 14,

1982 civil patrolmen from Xococ and soldiers came to Agua Fría and, based on the accusation that the inhabitants had fed the guerrillas, the civil patrolmen and soldiers executed 92 persons, among them women, children and the elderly.[37]

3384. Other villages suffered the same fate. For example, the population of Sesiguán, a village near Plan de Sánchez, fled to the village of Pacoc, in Chol municipality, Baja Verapaz, where shortly thereafter they were massacred.[38] This systematic persecution left open the single option of fleeing to the mountains, where the population continued to be persecuted and subjected to extreme conditions.

3385. In the cases recorded by the CEH, massacres were aimed against the Maya Achí population. *Ladino* communities, on the contrary, were victims of selective violence, directed against specific persons and not against villages or communities.[39] Thus it is possible to affirm that in the Rabinal area, massacres were massive acts directed specifically against the Maya Achí population.

3386. The existing ethnic conflicts between indigenous and *ladino* communities were exacerbated, which facilitated the violence against the Maya Achís.

3387. In 1981, a newspaper published an article with the following headline: "Rabinal inhabitants alarmed: two hundred *ladinos* kidnapped." The article read as follows:

> Two hundred persons who lived in villages of Rabinal, Salamá [sic] were kidnapped by "subversive" groups operating in the region ... they took the *ladino* peasants from their houses and carried them off to the surrounding mountains ... the only ones who were not kidnapped were the indigenous people who inhabit the area.[40]

3388. The article referred to the village of La Esperanza as the affected area, but there is no such village in Rabinal. Similarly, none of the testimonies gathered by the CEH refer to a massive disappearance of *ladinos* from the zone. This was, without a doubt, a false news report.

3389. Another example is the conflict that took place between the *ladino* community of Chirrum and the Maya Achí community of Chichupac. In this conflict the Army managed to get the *ladinos* to inform on and turn in their Maya Achí neighbors, and to plunder their community.[41] A witness sums up as follows:

There was a Machiavellian plan about all this, because you could see it … It was about eliminating from the roots everything that is indigenous … [To do so] conditions were created to bring to the surface the latent racism of the ladinos.[42]

Scorched Earth Policies

They destroyed our houses, they robbed our possessions, they burned our clothes, they took away the animals, they cut down the *milpa* [corn fields], they persecuted us day and night….[43]

3390. The killings that took the form of massacres were accompanied by the destruction and burning of property. In the north of Rabinal, the region near the Chixoy dam was completely razed. In that area, ten communities were destroyed: Río Negro, Los Encuentros, La Laguna, Agua Fría, Comalmapa, Jocotales, Chitucán, Los Mangales, Pacaal and Hacienda de Chitucán. The aim was the destruction of all the communities near the Chixoy river basin. Thus, one of the perpetrators recalled that "When the upstream villages were destroyed, then we slept easily."[44]

3391. The southern (downstream) communities were also affected, because after the massacres the Army returned to continue its destruction, for example in the massacres of Plan de Sánchez,[45] Chichupac,[46] and Xeabaj. A civil patrolman explains these forays:

The second task was to destroy the milpa and the cane [fields] of those who fled to the mountains, Chichupac, Xeabaj, and Chuateguas. The Army said to take away everything, that it was for them. There were people who took advantage; but others said "poor people." If they came across people they killed them right there.[47]

3392. Intentional destruction of dwellings, work implements, harvests, and domestic animals undoubtedly caused hunger, cold, and sickness. The killings and the destruction of goods were carried out simultaneously or in succession against the same communities. Both actions formed part of a common pattern of acts against the group: those who fled and thus saved themselves from the massacres should not be left anything for their subsistence. There were thus two choices for the communities: a quick death by machete or bullet, and a probable slow death, from hunger or illness. A witness explains:

"I said to myself: I'll die here from hunger but not from bullets."[48]

Forced Displacement

3393. As a result of the repression, especially the massacres, many communities abandoned their villages and fled to the mountains or to urban centers. Generally, the population tried to stay in the mountains nearest to their village, with the goal of returning to their community once the Army left, until the Army's harassment became unbearable and the population decided to leave for other regions.[49]

> Every time the Army arrived I would hide in the mountains with some 30 Achí families. This went on for two whole years. We would plant and the soldiers would destroy the crops. We couldn't prosper living like this. So I had the idea of going to live in Trinitaria to save my life.[50]

3394. Despite the municipality's mountainous topography, which means that most cultivated land is on a steep slope, the lack of vegetation limited the possible places of refuge for the displaced. For this reason, in Rabinal only part of the population sought refuge in the mountains. Others went to the South Coast and still others to nearby villages and to urban centers like Cobán or the capital.[51]

3395. During forced displacement, the population was subjected to conditions which provoked their death, since they were very weak and lacked food, and thus were easy prey for disease or death by starvation:

> I spent four years defending my life. We tried to plant cornfields...the Army cut down the corn, all our crops, they cut it all into bits, so that we would die of hunger.... We had no medicines, or clothes or anything. We ate the roots of unknown vines, palm roots ... we hunted animals ... and that is how we got by.[52]

3396. In addition to being subjected to harsh conditions, displaced populations continued to be persecuted during their forced displacement. For example, in the same area near the Chixoy river, the Army carried out bombing attacks against the displaced:

> They took refuge along the whole length of the Chixoy River, perhaps two weeks in each place, they always changed their location several times because if they didn't ... a fire is enough of a signal for the military.... In 1983 ... from there, from Rabinal, they bombed the whole area around Río Negro from airplanes.[53]

3397. This situation left the population with no option: in their communities they were executed or if displaced, they were also persecuted by the Army or died of hunger, sickness and cold.

Militarized Resettlement

3398. The third phase of the scorched earth strategy was the resettlement of the population under military control. In Rabinal, the population turned itself in to the Army to take advantage of successive amnesties:

> During three years the village practically disappeared. Some went into the mountains, some migrated to where the Army was. In 1985 they gave us the right to return here. We claimed the amnesty; most of us came to see the priest ... so that he could speak for us to the military outpost. The outpost sent a note for the local military commissioners. [54]

3399. One of the amnesties was declared at the end of 1982. Immediately, the Army and military commissioners let the village populations know that they could return:

> When Ríos Montt became President, he gave the amnesty, so they used small planes to drop leaflets all over Río Negro, which said "let all the people who are refugees turn themselves in because the new government no longer kills people."[55]

3400. In Rabinal, most of the population returned to its original communities; there were only two resettlement villages, San Pablo and Pacux. People from Canchún and Chitucán were sent to the first, and those from Río Negro to the second.[56] However, the fact that there were no "model villages" did not mean less military control. Militarized resettlement was a constant in all the villages. The population was forced to form civil patrols[57] and the Army occupied all positions of power. The following testimonies reveal this:

> The only government presence that was efficient, executed, evaluated, and revised in light of the evaluation was that of the Army, and it was carefully designed.[58]

> "That's fine," the judge told me, "look, Don Juan, you have to wait between 15 and 20 days because I have to send an official document to the [military] zone."[59]

3401. In other words, the population continued under Army control and again suffered acts that had no other purpose but to perpetuate terror and deter any possibility of autonomous community reorganization.

Acts against the Foundations of the Group

3402. Next we analyze acts carried out with the purpose of attacking the foundations of the group. Among these are the attacks against especially vulnerable sectors of the population, torture, the obligation to act against other members of the same community, and sexual violence.

Killings of Civilian Population, Especially of Vulnerable Persons

3403. During the massive repression, children, women and old people were direct victims of violence. In 1982, in at least four massacres, killings were aimed at these sectors.

> They kicked the children to death. The children screamed and screamed, and then they were silent.[60]

> With respect to the children, it wasn't very hard for them because they were children. The civil patrolmen came to where the children were ... they sat them down, they tied them up and hung them, to carry them, they let them fall to the ground, they grabbed them by the feet and smashed them against the rocks.[61]

3404. In some cases, the massacres were predominantly of children, like the second massacre in Río Negro, in which 107 children died,[62] or the massacre of Agua Fría, where 35 children who had fled from the massacre of Los Encuentros were executed.[63]

3405. Generally, women and children were excluded from the war itself since they were non-combatants, especially the young children. But in the case of Rabinal, where the goal was not to defeat the enemy but to annihilate, no distinction was made between civilians and combatants; women, the elderly, sick people and children all became military objectives.

Torture

3406. Massacres and other human rights violations were carried out with conspicuous violence, generating public commotion in entire communities.[64] One example was the massacre that took place in the municipal seat of Rabinal on September 15, 1981.[65] This massacre, the first of the large ones, aimed to eliminate real or perceived enemies, but was also designed to create a general cautionary effect. By witnessing "the punishment" of supposed guerrilla collaborators in the central square on Independence Day, the municipality's entire population knew what could happen to them if they did not unconditionally support the Army.[66]

3407. Events where people were executed in front of their entire community were not isolated. They were systematically repeated in different places. Thus, in Panacal:

> On December 4, 1981, the patrolmen from Xococ and soldiers from the military post at Rabinal, carried ropes and spiked clubs and they were yelling and pulling, calling for the men to come out of their houses, they gathered them together, they tortured

some of them, they cut off their ears, their nose and they poured salt in the wounds. They took them to La Lagua and executed them there.[67]

3408. In the same way, members of the Chichupac[68] and Nimacabaj[69] communities were kidnapped, tortured and executed while their family members and neighbors listened to the screams.[70]

3409. Exemplary punishment also consisted in displaying cadavers in public places. Thus, in September and October of 1981, dead bodies appeared in the communities of Pachalum, Pantulul, Rabinal proper, San Juan, Nimacabaj, Vegas de Santo Domingo, and Chiac.[71]

3410. These events constitute acts against the foundations of the group. They were aimed at breaking any form of organized resistance in the community and at forcing the community to assume new patterns of conduct that constituted attacks on their identity. In addition, torture caused permanent psychological damage to group members.

Forcing Members of the Group to Act against Fellow Members

> I was living in pain, I didn't work calmly, those of us in the civil patrols were indigenous, and they made indigenous people fight against other indigenous people.[72]

3411. The Army used Civil Defense Patrols to carry out killings in some cases. According to CEH data, patrolmen acted in the four massacres with the greatest marks of cruelty: Plan de Sánchez, Río Negro, Xococ, Los Encuentros, y Agua Fría.

3412. It is important to stress the use of the patrolmen to commit massacres. In addition to implicating them in the killings, using them was designed to fragment communities. The Army forced one village to act against the neighboring village:

> We called the people of Río Negro. For a whole day and a night, men women and kids were put into a house. We had to obey the order. If we didn't comply, the same civil patrolmen would say "kill 'em, boys." We had no choice but to comply, it wasn't voluntary.... At about 11 p.m., with the poor people already dead, they went to bury them. If we hadn't obeyed, our own people would have killed us. They had no pity. That situation was hard."[73]

3413. From that moment on, two neighboring villages belonging to a single ethnic group, which had lived together without problems for years, became enemies. An informant explains:

We don't trust each other any more, it's as if the people became more evil, they have no respect. The people from the time of the civil patrol, it's as if they liked using weapons, they began to do incorrect things. The violence split us up, we have no communication any more ... there is no friendship.[74]

3414. The documentation collected by the CEH indicates that the use of the patrolmen to commit executions against neighboring communities formed part of a predetermined plan which had, among other goals, that of dividing the communities. This constitutes an indicator of the intent to destroy the foundations of the group.

Sexual Violence

They made sure to kill her in different ways.[75]

3415. Collective and public rape of women was part of the pattern of action during the massacres. Before killing them, they were raped. Women were the victims of this specific form of violence against them, simply because they were members of the perceived enemy group. This happened in Río Negro, in Plan de Sánchez,[76] and in Agua Fría.[77]

3416. This conduct was repeated in daily life. Soldiers, judicial police, military commissioners, and patrolmen used sexual violence against women as a mechanism of control and psychological torture of the population.

The women were threatened, they had to stay at home because if they didn't they would be raped ... both the Army and the patrolmen convinced the women that the rapes were their own fault, because they had left their houses and were in the street, or had gone to the market or to ask about their husbands at the military post.[78]

3417. Rapes also seriously injured female reproductive organs, especially in the case of girls and adolescents, who were the main victims of these acts:

They separated the young women out from the men and the adult women, who were sent home; they said that at home there was soup waiting for them, it was a trick of the Army.[79]

3418. In addition to the physical consequences, the mass rapes had a symbolic effect, since Mayan women are responsible for the social reproduction of the group. Women embody the values that must be reproduced in the community,[80] and they were soiled:

The poor women screamed when they were in their hands; as though they were horses, they no longer showed any respect for the women.... [81]

Forced Transfer of Children

3419. In some communities like Río Negro or Pacux, children were forcibly transferred to other communities, where they were given a new identity. In the case of Río Negro, during the massacre by the patrolmen of Xococ, they carried off eighteen children who had witnessed the death of their family members.[82]

3420. Both Río Negro and Xococ are Achí villages, so the children continued to use their native tongue, in circumstances apparently similar to those of their original community. However, their identity was broken through other means, as the children were subject to intense militarization. They describe it thus:

> Every night I would go sleep with the patrolmen. When a child turned ten years old, he had to go sleep with the patrolmen.[83]

> From the time one turned 15 years old, he had to go to the Army, because the education there is good.[84]

3421. In addition, the children suffered serious psychological trauma by being forced to live with the persons whom they had seen kill their parents and siblings.

3422. In the community of Pacux, there was also forced transfer of children; they were taken away from their parents on grounds that the parents could not maintain them and taken to the House of the Nazarene, an orphanage administered by evangelical pastors. After two years the parents complained because their children were being turned into evangelicals and through the intervention of the local priests the children were returned.[85]

3423. In this manner the social reproduction of the group was disrupted, since the children grew up in a different cultural milieu, and relationships between the community and its children were broken.

Conclusion

> The root of all this comes from the high command, we can't complicate even more an already complicated situation.[86]

3424. In the judgment of the CEH, the totality of human rights violations carried out by the State against the Maya Achí population during the years 1980-1983 leads to the conclusion that acts of genocide were committed. These acts were inspired by a strategic determination also of a genocidal nature. The goal of the military campaign carried out in the Rabinal area was the partial destruction of the Maya Achí people. This was seen as a necessary prerequisite for maintaining absolute control over a militarily strategic area and for separating the guerilla forces from their presumed social bases.

3425. The State made this determination because it considered the Maya Achí population to be a base of support, or a potential base of support, for the guerrilla movement. This perception that wholly identified the Maya Achí population of Rabinal with the guerrilla forces, at one point led to a campaign to partially annihilate the Maya Achí people of Rabinal, who found themselves totally defenseless.

3426. The intent to destroy the group, in whole or in part, with which these acts were carried out, can be discerned from the repeated nature, their massive scale, and from the fact that these acts were aimed in a discriminatory manner against the Maya Achí people.

3427. To reach its objective, which originated in counterinsurgent motives, the Army stimulated latent racism and exacerbated interethnic conflicts through acts of psychological warfare.

3428. The massacres carried out in the communities of Xococ, Río Negro, Los Encuentros, Agua Fría and Plan de Sánchez, in which children—including newborns—women and old people were killed, demonstrate the pattern of aggression which characterizes genocidal acts, since the victims were selected based on their membership in the group.

3429. A similar pattern can be seen in the acts of repression aimed at the communities of Chautegua, Panacal, Nimacabaj, Chipuerta, Pichec, Chicupac, Vegas de Santo Domingo, Chitucán and Xeabaj: massive repression, generally against the men and especially against the leaders of the group, who were also part of the defenseless civilian population.

3430. The sequencing, repetition and massive nature of the brutal acts to which this ethnic group were collectively subjected, demonstrate the affirmative intent to destroy it in whole or in part. This occurred through the systematic persecution of certain communities, like Río Negro, along with the systematic persecution suffered by the displaced population, those who remained in their communities, and even those who turned themselves in to the Army. In the municipality of Rabinal these acts affected only the Maya Achí group. This further convinces us of the genocidal nature of these acts, since they are discriminatory.

3431. This military campaign left a balance of at least 3,637 people dead, among them women, old people and children, of whom 98.8% were Achí. Thus, 16% of the population became victims, suffering serious human rights violations, including torture, rape and enforced disappearance, together with the killings, other acts causing serious bodily or mental harm, and measures that prevented births within the group.

Notes

1. Collective testimony, Xococ. (T.C. 363)
2. CEH database *Muestra de 7109 casos registrados* [Exhibit of 7,109 registered cases].
3. Narciso Cojtí, "Estimación de Cifras Poblacionales por área Lingüística." [Estimates of population figures by linguistic area], Proyecto Aprendamos con Prensa Libre [Project: Let's Learn with *Prensa Libre*], 1995.
4. Interview of the CEH with the FAR [Fuerzas Armadas Rebeldes].
5. Julio César Macías, *La Guerrilla fue mi camino* (Guatemala: Piedra Santa, 1997), p. 39. [Macías refers to the FAR—Fuerzas Armadas Rebeldes—which was the country's earliest guerrilla movement and included the "13 of November Movement", the Communist Party (PGT), as well as other leftist groups.]
6. Witness (member of EGP), CEH (T.C. 128).
7. A witness explained: "I was a chief of military commissioners since 1981.... There was propaganda that the subversives would come by to drop off.... They distributed flyers." C 9213, March 1981. Rabinal, Baja Verapaz. Also see Ejército Guerrillero de los Pobres (EGP), *El Informador Guerrillero,* biweekly publication, No. 4, from Feb. 16, 1982 to March 15, 1982, p. 1, and No. 5, from March 16, 1982 to April 15, 1982, p. 2.
8. C 9157, March 1982, Rabinal, B.V.
9. C 9098, February 1982, Rabinal, B.V.
10. "A German came and told me that he had problems with a community that was there near the river ... they didn't want the project to continue.... The INDE had been deceiving them for around six years, telling them they were going to give them, they were going to buy them lands, they were going to build houses for them in Rabinal..." Witness (retired high-ranking military officer), CEH (T.C. 108).
11. Study on genocide carried out for the CEH by the American Association for the Advancement of Science.
12. C 9166, Jan., 1982, Rabinal, BV. Also see press reports from Dec. 3, 1981 from *La Hora* newspaper which discusses the execution of the assistant mayor of Vega de Santo Domingo and his companion.
13. Ibid.
14. C 9155, 1981, Rabinal, B.V.
15. Witness (Achí community leader. The case took place in Pacux, Rabinal, 1983.) CEH. (T.C. 54)

16. C 9160, Sept. 1981, Rabinal, B.V.
17. CEH database.
18. Witness (religious figure), CEH (T.C. 136).
19. In the era of the massacre the base was located on the edge of the town, near the cemetery. After these events, the base became mobile, possibly because of a change in counterinsurgency strategy. Equipo de Antropología Forense de Guatemala (EAFG). *Las Masacres en Rabinal* [Guatemalan Forensic Anthropology Team, *Massacres in Rabinal.*] 1995, p. 115.
20. C 9213, March, 1981, Rabinal, B.V. The CEH registered 204 victims, although some witnesses state that between 500 and 800 people were executed.
21. C 9256, Jan. 1982, Rabinal, B.V. The Armed Forces of Guatemala and military commissioners arrived with a list in Pichec; after the celebration of New Years' day, they gathered people in a school and executed 32 Achí men.
22. C 9329, September 1981, Rabinal, B.V.
23. C 9256, January 1982, Rabinal, B.V.
24. C 9223, September 1981, En Nimacabaj the Armed Forces of Guatemala executed 12 persons and disappeared 12 more.
25. C 9252, November 1981. Military commissioners executed nine Achí men and one Achí woman.
26. C 9463, December 1981. The Armed Forces of Guatemala killed ten people.
27. C 9307, January 1982. Thirty-two people died. Soldiers committed the massacre; they arrived with a list and locked the people in the health clinic where they tortured them. That day the soldiers distributed toys in the community to gather people together.
28. C 9253, December 1981. Soldiers, civil patrolmen and military commissioners from Xococ and Vegas de Santo Domingo captured 58 people, took them to La Laguna, tortured and executed them. According to testimony gathered by the Pro Justice and Peace Committee: "They went through the villages calling the men to go do a task, that they should bring sticks and rope.... [In the soccer field of Panacal] they tied up those who had been forced to follow the soldiers ... they cut out Viviano Xitumal's tongue; they poked others' eyes out, and they cut off the ears of others; they cut a piece of cheek off others.... they yelled at them that they were 'shitty Indians, Indians with no job, sons of bitches, damned Indians, piece of shit Indians....' Then they were brought to the meadow of the lagoon of Vegas de Santo Domingo ... the number killed was 52 or 62 ... just from being kicked to death." In this testimony the massacre is dated February or March 1982.
29. C 9098, Feb. 1982. The Armed Forces of Guatemala and the civil patrolmen of Xococ executed 74 persons, 55 men and 19 women, Achís. Massacre of the population of Río Negro in Xococ.
30. C 9156 March, 1982. The Armed Forces of Guatemala and civil patrolmen from Xococ executed 177 people, 70 women and 107 Achí children in Río Negro.
31. Ibid. The Armed Forces of Guatemala executed 79 persons and disappeared 15 in the community of Los Encuentros, all Achís.
32. C 9075, July 1982, Massacre of 268 people in Plan de Sánchez.
33. C 9099, Sept. 1982. Members of the Armed Forces of Guatemala under the command of lieutenant Díaz and civil patrolmen from Xococ executed 92 persons including men, women and children, all Achís.
34. C 9075, July 1982. Rabinal, Baja Verapaz, Massacre of Plan de Sánchez.
35. Thus, the guerrilla forces were A'ques, which means devil in Achi. Witness (religious leader), CEH. (T.C. 136).
36. "When the civil patrolmen transferred the women from town to the place where the clandestine cemetery now is, they kept saying ox, ox, ox to them." Testimony

of Margarito, a survivor of the massacre of Río Negro, published by the Sectores Surgidos por la Represión y la Impunidad (Sectors Born out of Repression and Impunity), April 1994. Along the same lines *see* (T.C. 363), survivor of the Río Negro massacre. Also, before the massacre of Plan de Sánchez, "the Armed Forces of Guatemala hung a long banner that said 'Fattened pigs sooner or later have to die.'" C 9075. July 1982, Rabinal, Baja Verapaz, Massacre of Plan de Sánchez.

37. CI 10. Between March 1980 and September 1982. Rabinal, Baja Verapaz.

38. C 864. Nov. 1982. Rabinal, Baja Verapaz.

39. The Forensic Anthropology Team of Guatemala comes to the same conclusion: "with regard to the ethnic composition of the victims, in most indigenous communities there were collective massacres, while in communities made up of ladinos, for example Chirrum, Toloxoc and San Luis, the crimes were committed selectively: there were individual assassinations, most of them committed by insurgents, and also the execution of a religious leader of Chirrum by paramilitary elements." Equipo de Antropología Forense de Guatemala (EAFG). *Las Masacres en Rabinal.*, p. 203.

40. *Prensa Libre*, Guatemala, Oct. 10, 1981, p. 12.

41. "Thirty-two men from Chichupac were pointed out to the Armed Forces of Guatemala by 15 persons from the neighboring community of Chirrum. Their names were on a list, and they were turned over to the Armed Forces of Guatemala where they were tortured and killed. The Armed Forces of Guatemala took all the animals, and the inhabitants of Chirrum stole their things in front of the people of Chichupac. Chirrum was composed of *ladinos* and Chichupac by indigenous people." C 9094, Jan., 1982, Rabinal, Baja Verapaz.

42. Witness (religious personnel), CEH (T.C. 32).

43. Testimony from REHMI 5339, declarant, Achí man, Plan de Sánchez.

44. The testimony is from an ex-civil patrolman from Xococ, this community was located south of the nine communities that were destroyed. Community Report, p. 5.

45. "In the following weeks the soldiers kept on returning and destroying the roof tiles. Two months later they destroyed the houses and began to mess with [destroy] the planted fields as well." C 9075. July 1982. Rabinal, Baja Verapaz, Massacre of Plan de Sánchez.

46. The same thing happened after the massacre of Chichupac: "We fled the house because we didn't have a house, since it was burned. I left town and went to the coast to earn a living for the children." C 9094. January 1982, Rabinal, Baja Verapaz, Massacre of Chichupac.

47. C 9155, 1981. Rabinal, Baja Verapaz. Also see C 9156, survivor of the Río Negro massacre, who recalls: [After the Río Negro massacre], yes, the next day they came to set fire to the houses. The next day we saw them bombing the houses. The third time they came to take the animals. They ate the grilled meat in front of us and left us only the bones. We ate worms because there was no food.... In all God's houses there was nothing left, they even broke the grinding stones."

48. CI 10, March 1982, Río Negro, Alta Verapaz.

49. In this regard, see CEH, "Desplazamiento, Sobrevivencia y vida en las Aldeas Modelo, Estudio de una Comunidad Ejemplar" [Displacement, survival and life in the model villages, Study of a typical community], p.8.

50. C 11385, May 1982. Rabinal, Baja Verapaz.

51. Witness (religious figure) CEH. (T.C. 136).

52. C 9156. March 1982, Rabinal, Baja Verapaz.

53. Witness (Achí leader), CEH, (T.C. 216)

54. C 9075, July 1982, Rabinal, Baja Verapaz, Massacre of Plan de Sánchez.

55. Witness (Achí leader), CEH (T.C. 216).
56. Witness (religious figure), CEH (T.C. 136).
57. C 9075. July 1982, Rabinal, Baja Verapaz, Massacre of Plan de Sánchez.
58. C 9157. March, 1982. Rabinal, Baja Verapaz, Massacre of Río Negro.
59. C 9156, March 1982. Declarant, father of one of the children from Río Negro who were forcibly transferred to the community of Xococ.
60. C 9075 July 1982, Rabinal, Baja Verapaz, Massacre of Plan de Sánchez
61. C 9156, March 1982. Rabinal, Baja Verapaz, Declarant a survivor of the massacre in Río Negro.
62. CI 10, March 1980 and September 1982, Rabinal, Baja Verapaz.
63. C 9099, September 1982, Rabinal, Baja Verapaz, massacre of Agua Fría.
64. Along these lines, see Equipo de Antropología Forense de Guatemala (EAFG). *Las Masacres en Rabinal*, p. 161.
65. C 9160, September 1981. Massacre of Rabinal, Baja Verapaz, where a civil patrolman tells what happened to those who tried to escape: "they burned his eyes out with a hot coal and they put gunpowder on his belly button to make him explode, the man was still alive and they gave him a coup de grace."[shot him in the head]
66. A witness explains: "When we got to the park, it was full of people who had come from all the villages; the military commissioners had told them a week earlier to come.... Then a really angry man began to speak.... 'You'll see what happens to you if you keep backing the subversives, we've warned you before, but if you don't listen, you'll be punished; so he said, and all the people got very nervous." Interview R-90-5, cited in Equipo de Antropología Forense de Guatemala (EAFG). *Las Masacres en Rabinal*, p. 161.
67. C 9253. December 1981, Rabinal, Baja Verapaz. Collective testimony CEH.
68. C 9307. January 1982, Rabinal, Baja Verapaz.
69. C 9223. September, 1981, Rabinal, Baja Verapaz.
70. "We are going to say a rosary to help them, because they are screaming, so that the pain passes quickly." Informant No. 7, formal interview 1-0-Rabinal, cited by Equipo de Antropología Forense de Guatemala (EAFG). *Las Masacres en Rabinal*, p.210.
71. Knowledge of the justice of the peace of Rabinal.
72. C 9165. 1982, San Miguel Chicaj, Baja Verapaz.
73. C 9098, February 1982, Rabinal, Baja Verapaz. Declarant, Achí patrolman of Xococ. Also see C 9154, November 1981, Rabinal, Baja Verapaz. When the patrolmen did not turn over names, the Armed Forces of Guatemala distrusted them and executed them.
74. C 9169. October 1984, Salamá, Baja Verapaz.
75. C 9364, September 1982, Rabinal, Baja Verapaz.
76. "The women were taken to the house where the chapel is now, before there was an adobe house; they raped nineteen women. They tore their skirts, they hit them in the legs. The soldiers made fun of them and accused them of being guerrillas." C 9075, July 1982, Rabinal, Baja Verapaz, Massacre of Plan de Sánchez.
77. "The military raped women of twelve and thirteen. The women could do nothing because there were lots of soldiers who were waiting in line and raping them in turn. First they raped them and then they killed them." C 9099, September, 1982, Rabinal, Baja Verapaz, Massacre of Agua Fría.
78. C 9306, January 1982, Rabinal, Baja Verapaz.
79. C 9075, July 1982, Rabinal, Baja Verapaz.
80. Witness (religious figure), CEH (T.C. 136).
81. Testimony REHMI 536, Rabinal, Baja Verapaz.

82.   CI 14. Forced transfer of the child survivors of the massacre of Río Negro. 1982-1984.
83.   Ibid.
84.   CI 14, March 1982. Río Negro, Baja Verapaz.
85.   Witness (religious figure), CEH (T.C. 136).
86.   Witness (collective interview in Xococ) CEH (T.C. 363).

Region III (Maya K'iche' People): Municipality of Zacualpa, K'iché

3432. The municipality of Zacualpa is one of the 23 municipalities that comprises the department of Quiché. It occupies an area of 336 square kilometers[1] and in 1982 contained a population of 13,743 inhabitants.[2] Seventy-eight percent of the population lived in rural areas and 22% in urban centers. 12,369 people there, or 90% of the inhabitants, were descendents of the Maya K'iche', and 1,374 or 10% are ladino.[3]

3433. The Maya K'iche' lived in six departments, Sololá, Totonicapán, Quetzaltenango, Quiché, Suchitepéquez and Retlhuleu and numbered 925,300 in 1972.[4] To determine if there were acts of genocide against the Maya K'iche', the research was limited solely to those Maya K'iche' living in the municipality of Zacualpa. This research decision was made because of the high levels of violence documented there by the CEH. Also, Zacualpa was under military control. The Army operated a detachment there with jurisdiction over the region, whose leadership was responsible for the majority of human rights violations in the area.

3434. The territorial limits of Zacualpa are San Andrés Sajcabajá and Canillá to the north; Joyabaj and Cubulco (Baja Verapaz) to the east; to Joyabaj and Chiché to the south, and Chiché, Chinique and San Andrés Sajcabajá to the west.[5] Zacualpa is located in a strategic area since it connects the municipalities of San Martín Jilotepeque and San José Poaquil in Chimaltenango to the central region of Quiché and Baja Verapaz. Zacualpa's borders and geographic location are particularly important in that they partially explain the intense repression there. In 1981, Zacualpa had a town, three villages, eight housing developments, two distinct regions, an archaeological site and two farms. The rural communities were known to be totally isolated and out of touch with the municipal capital.

3435. Various historic interethnic conflicts existed in Zacualpa between people from the villages who were mostly indigenous and people from the municipal capital, where the *ladinos* live. One witness explains the interethnic conflict:

> "If there are problems between the indigenous and the *ladinos*, it would be that there is a lot of discrimination. As I told you before, the *ladinos* are in the town. It's the *ladinos* who hold local power.... "[6]

3436. For example, in the 1970s, the first Maya K'iche' mayor abolished forced unpaid labor requirements for indigenous people, who had been obliged to work for 30 days in the county seat each year.[7]

3437. During the 1960s, the local population in Zacualpa organized in peasant leagues to demand their rights, especially labor rights.[8] The Peasant Unity Committee (Comité de Unidad Campesina, CUC) was formed in the 1970s. A large number of workers joined this organization and issued a series of demands, including a minimum wage and better working conditions in the Costa Sur farms.[9]

3438. On a separate note, the Augusto César Sandino guerrilla front of the People's Guerilla Army (EGP)[10] operated in the area since 1979.[11] The EGP undertook several propaganda campaigns, among them a rally in the plaza of Zacualpa in January 1981.[12] The CEH also documented two Army campaigns against the EGP's Augusto César Sandino guerrilla front: one in 1981 when four helicopters bombed the foot of the Chuacús Mountains; and another in 1982 when the Army confronted a guerrilla group that had suffered two defeats.

3439. The municipality's strategic location and the guerrilla's presence in the area were the principal reasons the Army labeled the Zacualpa population as the enemy, and consequently as a target for elimination.

3440. According to the CEH's findings, at least 1,215 people's human rights were violated.[13] This constituted 11.5% of the municipal population.

3441. However, the Army did not label all of the population as the enemy—only the Maya K'iche' population. 99.2% of the victims were Maya K'iche' and 0.8% were *ladino*. This shows that repression in the area was not random. Victims were selected on a discriminatory basis according to their ethnic background, even though it may have been for ostensibly military-political reasons.

Facts

3442. The investigation found the following: First leaders were killed, then massacres took place with scorched earth operations, and finally forced displacement. This sequence is explored below, and corresponds to the actual evolution of events in Zacualpa, from selective executions to mass operations that generated forced displacement. All three phases were characterized by systematic human rights violations.

Killing Leaders

3443. In Zacualpa the repression affected religious, political and rural development leaders. The main victims of the selective repression were the members of Acción Católica,[14] Mayan priests,[15] CUC members,[16] members of committees for community development[17] and members of the cooperative.[18] (Later on, groups of victims were selected on the basis of their leadership, often with numerous people executed at the same time[19] or with their families.[20]) Executions of leaders took place according to a victim selection process, often based on lists:

> We already knew that there were lists, Fidel was worried because he had already been threatened and because he was a leader because of his post in the cooperative. The same day that the Army arrived he was going to flee. While he was leaving he ran into some soldiers who took him away, they killed him in the Boquerón.... They destroyed the cooperative and burned some houses.[21]

3444. The municipal mayor Nicolás Barrera Cux, a K'iche',[22] who had been elected for the period from 1981-1982, was disappeared by para-militaries on March 25, 1982.[23] The Army replaced him with a *ladino* mayor.[24] According to one witness, in this case and in other similar ones, the repression was directed against "various indigenous members ... who were part of a generation of indigenous people that began to stand out and lead in the political life of the place."[25]

3445. Disappearances of leaders deeply affected community life. Social organizations, especially political, religious, and cultural organizations, disappeared from the community. Leaders were replaced by military commissions and patrol leaders. The Army named functionaries to replace democratically elected leaders. By attacking leaders and cracking down on all forms of communal organization, the Army attacked the foundations of the Zacualpa Maya K'iche' community.

Massacres

3446. The CEH documented at least 800 victims of extra-judicial executions in Zacualpa,[26] 80% of whom died in massacres between 1981-1983. Military and paramilitary forces first appeared in Zacualpa in 1980, but mass violence only began in 1981 when a military detachment installed itself in the local church.[27] After that, the violence increased steadily. The period of greatest intensity occurred during March, April, and May of 1982 when nine massacres were perpetrated, four of which were indiscriminate.

Selective Massacres

3447. One of the first massacres in Zacualpa took place on May 8, 1981 in the municipal capital, when masked armed men in civilian dress captured and executed seven people.[28] The victims' corpses were abandoned on a bridge linking the communities with the municipal capital—the most frequented place in the area. The incident was designed to terrorize the population in rural areas as well as in urban centers. According to one witness, the victims:

> Had their tongues cut off, wires were placed in their ears, then they were shot and left abandoned in that place. Their bodies showed various gunshot wounds, one on top of the other.... The bodies showed up later. They showed up on the bridge, at the entrance to the town.[29]

3448. Some of the massacres were selective, following a selection process for executing people. These kinds of massacres generally followed a pattern: after public or anonymous identification by means of lists or "signalers," victims were sent to a detention facility, and then to nearby public places where they would be tortured and assassinated in an extremely cruel manner preventing the burial of the corpses. This is how the massacres of Chichá,[30] Chuchucá,[31] Tunajá,[32] and Xicalcal[33] unfolded.

> On January 12, 1982 an unknown military contingent arrived and called a meeting of the community. When nearly all of the community had arrived, one of the military took out a list of names.... That day, during the meeting at around noon, they began to kill various members from the community.[34]

3449. The first selective massacres were directed against members of the Committee for Peasant Unity (CUC) or members of Acción Católica. Afterwards, once the Civil Defence Patrols (PAC) were formed, the massacres changed. People were executed for not joining patrols or for being accused of not wanting to join. For example, in El Tablón, four patrolmen were killed,[35] as were others in Turbalá.[36]

3450. Because the survivors were terrorized, they often did not dare to claim their family members and bury the dead. The public display of victims and impeding a proper burial was a way of dehumanizing victims and breaking the ties between those executed and survivors.

Indiscriminate Massacres

3451. Later, massacres against entire families began. Here the army executed men, women, children, and the elderly, often inside their houses, which were then burned. This happened in Tzimatzatz, where soldiers apparently from Tarea Gumarjac executed 26 people, including seven children and one pregnant woman. The soldiers selected eight men at first among those who had been at a religious service. They executed the men and then completely eliminated two families.[37] The same thing occurred in Potrero Viejo where the Army executed all the members of a family,[38] and in Tunajá, where soldiers massacred seven people, three of them children.[39]

3452. In other communities, massacres were directed against all of the people that the soldiers or patrolmen found in the villages, regardless of age or sex. People were executed merely for being in the town. The CEH documented four cases of indiscriminate massacres: one in Piedras Blancas with 88 victims;[40] another in Arriquín[41] where soldiers executed between 83 and 140 people; and three more in San Antonio Sinaché,[42] with the first massacre claiming between 108 and 210 victims, the second killing 45 victims, and the third executing 39 people.

3453. Soldiers would arrive in the morning, surround the community, search from house to house, rape the women, and then kill them with everyone else in the place. In some cases they would also torture victims before executing them. Afterwards they would burn homes with people inside who had not yet finished dying. In some instances they stayed in the community and celebrated the killing.[43] For example as in Piedras Blancas:

> It was a Sunday, at four in the morning when they arrived.... It was the Army, they were going to finish the village of Piedras Blancas. They burned the people in their houses while they were asleep, men, women, children, everyone together.... They stabbed them and then flung them into the flames while they were still alive, that's how about 80 people died, among them children, women and the elderly. However, in other houses the soldiers tortured the victims by cutting off their tongues before killing them.[44]

3454. Various communities suffered more than one massacre. The CEH documented at least three massacres in Tunajá, Chuchucá, and San Antonio Sinaché.[45] In the latter case, the decision to exterminate was evidenced by the fact that there were three military operations against the same village. During the first massacre, the Army killed the women and children after sending the men to sweep other villages. In the second massacre they orchestrated the killings to target those who had fled previously, executing children, the elderly, women and men. In the third massacre, they tortured and executed 30 men.

3455. In some cases the massacres were part of a larger military operation. This was the case with the first Chuchucá massacre, the first San Antonio Sinaché massacre and the Arriquín massacre. All three took place only a few days apart from each other: on the 12th, 16th, and 19th of March 1982. In each massacre, the Lieutenant from the detachment participated. Also, after the second San Antonio Sinaché massacre, the Army went to Turbalá on May 15 where soldiers killed at least nine people.[46] Later, on May 18 the soldiers moved to Chuchucá where they executed nine people. The Army arrived with between 50 and 60 soldiers.[47]

3456. The massacres were executed as part of a military plan targeting the non-combatant civilian population. In all cases, military attacks were carried out without any form of resistance or combat. Military units acted when they knew they would have the upper hand. They would enter communities in the morning when most inhabitants were at home and stay for several days, probably to decide movements following the events. For example:

> The second platoon of soldiers entered through another sector of the community and apprehended one person.... There was a third platoon that entered by another sector and took a few people. These people were held with the others taken at worship.[48]

> The soldiers followed their route to the center of the village, they stayed for two nights, and the third day they left in the morning to search the Pacoc and Chuchucá communities.[49]

3457. This is evidence that the acts against the Zacualpa civilian population occurred *en masse* as a result of previously planned military operations. The massacres affected at least 99.2% of the Maya K'iche' population and 0.8% of the ladino population. This is also evidence of direct discrimination against an ethnic group.

3458. To achieve its strategic objective, the Army incited interethnic conflict and created conditions for these conflicts to erupt openly. In the community of San José Sinaché, for example, pre-existing antagonisms between the *ladinos* and indigenous people were exacerbated:

> Peasants from the neighboring *ladino* communities, such as Capuchinas and Chinique, accused the people from San José Sinaché of being guerrillas, reinforcing the ethnic and land conflict that had existed before.[50]

3459. The clearest case of incitement to inter-ethnic conflict was in Arriquín, a community where historical rivalries have long centered around issues of discrimination and land.[51] According to testimonies, the *ladino* population was alerted prior to the massacres and fled before the killings. Moreover, the *ladinos'* houses weren't affected:

> Afterwards they passed to the following house, which was Pedro Gutiérrez Chingo's, and they burned it because he was indigenous. Next, another house about 20 or 25 meters from Pedro Gutiérrez'; but since it belonged to a *ladino* they didn't burn it and they stopped there. They didn't continue because the rest of the houses belonged to *ladinos*.[52]

3460. This situation shows that the military and the PACs' actions were based on a plan that specifically distinguished the neighborhood's socio-cultural composition. In this case, violence was discriminatorily directed against the Maya K'iche' population.

Scorched Earth Policies

3461. From 1981 onwards, massacres were combined with the destruction of goods, especially the burning of people's houses, as happened in Tzimatzatz, where victims' homes were burned as a part of the killings.[53] In 1982 the partial destruction of houses evolved into the complete razing of villages. For example, in San Antonio Sinaché, the Army burned houses, grain stores, and community farms:

> Let's burn everything. They're the guerrillas' houses, they would say. Then they began to burn the whole harvest, all of the corn, the beans, the seeds. They burned the clothes, the *huipiles* (traditional clothes), the shirts. Just as it happens to one family, so it happens to everyone in the community.[54]

3462. The CEH documented the burning of houses, clothes, tools, grinding stones and grain stores in the communities of San Antonio Sinaché,[55] Tzimatzatz,[56] Turbalá,[57] Piedras Blancas,[58] Chuchucá,[59] Chichá,[60] and Trapichitos.[61]

3463. One fundamental characteristic of this destruction in the indigenous communities was its cultural impact. For the Maya K'iche', a millstone represents a link to the genealogical family tree. Besides being a necessary utilitarian object, it also has a subjective value that represents familial continuity in a specific place where one's identity is formed.[62] Its destruction affects the group's basic beliefs.

3464. Along with the physical destruction of the villages, soldiers and patrolmen looted the communities.

> This year [1982] was the worst. There was a lot of hunger. The soldiers destroyed our dwellings. They knocked them over with pick-axes, they did not burn them as in other places. They stole the harvests and the animals and destroyed the corn, bean and fruit tree plantings. They burned part of the forest.[63]

3465. Looting was documented in Xicalcal, Pacoc, Chuchucá, El Tablón, Potrero Viejo, and San Antonio Sinaché. By depriving people of basic elements of survival like corn, looting produced hunger. Destroying dwellings and denying the protection of a roof also created a sense of helplessness.

Forced Displacement

3466. A large portion of the population of Zacualpa abandoned their villages at least temporarily to save their lives. Generally, when the Army neared, people left for ravines or forests where they would stay until the village was clear:

> In May the Army continued to come to Turbalá. The people were displaced for a few days and returned to their houses. That is to say … they would come and go. This situation lasted about six months until it was possible to establish oneself in a stable manner. Others decided to migrate to the Costa Sur.[64]

3467. According to community interviews, the communities of Xicalcal, Tzimatzatz, Turbalá, San Antonio Sinaché, Arriquín, Trapichitos, Chuchucá, Pacoc, Chichá, and the municipal capital of Zacualpa were displaced.[65] This means that villagers abandoned at least ten of the 16 municipal population centers to save their lives.

3468. Unlike communities that permanently abandoned their villages, the displacement in Zacualpa was only temporary. The community that suffered the most prolonged displacement was San Antonio Sinaché, which spent six months in the mountains. Because of this, the region wasn't marked by the processes of displacement, capture, amnesty, or relocation. However, after 1980, tracking groups that later became part of the patrols (PACs) were installed in the communities as one facet of military control over the population.[66]

3469. During their displacement, people suffered conditions that led to death by starvation, sickness or cold.

3470. Some communities were persecuted during their displacement. One of these was San Antonio Sinaché. During the May 18, 1982 massacre, while the population sought refuge in the forests, it was attacked by the Army with grenades. Upon their taking refuge in some caves, soldiers sharpened poles into points, to force the refugees out and execute them. The victims were totally defenseless, especially the children. Even though the Army could easily have detained them after forcing them out of their hiding places, the soldiers still assassinated them:

> On the 18th they chased all of us there. They were killing children.... They died un-der rocks where they thought were caves, underneath a rock and when the soldiers arrived and they couldn't get the people out, they looked for sticks and sharpened them and goaded them....[67]

> The soldiers sharpened a stick and shoved it up the women's asses, they stuck it in their stomachs ... at the same time they took their lives.[68]

> The soldiers had no respect for age, they had no interest in detaining people, if that was the case they could have captured the old people and the children, but they didn't, they wanted to finish off the people in the community.[69]

3471. The persecution during the displacement shows the desire to exter-minate. There was nowhere safe to hide. The Army tirelessly chased after non-combatants, who were eliminated without any means of defending themselves.

Acts against the Group's Beliefs

3472. This section examines acts[70] carried out against the group's beliefs, namely attacks on the vulnerable population, torture, and rape.

Killing Vulnerable People

> In one of the beds, there was a baby that was scarcely eight months old ... a soldier took it in his arms and the other soldier put the barrel of the gun in its mouth and with one shot, blew off the top of the baby's skull.

3473. In seven of the massacres documented by the CEH, the Army at-tacked men, women, children, and the elderly. In some cases, the Army expressly targeted the vulnerable population: women, children and the elderly. For example, this was the case in San Antonio Sinaché where they ordered the men to patrol the mountain before starting the massacre:

> They sent us to patrol, there on the hill. They took the men aside and told them to go and patrol then they entered the houses and killed the families; my dad, my mom and my wife with all the kids.[71]

3474. Likewise after the Tunajá massacre, a two-year-old child was unable to flee because his parents had put him down. He stayed on the side of the road.

> A neighbor from Tunajá who was hiding among some pine trees witnessed a soldier passing who beheaded him with a machete.[72]

3475. The killing of vulnerable persons, especially children, shows the intent to destroy the group. These killings did not target guerrillas or supposed collaborators. They were directed against everyone belonging to the group under investigation: victim selection was based on ethnicity.

> "They accused all of us of being guerrillas…. I can't understand why they would kill a child that was barely a month old."[73]

Torture

> But since they were asking her in Spanish and she would answer in K'iche', they would give her even worse. They'd hit her more. They would say to her: "Damned Indian," and they would pistol-whip her.[74]

3476. The CEH documented 217 cases of torture from 1981-1983 in Zacualpa.[75] After the military installed a detachment in 1981 in the municipal capital, and created patrols (PACs) in most rural communities, the use of torture expanded in Zacualpa. Military officials even forced the community's own patrolmen to commit acts of torture. Torture represented a new way for the Army to act against the population. Torture also became part of massacres: victims were first tortured and then executed.

3477. In the municipal capital of Zacualpa a detachment installed itself on the site of the church and convent. This place was converted into a torture center, as one ex-soldier explains it:

> By the third day there, he saw lots of people in the convent…. There were about 200 people complaining that they had been tortured…. One evening during the 15 days that the company was in Zacualpa, the official in charge of the company ordered that

they eat quickly, then gave them their combat gear and a blanket. They went to place near Zacualpa about two kilometers away by way of the old field road. There, they assassinated all the people that he had seen in the convent.[76]

3478. There were torture centers in almost every community. The patrolmen would dig holes in the villages as places to punish those people who were pointed out as having supported the guerrillas or not wanting to join the patrol. Thus, in the Pasojoc community:

> The patrol from Joyabaj ... built a hole in which to torture. When someone didn't complete the chief's orders they were placed in the hole and water was poured over them and they were left there for a day. Those were the Army's instructions....[77]

3479. In addition to "the hole," the Army forced patrolmen to perpetrate acts of violence against their own people, as a way of forcing them to enter into the patrol and to keep them terrorized. Typically, a number of patrolmen would gather for maximum impact, sometimes from various communities. They would point out those accused of refusing to patrol or of collaborating with the guerrillas. Under threat of death, the Army would coerce patrol members to torture and execute those people. Deaths had to be slow, thus exacerbating the suffering of victims and their physical executors.

> With everyone together, they would call out those that were on the list. They separate the victims and take them to a wooded area and tie them up. Then the soldiers ordered the patrolmen from Tunajá to give a machete blow to each of the people that were tied up. One patrolman refused to torture his neighbors, he was kicked and badly beaten by those from Cruz Chich.[78]

3480. This pattern, which was followed in Turbalá,[79] Trapichitos,[80] Pasojoc,[81] Tunajá, and San José Sinaché,[82] demonstrates how the Army treated the population. First the Army created the PACs, and then used them to implicate civilians in the repression, turning them against their own communities and families.

3481. In addition to executions, acts of violence caused severe, permanent mental damage to the members of the group, both those that were forced to carry out the torture and execution, and also those who were forced to witness the events.

> We feel grief ... because all of a sudden they struck us too ... and we grieve for those who had died.[83]

> He'll never recover from the fact that they killed his dad, since they let him go, even though tortured, so he feels that if he had been in the house he would have been able to defend his dad, talk to the soldiers, so that they wouldn't have killed him.... We

can't take away that grief, that pain, the guilt over the death of his dad, he's always
very sad and he can't recover.[84]

3482. Finally, these acts were directed against the group's fundamental
beliefs because the Army forced civilians, neighbors, and relatives to confront one another. The acts were carried out in front of numerous people,
which led to feelings of terror even in neighboring communities.

Sexual Violence

3483. The CEH documented 17 cases of sexual violence in Zacualpa.[85]
In at least three massacres, women were publicly and collectively
raped. Cases of public rapes were also documented in San Antonio
Sinaché, Arriquín, and Potrero Viejo.[86] In these cases, sexual violence
was one element in massacres. Generally, the soldiers entered the
households, gathered the women, raped them, executed them, and
then burned the houses. One former soldier explains it in the following manner:

> They went to Potrero Viejo, which is situated about a kilometer and a half from
> Zacualpa. They found arms and guerrilla uniforms. Before that they surrounded the
> village and many children were assassinated.... In that instance, as in many others,
> the soldiers raped the women from the community.[87]

3484. Beyond the rapes that occurred during the massacres the women
from Zacualpa suffered on a daily basis for their supposed links to the
guerrillas. Soldiers and patrolmen frequently committed acts of sexual
violence:

> He was a rapist, he threatened the lives of widows and then they had to accept. He
> arrived at their houses and said to them: "You're cooking for the guerrillas that's why
> you don't have husbands, and they would rape them right there in their houses."[88]

3485. Along with the rapes, the Army members and the patrolmen committed extreme acts of cruelty such as fetal extraction:

> They raped her [the woman who was 7 months pregnant (CEH)], they opened her
> stomach with a knife and removed the fetus, that's how we found her later on.[89]

Conclusion

3486. The CEH finds that most crimes committed by military forces
against the Maya K'iche' from 1981-1983 constituted genocidal acts.
They were inspired by a strategic assessment that was also genocidal in
nature. The Army designated the indigenous population as the social base
for the insurgency movement and consequently identified them with the

internal enemy. The objective of the military campaign in the Zacualpa region was the partial destruction of the Maya K'iche' people.

3487. The identification of the Zacualpa Maya K'iche' with the internal enemy translated into the planning and execution of the massacres in Arriquín, San Antonio Sinaché, Piedras Blancas, Tzimatzatz and Potrero Viejo, which affected the entire community, especially women, children and the elderly—because they belonged to the ethnic group being investigated.

3488. Killings were similar in the neighboring communities of Chichá, Chuchucá, Tunajá, Turbalá, Xicalcal, Pajoso and Pacoc in which men (typically group leaders) were tortured and rapes were carried out.

3489. Army and patrol actions against the Zacualpa civilian population were planned. The general plan of action began with sweeps of the area in anticipation of the killings. Large contingents of soldiers and patrolmen participated in the sweeps under direct orders from the head of the Zacualpa military detachment. They began the action by surrounding the area to prevent escapes and to increase the number of victims.

3490. According to CEH data, killings took place in twelve of the sixteen population centers in Zacualpa and the population was displaced from ten centers. This reveals the pervasive nature of violence committed by the Army.

3491. No CEH documentation on violence in Zacualpa uncovers any indiscriminate massacres of the *ladino* population. In some cases the *ladino* population was alerted so that they could abandon the community before the killings, as was the case in Arriquín. Additionally, 1.1% of the documented victims were *ladino* and 98.9% indigenous. This percentage contrasts with the ethnic distribution of the municipality and shows that the Army did not randomly select their victims. Rather, the Army directed its actions discriminatorily against the Maya K'iche' population.

3492. The military campaign killed no less than 1,473 persons, among them women, children, and the elderly. 98.9% of these victims belonged to the Maya K'iche' group. In addition, 8.6%[90] of the population suffered other severe human rights violations such as torture, rape, forced disappearance, acts to impede births, and other acts designed to inflict severe harm to the physical and mental integrity of the group.

Chart I
Massacres Documented by the CEH in the municipality of Zacualpa, Quiché

Case number		Date	Community	Number of
1.	2927	03/81	Potrero Viejo	8
2.	16238	29/0781	Tzimatzatz	26
3.	2392	08/81	Zacualpa	6
4.	16264	01/08/81	Chichá	5
5.	16223	05/08/81	Chuchucá	7
6.	16458	07/10/81	Tunajá	6
7.	529	1982	Zacualpa	200
8.	2923/2925	15/01/82	Chuchucá	7
9.	16222/16262	12/03/82	Chuchucá	11
10.	2756	16/03/82	San Antonio Sinaché	108-201
11.	16202	19/03/82	Arriquín	83-140
12.	16645	25/04/82	Piedras Blancas	80
13.	16640	05/05/82	Tunajá	12
14.	16224	18/05/82	Chuchucá	9
15.	16150	18/05/82	San Antonio Sinaché	45
16.	2576	18/05/82	Turbalá	9
17.	16286	29/05/82	Chichá	10
18.	16289	30/05/82	San Antonio Sinaché	39
19.	16012	10/07/82	Xicalcal	5
20.	16200	28/01/83	Pasojoc	12
21.	16200	28/01/83	Tunajá	7
22.	16451	25/03/83	Tunajá	5
23.	16004	10/04/84	Pasoc	7

Chart II

Year	Forced disappearance	Extrajudicial execution	Death because of displacement	Deprivation of Freedom	Torture	Sexual violence
1881	17	94	1	22	38	
1982	60	340	76	56	155	15
1983	20	283	6	5	24	3
Total	97	717	83	83	217	18

Source: Database, court date, September 4, 1998

Notes

1. Fundación Centroamericana de Desarrollo [Central American Development Foundation], *Diagnóstico y Plan de Desarrollo del Municipio de Zacualpa, Departamento de Quiché* [Analysis and Development Plan for the Municipality of Zacualpa in the Department of Quiché], Guatemala, 1995, p. 13.
2. Instituto Nacional de Estadística [National Statistics Institute]; 1981 Census. The data from the 1981 census has been questioned since that year was part of the worst period of the armed conflict. Because of this, the data will be replaced by that which was gathered by the CEH Database.
3. Instituto Nacional de Estadística, 1981 Census.
4. Narciso Cojtí, "Estimación de cifras poblacionales por area lingüistica," [Estimates of Population Figures by Linguistic Area]. Proyecto Aprendamos [Project Let's Learn] with *Prensa Libre*, 1995.
5. Fundación Centroamericana de Desarrollo, *Diagnóstico y Plan de Desarrollo del Municipio de Zacualpa, Departamento de Quiché*, p. 15.
6. Witness (K'iche' leader from Catholic Action or *Acción Católica*). (T.C. 277).
7. One neighbor from Arriquín says: "before the violence we already had problems, because the *ladinos* don't want to work, they only want the indigenous to work for them." C 16201. October, 1981. Zacualpa, Quiché.
8. CEH Collective Testimony from the community of Tzimatzatz, Zacualpa, Quiché CEH. (T.C. 355).
9. For more about the Zacualpa organizing process, see C. 16201. October, 1981. Zacualpa Quiché, CEH Collective Testimony, community of Pasojoc, Zacualpa, Quiché. (T.C. 357).
10. CEH Document, *La Estrategia politico-militar del Ejército Guerrillero de los Pobres*, EGP [Military-Political Strategy for the Guerrilla Armed Forces of Guatemala of the Poor].
11. CEH Collective Testimony, Aldea de Trapichitos, Zacualpa, Quiché. (T.C. 359).
12. CEH Collective Testimony, Zacualpa, Quiché. (T.C. 355).
13. CEH Database, *Muestra de 7,109 casos registrados [Exhibit of 7,109 registered cases]*, September 4, 1998.
14. C 2908, 1980, Quiché. C. 2928, July, 1980, Zacualpa, Quiché.
15. C 16463, November, 1982. Zacualpa, Quiché.
16. C 16218, March, 1982, Zacualpa, Quiché. C 2392. August, 1981. Zacualpa, Quiché.
17. C 2923, January, 1982. Zacualpa. Quiché.
18. C 16201, October, 1981, Aldea Arriquín, Zacualpa, Quiché.
19. C 16223, August, 1981, Zacualpa, Quiché.
20. C 16640, May 1982, Zacualpa, Quiché.
21. C 16201, August, 1981, Zacualpa, Quiché.
22. Nicolás Barreras Cux was one of the first K'iche' mayors elected in the municipality. Prior to the 1970s, *ladinos* had been the only ones in local power. C 16307. March, 1982. Zacualpa, Quiché.
23. The disappearance happened in the following manner: "It was a Saturday, the mayor and his wife were busy building a thatched roof for their business; at that moment a white pick-up truck appeared and the riders who were heavily armed put them in the bed of the truck where they were holding the Municipal police chief and two businessmen. They took them via the asphalt road that leads to Joyabaj. Upon arriving at Tunajá they assassinated the three people, left the wife to go free and took him to Joyabaj. They never had any news of what happened to him in this encounter." C 16307. March, 1982. Zacualpa, Quiché.

24. C308, July, 1982, Zacualpa Quiché.
25. CEH Witness (K'iche' leader). (T.C. 53).
26. CEH Database, *Muestra de 7109 casos registrados*, September 4, 1998.
27. This is how one witness explains it: "Between March and April, I remember that Zacualpa was paralyzed, the market wasn't even there anymore, the people no longer came to the plaza, then, when the military came to the convent, everything suffered because there were no more people." K'iche' member of Acción Católica. (T.C. 277)
28. This is how one witness narrates it: "That day I was leaving on a trip, it was in the early morning, it was still dark, various armed men (30 more or less) approached, wearing plain clothes and masks, they seized and took them [two men]; on the road they met five people and they also captured them." C 16315. May, 1981. Zacualpa, Quiché.
29. Ibid.
30. C 16264, August, 1981, Zacualpa, Quiché, Massacre in Chichá.
31. C 16223, August, 1981, Zacualpa, Quiché, Massacre in the Chuchucá community.
32. C 16458, October, 1981, Zacualpa, Quiché, Massacre in the Tunajá community.
33. C 16012, July, 1982. Zacualpa, Quiché. Massacre of five persons in the Xicalcal community, they were members of the Comité de Unidad Campesina (CUC) [Committee for Peasant Unity].
34. C 16673. January, 1982. Zacualpa, Quiché.
35. C 13015. May, 1982. Zacualpa, Quiché. In 1982, five victims were killed, El Tablón.
36. Members of the Armed Forces of Guatemala and the PACs from Turbalá destroyed belongings of the members of the Committee for Peasant Unity (CUC), they look for them on a list that the soldiers had of people who didn't want to be on the patrol. The following day they captured and summarily executed five men, each accused of collaborating with the guerrillas because they had not wanted to be on patrol. C 2576. May, 1982. Zacualpa, Quiché. Massacre in Turbalá.
37. The incident happened in the following manner: "It was July 29, 1981, a group of religious people from the Church of the Prince of Peace was in the chapel at approximately 3 pm attending a religious service. A group of soldiers arrived by surprise and surrounded the chapel they entered and selected eight people from those present, they took them on foot for about 2 kilometers to the center of the village they shot at them at point blank range and beheaded them and finally shot at them again." C 16238. July, 1981. Massacre that affected 21 victims in the Tzimatzatz community, Zacualpa, Quiché.
38. C 2927, March, 1981. Massacre in Potrero Viejo, Zacualpa, Quiché.
39. C 16640 May, 1982. Massacre in the community of Tunujá, Zacualpa, Quiché.
40. C 16646 April 1982. Massacre in Piedras Blancas, Zacualpa, Quiché.
41. CI 80, Massacre in Arriquín, March, 1982.
42. CI 78. Massacres in San Antonio Sinaché. March May 1982.
43. "They took the food away with our neighbors, from our community, there the patrols, the Armed Forces take their food, they take all of the chickens from the neighbors' houses, they make a good soup in the chapel, they start at 3 in the afternoon until 7 or 8 in the evening." C 16289. May, 1982. San Antonio Sinaché, Quiché.
44. C 16646. April, 1982. Zacualpa, Quiché.
45. Chart 1.
46. C 2576, May, 1982, Zacualpa, Quiché.
47. C 16224. May, 1982. Zacualpa, Quiché.

48. C 16238, July, 1981, Zacualpa, Quiché.
49. Ibid.
50. C 16053. May, 1982. Zacualpa, Quiché.
51. "Arriquín is a very polarized community, there has been a rivalry since the arrival of the *ladinos*. Before the violence there were already problems between indigenous and *ladinos*, they [the *ladinos*] wanted the indigenous to work for them and they would keep the best lands on the edge of the river and increase their herds." CI 80 March 1982. Arriquín Quiché.
52. CI 80 March 1982. Arriquín, Quiché.
53. C 16238, July, 1981, Zacualpa, Quiché.
54. C 2756. March, 1982. San Antonio Sinaché, Zacualpa, Quiché.
55. Ibid.
56. C 16238, July, 1981, Zacualpa, Quiché.
57. C 2576, May 1982, Zacualpa, Quiché
58. CEH Witness (collective interview with the Piedras Blancas community, Zacualpa, Quiché). (T.C. 356).
59. CEH Witness (collective interview with the Chuchucá community, Zacualpa, Quiché). (T.C. 361).
60. C 16286. May, 1982, Zacualpa, Quiché.
61. CEH Witness (collective interview with the Trapichitos community, Zacualpa, Quiché). (T.C. 359).
62. C 16323. May, 1982. Zacualpa, Quiché and C 16098. November, 1982. Zacualpa, Quiché.
63. CEH Collective Testimony, community of Xicalcal. (T.C. 354).
64. C 2567, May, 1982, Zacualpa, Quiché.
65. C 16315, May, 1981, Zacualpa, Quiché. "Between 1981-1982 all of the population of Zacualpa migrated, it was left totally empty, there was only one family that revisited in the most violent period. During this period they looted the houses, what little the people had was stolen."
66. Infra, III.B.
67. C 16150. May, 1982. Zacualpa, Quiché.
68. CI 78. Massacres in San Antonio, Sinaché, March-May, 1982.
69. Ibid.
70. C 16646. April, 1982. Zacualpa, Quiché.
71. C 2756. March, 1982. Zacualpa, Quiché.
72. C 16142 August, 1982. Zacualpa, Quiché.
73. C 16640. May, 1982. Zacualpa, Quiché.
74. C 16215. January, 1981, Quiché.
75. CEH Database, *Muestra de 7109 casos registrados*, September 4, 1998.
76. C 529. October, 1981. Uspantán, Quiché.
77. CEH Collective Testimony Zacualpa, Quiché. (T.C. 357).
78. C 16358. February, 1983. Zacualpa, Quiché.
79. C 16323, May, 1982, Zacualpa, Quiché.
80. CEH Collective Testimony, Zacualpa Quiché. (T.C. 359).
81. These acts continued throughout 1984. In Pasojoc, Lieutenant Chechá ordered the heads of the PAC to meet with the patrolmen from various communities to learn who didn't want to participate in the patrols, the "bad people." Upon receiving the order they signaled out four people and eight more from Tzimatzatz. "They're guerrillas, you will make 'justice' said the lieutenant to the patrolmen. They tied up the victims and the patrolmen were forced to execute them with sticks and machetes, slowly, because they had to go by each one and hit him with the machete without entirely killing him. Victim number one, no longer had a head, but he

was still alive, one soldier shot him twice. After the massacre, the Armed Forces of Guatemala ordered the patrolmen to bury the victims right next to the Pasojoc school." C 16200. January, 1984. Zacualpa, Quiché.
82.   CI 53. 1982. San José Sinaché, Quiché.
83.   Ibid
84.   C 16215. January, 1981. Zacualpa, Quiché.
85.   CEH Database, *Muestra de 7109 casos registrados*, 04/09/98, ETVDMET.xls.
86.   C 2881. July, 1982, Zacualpa, Quiché, C 16313, August, 1982, Zacualpa, Quiché.
87.   C 529. October, 1981. Uspantán, Quiché.
88.   C 16324. 1982. Zacualpa, Quiché.
89.   CI 80. March 1982. Arrinquín, Quiché.
90.   The definition of the Zacualpa region in this case corresponds exclusively to the municipality of Zacualpa, differing from the definition of the region of Zacualpa that appears in the Análisis Intermuestra of the AAAS that appears in the statistical annex of this report. For this document, the Zacualpa region includes the municipalities of Zacualpa, Joyabaj, and Chiche. Note that in both cases the same methodology of analysis and calculation was utilized.

Region IV (Chuj Maya and Q'anjob'al Maya Peoples): Municipalities of Nentón, San Mateo Ixtátány Barrillas, Huehuetenango

3493. The Chuj Maya and Q'anjob'al Maya live in the municipalities of San Mateo Ixtatán (north of the municipality of Nentón) and of Barrillas,[1] all in the department of Huehuetenango. The region occupies 2,459 square kilometers, and is largely composed of mountainous areas with some lowlands. According to the CEH's data collection,[2] in 1981 the Chuj-Q'anjob'al region had 64,679 inhabitants, of whom 83% were Q'anjob'al or Chuj Maya.

3494. In the history of Guatemala, the Chuj of San Mateo Ixtatán were always considered to be a rebellious people. This characterization dates back to 1876, when the Chuj of San Mateo Ixtatán were forced to cede some of their lands for the creation of the municipality of Nentón. The Mateans were able to preserve their communal lands in the high mountain regions of the *Cuchumatanes* by fighting in collective land disputes.[3] As a result, at the beginning of the century, laws were passed that in the neighboring towns the mayor and municipal councilor had to be *ladinos*.[4]

3495. Conditions of extreme poverty and forced migration to the South Coast generated permanent tensions in the communities North of Huehuetenango. The CEH recorded indications of constant indigenous uprisings there.[5] In San Juan Ixcoy, a municipality of San Mateo Ixtatán, a contractor from the South Coast plantations was executed on the night of July 17, 1898. Apparently in order to hide the crime, 30 other *ladinos* were also assassinated. The sole surviving *ladino* informed the Army immediately, which responded by killing 310 indigenous people. Afterwards began a great spoliation of the Mateans' lands[6] by *ladinos* and by the neighboring communities of Soloma and Chiantla. Also, however, some aggressions against indigenous people in the area occurred without an indigenous response, at least not publicly, for fear of being labeled "rebellious." According to the inhabitants of the region, the modern equivalent of calling the indigenous people "rebellious" would be to call these people "guerrillas."[7]

3496. During the 1970s, incidents were registered where the civil population confronted the Treasury Police (*Guardia de Hacienda*) and the National Police (*Policía Nacional*). For example: in 1974, the people of the village Coyá, San Miguel Acatán, stole uniforms and arms from ten agents of the *Guardia de Hacienda*. After that, the presence of the state in the village was gone. This marked the beginning of the time when this community was considered to be a village of "fighters."[8]

> Coyá was always a special village. People say that in Coyá there were people who know the secret of witchcraft. At least that is what the people of Coyá thought. They thought they were capable of winning the war and taking power from the Army. In fact, a couple of times they ejected the Army from the village. Because of that, they thought they were stronger and stronger, and thought that they could bewitch the Army with their wisdom, and that they knew the secret to bring down planes and stop weapons.[9]

3497. The Chuj-Q'anjob'al group was perceived not only as rebellious and as distinct from the *ladino* group, but also as antagonistic to authority and especially capable of organizing to defend the people's interests. The inhabitants of the plateau of Huehuetenango constituted one of the most important groups in the colonization of the Ixcán region.

3498. One of the hardest hit areas of Quiché was the municipality of Ixcán and inside Ixcán, a particularly affected area was the cooperative Ixcán Grande, colonized mostly by Chuj and Q'anjob'al. They suffered massacres and scorched earth campaigns. Indeed, Ixcán was one of the areas most affected by the war. The State invested many resources in undertaking different colonization and population control projects there. It opened the "transversal band of the North" that went up to the Xalbal river, which is the limit of the Ixcán Grande cooperative, and colonized the extreme North of Ixcán in joint projects of INTA and the United States Agency for International Development (USAID). Nonetheless, the area of the Ixcán Grande cooperative organized its own development, infused by some suspicion of the State and its institutions. The EGP guerrilla force initially installed itself in Ixcán near the Ixcán Grande cooperative, making the Government of Guatemala even more suspicious of people in the cooperatives. Probably together with the Ixil area and the area north of Huehuetenango, Ixcán Grande proved to be one of the three places most stigmatized by the army as enemy areas.

3499. During the armed conflict, the Chuj people defended a diverse array of cultural and economic interests: an example was the 1981 struggle of the Mateans to preserve their forests. Since 1977, the municipality of San Mateo Ixtatán had signed a contract with the company Cuchumadera for the

> sanitization, reforestation, maintenance and exploitation of forests, based on the urgent necessity of managing and maintaining the natural resources attacked by the pine weevil.[10]

> When the treaty between the Municipality and the company comes into force, the Mateans will oblige the authorities to hold an Open Assembly and explain the nature of the compromise.[11]

> Every member of the municipal corporation gave his or her testimony, revealing contradictions that resulted in the mayor's resignation during the same session.[12]

3500. Because of the threats that some inhabitants of San Mateo received, they organized a local committee to defend the forest, initiating a legal action against the company. As a consequence, damaging logging was stopped.

3501. These antecedents were important because they factored into the way in which the Army came to consider the Chuj Maya and Q'anjob'al Maya as internal enemies in the 1980s.

3502. Military Intelligence affirmed that the indigenous population of Huehuetenango was "very difficult to penetrate." Military Intelligence considered the *ladino* population as "more favorable because they had demonstrated their support for the Army and expressed their desire to see the bands of rebel agitators eradicated."[13]

3503. The perception of indigenous people from the North of Huehu-etenango as especially dangerous enemies was confirmed by Military Intelligence declarations, which described how the indigenous population had been shaped:

> Population transformed by subversion in its ways of thinking, feeling, and acting.[14]

> Our units have encountered great difficulty in penetrating the population as it is extremely difficult to understand or communicate between our people and the indigenous people of the place for linguistic reasons, and their origins and customs erect an insurmountable barrier against our efforts of rapprochement.[15]

3504. The notes on the origin, language, and custom constitute a description of what it means to be an ethnic group in and of itself.[16] What the Army called "origin" is affiliated to "history." In the case of indigenous Maya groups, this was associated with a culture oppressed and fragmented by the State, and hence capable of rising up *at any moment.* "Language" was seen as a marker of social cohesion. The [Army] perception of "us" and of "custom" was a determining factor in identifying a group. Military Intelligence identified and clearly defined this group as an inaccessible ethnic group set apart [from the majority] by insurmountable barriers—a crucial step in its identification as an enemy group.

3505. In its definition of the enemy, the analysis by Military Intelligence was even more stark, dividing the country in two: one, those areas inhabited by indigenous peoples: "the problem is even worse where the percentage of indigenous people is higher, who have openly manifested their aversion to the Army."[17] Regarding the areas inhabited by *ladinos*, Military Intelligence affirmed that "the situation is a bit more favorable where *ladinos* live. They have manifested their support for the Army."[18]

3506. The CEH gathered information that the guerrillas had elicited the sympathy of some communities north of Huehuetenango, particularly insofar as they proposed claims about age-old grievances around land and extreme poverty:

> We liked the message of the guerrillas because they were good politicians. They explained to us that in Guatemala only the rich had land, while the poor were the ones working the earth ... we will take away the land of the rich and distribute it amongst the poor, they told us.[19]

3507. However, Military Intelligence associated the guerrillas' ability to garner support with the "credulity of the indigenous people":

> ideologically they were instructed constantly and they spoke of their personal experiences ... they successfully and radically changed the indigenous population's way of thinking and feeling, erasing from their mind the concept of fatherland, family, and traditions, and badgering them constantly about their being exploited by the wealthy ... taking advantage of real or imagined dissatisfactions and all their doctrines about the conscience and morality of man.[20]

3508. Refusing to acknowledge the historical causes of dissatisfaction, Guatemala's agrarian problem, and its extreme poverty, Military Intelligence affirmed that the guerrilla movement's increasing success in mobilizing [the Maya population north of Huehuetenango] was because of the "gullibility" of the indigenous people rather than their historical grievances. Military Intelligence conceived of the indigenous population as a *"mass"* capable of rebelling all together. Thus, for the Army, the guerrilla movement was so vast that it included a total of 20,111 people in the area of Huehuetenango.[21]

3509. This affirmation contrasts starkly with the information given by the EGP [the Guerilla Army of the Poor], specifically from ex-combatants of the Ernesto Che Guevara Front (*Frente Ernesto Che Guevara*) who affirmed that they never had more than 52 armed men[22] in their moments of greatest strength.

3510. Guerrilla combatants' operational capabilities should have been measured by the intensity of combat, as dictated by international norms regulating armed conflict.[23] In line with this type of analysis, the CEH only recorded two cases of armed conflict in the area north of Huehuetenango. In these incidents, inhabitants of communities that were attacked tried to defend themselves with sticks, machetes and stones. In both cases, the attacks ended with a massacre of the inhabitants and there were no indications of casualties on the part of the Army.

3511. After identifying the Maya population north of Huehuetenango as its internal enemy, the Army carried out a number of distinct human rights violations. Our investigation into these abuses was limited to an area where there were indications that acts of genocide had been perpetrated. Investigations began by reviewing cases recorded by the CEH, then considered the frequency of cases of selective repression, and finally studied patterns in the three most violent military operations where the "foundations of the group"[24] were attacked.

3512. This area of study includes the North of the municipality of Nentón, the North of the municipality of Barillas, and the entire municipality of San Mateo Ixtatán. It encompasses approximately 180 square kilometers. In 1982 this area was home to a population of around 64,679 people.[25] In this same area, according to CEH data compared with data collected by REMHI, 15 massacres were carried out in a period of 83 days, between June 2 and August 25 of 1982. In all, 2,636 men, women, and children died. Seven of these massacres can be labeled as total massacres, where communities experienced sexual violence against all their women and the execution of all their children.

3513. Disappearances of people were also registered. In addition, 15 villages were destroyed, including the farms and goods indispensable for the civilian population's survival.[26] All this violence was preceded by innumerable acts of repression. Of these, some are included in this analysis: those that took place in 1980, 1981, 1982, and 1983. The Army clearly delineated an enemy area, as is confirmed by a high authority in the military:

> The concept of the Labor Gangs was that the Cuchumatanes in the North, they were all enemies.[27]

Facts

3514. The political violence [in this area] unfolded in three stages. The first was characterized by selective repression, directed primarily against community leaders, members of the Catholic Church, and deputy mayors. This type of violence was meted out starting in the 1970s. The second stage—from 1981 to 1983—was designed to destroy the communities and "eliminate their population." The political violence in this phase was massive and generalized. The third stage started in 1983. Abuse in this period was again more selective, but was characterized by persecution, displacement, population control, social and political reorganization, and "reeducation" or psychological campaigns to "reclaim" the population.

Killing Leaders

3515. During 1980-1983, repression was directed at the non-combatant civilian population generally. However, it is possible to pick out some categories of victims according to their participation in social structures. Development workers, members of cooperatives, deputy mayors, and traditional Maya authorities were the hardest-hit groups. The elimination of development workers increased the communities' vulnerability, preparing the scene for their annihilation. There were also multiple cases of disappearance and detention followed by assassination. All these acts were marked by the use of disproportionate force, extreme cruelty, and relentless ferocity.

3516. It is possible to identify the foci of violence against community leaders: the area of the Chaculá plantation and the area of Barillas. The *modus operandi* common to the majority of those cases was: [first] a public or anonymous warning, [second] detention, [and third, the] transportation of detainees to nearby detachments where they were ultimately tortured, assassinated, and disappeared. The latter crime prevented their burial.

3517. In the area of Chaculá, located between the regional capital of Nentón and the villages of San Francisco, Yalambojoch, and Campamento in the extreme north, the following events were recorded: In November 1980, members of the Mobile Military Police (*Policía Militar Ambulante* or PMA) captured four peasants in the path that led from the town of Nentón to Chaculá, tied them up, put grenades on their bodies and blew them up; they did not permit the remains of the victims to be buried.[28] According to the reports, it is possible that the victims were community leaders from the neighboring villages who were on their way to the municipality of Nentón, to denounce abuses by the owner of the Chaculá plantation.

3518. The Army assassinated a Maya professor from Nentón on August 24, 1982.[29] His house was probably destroyed. His family had to flee. Different reports mention cases of assassinations of teachers in the area: in the end of 1981 and during all of 1982 the educational system was paralyzed by assassinations and by threats against teachers.

3519. Religious leaders also became victims of repression, in particular those from the Catholic Church. Various catechists were assassinated.[30] On July 18 of 1982 a catechist from Nentón was assassinated. Soldiers dressed in *"camouflage,"* probably from the detachment of Nentón, captured him, tortured him, spearing his body with stakes until they killed him. They publicly exposed the corpse and forbade any burial.[31]

3520. In the area north of Huehuetenango selective violence traced a spiral. In the beginning, it struck a sector of the population simply suspected of sympathizing with the guerrillas, of belonging or being militarily active in a guerrilla group, or other groups opposed to the regime. Afterwards, violence became increasingly concentrated. It started with freezing the social stratification[32] of the enemy, then aggregated them by socioeconomic origin, by their condition as rural or urban populations, by their age and last, by their ethnicity. Here, the portion of the affected population was ever greater, surpassing the concept of activism or belonging to the guerrillas. The spiral culminated when the enemy was identified by ethnic origin alone:

Thus, in the Honor Guard (Guardia de Honor), we were there since that Mr. Ríos Montt took away from Maldonado Shaadd and Gordillo, and became the only Head of State. One time I was able to speak with him. . . . I said that we had the obligation to save the fatherland, that we had to finish with the guerrilla and that our hand would not shake when we had to kill, because there were orders. . . that we would not feel pity or sorrow because people looked so innocent, but that they were all guerilla fighters and that we just had to kill them.[33]

3521. In an official document, the Army very clearly analyzed the social, economic, political, and military factors that led them to consider a group identifiable by its ethnicity as an enemy:

The work of the Political Military Command (MPM) of the guerrillas has penetrated different social strata of these regions little by little. Every day it succeeds in getting more sympathizers, collaborators, and rebels. This work of ideological indoctrination is aided by printed propaganda and direct contact with the indigenous population, whom they convince, by exploiting socioeconomic and political factors to the hilt.[34]

3522. At this point in the conflict, the logic of violence was concentrated against the essential nature of the group. In 1981, a Chief Priest named Mamín was publicly decapitated, along with four other people.

On July 19, 1981, the soldiers of the Army killed my father in Chimban. My father was a Maya Chief Priest. He was 80 years old and had been living in Chimban for two years. Some 150 soldiers arrived in Chimban, coming from Soloma and Jacaltenango. Some 40 soldiers arrived at my father's house, they took out a hooded man, and that is how the soldiers took my father from the house. I followed the soldiers to the place where they killed him. First they interrogated him, saying that it was certain he was a guerrilla. Then they started stoning him, they split his head, afterwards they chopped him with machetes until he died. They cut one of his arms and the soldiers took the arm in all the neighboring villages to teach the people what happened to "subversives.[35]

3523. In the Guatemalan armed conflict, an 80-year-old like the aforementioned priest would have fallen outside any possible definition of combatant. Rather, his assassination was designed to intimidate, direct, or control the group. Moreover, the acts that followed his death, namely the mutilation of his body and the fact of showing his arm in all the neighboring communities, can only be associated with a "psychological operation" aimed at the destruction of the group's symbols.

3524. This proceeding marked the beginning of [a phase characterized by] acts of profound barbarity. An example is an event in the village Ojo de Agua, near the Chaculá plantation, where after being tortured, captives were shot and afterwards the corpses were trampled, making burials impossible.[36]

Recently people had opposed the abuses of the owner of the plantation. The CEH recorded a total of 46 cases of assassinations that took place in the area.[37]

3525. The second area which saw the most intense violence against community leaders was the area south of the municipality of Barillas. In August 1981, a group of over 150 soldiers and patrolmen arrived in Babeltzap, captured 11 people and took them to another nearby detachment camp where they shot the 11 victims. Thereafter the patrolmen were forced to destroy the bodies. Testimonies affirm that these eleven people were accused of belonging to the guerrillas. However, two of [the CEH's] three witnesses confirmed that the victims had not been part of the guerrilla movement, but rather had been assassinated because they were leaders of Babeltzap, a community which was constantly persecuted by the Army.[38]

Massacres and Scorched Earth Policies

The house in which they killed the women was an old house with lots of things in it. There was wheat in the granary. . . . So it was like *zacate* [a highly flammable plant] and the house caught on fire very fast. The fire killed the women and boys and girls and the elders. When they exploded the bomb it lit the whole house on fire. That is how it caught on fire. We could hear the screams of the women also after they fired the bomb. Only for a short while like one minute we could hear the women's screams. You could hear the screams of the children. There were a considerable number of children. It is certain that they burned them alive, the women and the children.[39]

3526. In Chuj and Q'anjob'al area in the north of Huehuetenango, the CEH recorded 19 massacres between 1981 and 1982, 80% of which were registered between the months of June, July, and August of 1982. Approximately 2,636 victims were executed there in three military operations.[40]

The Events of 1981

3527. On May 31, 1981, the Army entered the regional capital of San Mateo Ixtatán, massacring 35 people:

The Army entered the municipal capital of San Mateo, from Barillas. They got out of vehicles behind the town in the canton of Yoltán and from there they entered, setting fire to the first houses of the town, machine-gunning men, women, and children, massacring 35 people. They also killed the municipal treasurer and stole the money from the city hall, painting the letters "EGP ARE ASSES." The next day the same military men came back to the municipal capital to investigate the facts, which were registered in the municipal books as natural deaths.[41]

3528. The same day, before dawn, the Army entered into Yoltán, assassinating 49 people including men, women, children, and the elderly. They used machetes, machine guns and bombs on part of the community.[42] On June 27, another group of soldiers entered San Carlos las Brisas, where they sprayed ten people with bullets. After the assassinations they dismembered the bodies in front of the whole community.[43]

3529. On July 19 1981, about 300 soldiers from Jacaltenango entered into Coya, accompanied by aerial forces. They fell on the population with machine guns and bombs. Apparently the population tried to defend itself with machetes and sticks. Again on September 28 the Army entered into Coya, killing various people with knives and bullets, and massacring 19 people in the El Rosario mine.[44]

The Events of 1982

3530. In June 1982 the army began to quarter a great number of troops in different places. They may have been reinforcements for the detachments of Nentón, Barillas, Ixquisis and Jacaltenago. According to REMHI, some 3,000 soldiers had arrived in Huehuetenango by mid June 1982.[45] In that period, it is possible to identify three military operations where the majority of indiscriminate acts of violence were committed.

3531. At the end of June a reconnaissance patrol in the area went from Nentón to San Miguel Acatán. At the same time, troops coming from Nentón travelled in the area North of San Mateo Ixtatán, passing through the village Yulaurel. They then went down to the villages of Patacal, Octé and Bulej. The soldiers did not cause major damage on these patrols. However, the execution of these reconnaissance operations allows for conclusions to be drawn about planning or premeditation of the later acts by the Army.

3532. There is no doubt that this operation was a reconnaissance patrol sent out to obtain information for Military Intelligence, to assist in the preparation of later military operations.

3533. The facts confirm this theory. The three most violent operations registered in this area began on June 26. The ultimate intent of these three operations transcended the physical elimination of individual people as possible enemies or armed combatants. The intent of these three operations was to destroy the group, killing men, women, and children, raping women and killing them thereafter. The bulk of the [Army's] resources, time, equipment and men were used to prevent the victims from escaping and to exacerbate their pain before killing them. Moreover, [the Army] forced civilians to collaborate in these violations in order to make them responsible and create a sense of guilt that would break their communities' social structures.

3534. On June 26, soldiers from Barillas patrolled an area off of a road from Barillas to Santa Eulalia. The villages of that zone bad been abandoned probably because they had heard of the Army's impending arrival. However, we do know of the massacre of a family in the village Balli, where all the houses were also burned.

> The same soldiers that massacred in Balli moved to Quikil where they killed about 50 people…. By the dawn of a day in 1982 [June 28, 1982] about 60 soldiers were already in the community. The mass killing began sometime around ten in the morning. Approximately 50 people died, many from my family.[46]

3535. The soldiers moved on to the village Puente Alto where they massacred inhabitants on the 4th or the 6th of July. The massacre of the Puente Alto village is representative of the intent to destroy a group in its entirety. The facts show that in this massacre, all possible methods were used to encircle the inhabitants of the village, torture them, and assassinate them, leaving a death toll of 350 victims. According to testimonies, one day before the massacre, the Army assembled the villagers of Ballí and Puente Alto. Witnesses confirm that before the massacre, the village had about 600 inhabitants. Now there are only 30 inhabitants originally from the village.

> On July 6 the Army came to the far part of Puente Alto and declared that the next day there would be a meeting at eight in the morning, and that men, women, and children should come. Because I was a child I entered the church with my mother, which was where the women were gathering. They took out the women under 17 and raped them. After that a man whose face was covered said, "let's give them three minutes so that they can see what they won't ever see again." Then he said: "This firewood will serve to turn you into cooked pork rind." All the people screamed. Then he said: "wait just a minute," and they began to machine gun. Afterwards they poured gasoline and set us on fire. When a baby who was being burned woke up, it screamed. I don't know how I managed to run out. I ran to the mountain and gave myself up to a detachment to tell them that I was not a guerrilla.[47]

3536. From July 12 to 17 in 1982, the soldiers returned to the area north of San Miguel Acatán, this time massacring the communities of Sebep (30 to 40 victims).

When they had rounded up all the men, a masked man appeared. He forced the men to get into lines. Then this man passed between the lines signaling at various men in the community. So they took out 30 men. Afterwards, the soldiers picked some 30 patrolmen and taught them how to kill their neighbors. The lieutenant said, if you don't want to kill them, we will kill you. That is how they beheaded some of them, and others had different parts of their bodies cut off.[48]

3537. The soldiers went on to Yocultac where nine victims were reported. In Yocultac the troops probably divided themselves into two platoons. One went towards Bulej, then to Campamento, Yalambojoch and San Francisco, where they received reinforcements: a helicopter, a captain, and four officials.[49] In San Francisco they massacred approximately 350 people. They went house by house, forcing all the inhabitants to get out.

Afterwards they regrouped the women and the children in the church, and the men and the elderly in the auxiliary city hall. Afterwards they asked for some oxen, asking that they be from the peasants and not from the boss. They assured everyone that they were going to organize a party. At two in the afternoon they began to take out the women in groups of ten and 20, some escaped to their houses where they were raped and burned alive along with the houses. They began to take out the children in groups, killing them with blows. They tortured the elders, forcing them to lie on the floor and passing a machete along their necks several times until their throats were slit. They stripped the men naked, made them get out, and killed them. Apparently at the end of the massacre they grilled the meat of the oxen and ate it, then burned the village before leaving.[50]

3538. After committing the massacre of San Francisco the soldiers returned, heading south, taking as a prisoner the administrator of the plantation of San Francisco. They stayed four days in Yalambojoch, forcing the people to participate in various meetings to organize the patrol. On the next day they made a ditch and put bombs in it, which they blew up. Many women fled. Some 200 soldiers went in the direction of Yaltoya and found women there whom they raped and killed.[51]

3539. Apparently the other group of soldiers had similar orders, but in a second direction —that of the communities of Petanac and Sebep, where indiscriminate massacres were carried out:

The soldiers surrounded nearly all the houses (probably urban ones), profiting from the fact the people were gathered in the center, brought the men to a house, tied their hands behind their backs and left them linked to each other with a rope. Afterwards they encircled a house. They made the men go in the house one by one, killing them as they entered. The women they locked up with the children and the elders in another house, put a bomb in the house and burned them alive. One tried to escape from the great flames, they shot her and took out her heart, I saw something yellow in her breast, there was a lot of blood, I was about four or six meters away.[52]

3540. On the 22nd of June or July 1982 four helicopters landed in the village Sacchén, carrying approximately 50 soldiers. They went along a path that goes from Guatemala's northern border with Mexico to the plantation of Sacchen, passing through the villages of Xoxlac and Momonlac and killing 80 people, mostly people that they met in their path.

In the end they arrived at the village Nucá[53] and Cananá,[54] where they massacred 14 people. According to testimonies collected by CEH, the villages of Xoxlac, Yalanhuitz and Sacchén stayed abandoned and were razed afterwards by soldiers and civil patrols from Pojom, San Mateo Ixtatán.

Forced Displacement

3541. A vast majority of the communities in the region suffered forced displacement. The displacement ranged from four to six weeks in some cases, to much longer periods of two years in other cases.

3542. By 1983, 43,000 refugees were officially registered, 53.48% of whom came from Huehuetenango. Refugees who had escaped from the area north of Huehuetenango were located as follows: 21% in the Mexican province of Chiapas or about 4,830 people; 9,807 refugees in the woods of Independencia and Trinitaria (46.5% of whom were Q'anjob'al, and 34.4% of whom were Chuj); and last, another 8,363 in the forest of Margaritas (95% of whom were Q'anjob'al and 4.5% of whom were Mam).

3543. After massacres, the population had no choice, they could turn themselves in to the Army, which entailed running the risk of being killed or losing many members of their family, or they could try to survive in the mountains in very difficult conditions. The militarization that followed the phase of great repression probably kept most of the population from considering the second option.

> We lived three months in the mountain. There were 150 people living behind the community of Morelia. Life was hard. We often wanted to cry. There were people who died, who could not endure the difficult conditions, living under the rain.[55]

3544. The process of seeking refuge was marked by continued violence for most refugees. According to testimonies collected by the CEH, some communities that returned through the repatriation process suffered different reprisals, including torture and the deprivation of freedom. Moreover, they were forced to negate their cultural identity, and to divide up into small groups and settle in areas under military control, far from their places of origin.

3545. The Army in Guatemala persecuted the people who fled. For example, the community of Babeltzap was constantly harassed. The village was burned to the ground on two occasions, and suffered a massacre that ultimately led to the displacement of its inhabitants to the village San Felipe. After that, the Army forced the inhabitants of the village San Felipe to expel the people from Babeltzap by making numerous radio announcements.[56]

3546. In 1983 alone, 52 incursions by the Army were registered in refugee camps in Chiapas, Mexico.

> The helicopters flew over the path several times. When that happened, we all had to hide in the trees, to sleep at night in the mountains, because we knew that the Army was following us.[57]

3547. Children, babies, and the elderly were the groups most affected by displacement:

> There we stayed in the forest, suffering fear, hunger, thirst and cold. Many died there. Especially the poor babies couldn't survive.[58]

3548. Ultimately, the Army prevented the return of displaced populations by developing three obstacles:

Militarized Resettlement

3549. On September 6, 1984 the first group of 28 families from the Pacayal colony or from Pacayas, was repatriated to Xoxlac, Barillas. They were sent directly to the Military area No.19 of Huehuetenango, where they were beaten several times. Finally on September 29 they were sent to Xoxlac. Similar processes happened for at least the following communities: Puente Quemado, Campamento Salamay and El Aguacate.

Acts against the Foundations of the Group

> People said, hopefully they never overcame us; the women said that the soldiers spat on them in their face and accused them of being guerrillas when they tried to defend their husbands. When they looked the soldiers in the eyes, that is the fundamental question for me—the Indians, especially Indian women, must lower their heads when someone looks at them.... Looking at them [the soldiers] with hate when they had them tied up and were raping them, lowering their heads was a challenge. Not touching them but attacking their dignity through their gaze and their dignity.[59]

Mass Killings of Civilians, Especially the Most Vulnerable

3550. During the massacres carried out in the area North of Huehuetenango the Army victimized the most vulnerable members of the community, especially girls, boys, and elderly. This was clear in their direct attacks against these groups, by torturing them, assassinating them, and forcing them to participate in acts of violence or to witness them. This forced witnessing of abuses constituted a permanent trauma for many people, especially children.

> What we have seen has been terrible. Burned bodies, women with their bodies pierced by stakes and buried as if they were animals ready to cook like grilled meat, bent over double, and children massacred and stabbed with machetes, and women also killed like Christ.[60]

3551. The CEH recorded at least seven massacres where all the children were executed. It is difficult to determine how many children died because in many cases they were executed together with their parents and families. However, the CEH confirmed no less than 268 cases. Killing children was not an excess or an accident: these were premeditated assassinations. The following testimony explains how this type of violence happened in Sebep, Cananá and San Francisco.

> They took out the boys and girls by grabbing their feet and hitting them like bags against a wooden column. There were pieces of the small ones' brains stuck like corn paste. When they finished they threw them in the house and went to look for the others in the church.[61]

3552. In the massacres in Puente Alto, Petanac, Coyá and Piedras Blancas Barillas they locked up women and children in houses and burned them:

> They gathered the women with the children and locked them up in a house. Then they set fire to the house until they died. Four children escaped from this mass killing. Some 50 or 60 children died that day.[62]

3553. In the displacement the Army attacked women, some of them pregnant, and killed them because of injury by repeated rapes. Others were executed by assaults with knives, or by having fetuses cut out of their stomachs.[63] These attacks gave no military advantage to the Army, and thus cannot be interpreted as actions against the guerrilla movement. A newborn child cannot be a combatant or a guerrilla collaborator.

Torture

3554. Forcing individuals to witness executions, forcing them to torture members of their own community, or to carry out massacres based on age, gender, or social role in the community, all constituted patterns of collective torture. For example, in San Carlos Las Brisas Barillas, on June 27, 1981, the Army gathered some 200 patrolmen and military commissioners from the area of Barillas:

> Right after they had organized us into the PACs [Civil Defense Patrols] there was a massacre in San Carlos las Brisas. I remember that the day of June 27, 1981 at three in the morning, the order arrived from the detachment of Barillas, to leave immediately for Amelco in a sweep to remove ten guerrillas. All the PACs of the area received the order to go.[64]

3555. Afterwards, in the detachment of Barillas, the ten accused were tortured and sent to San Carlos las Brisas to be publicly executed. It seems that the accused were from that community:

> In the detachment the ten guerrillas were tortured to obtain information.... The lieutenant told us: "Because of their guilt you have to patrol and suffer. Now, what do you want us to do with these fuckers." Then the lieutenant decided that we should bring them to San Carlos las Brisas, while he went ahead in a car. "Bring the fuckers but you need to hit them hard along the way." The alleged guerrillas were dressed like me, like civilians. I don't think that they were guerrillas.[65]

3556. The officer psychologically and socially damaged the community, forcing it to be present and making it responsible not only for torture but also for the destruction of corpses. The act described below damaged the entire community: the ten who were tortured and assassinated; those who were forced to torture and kill; and those who were forced to watch, especially children.

> The ten arrived nearly dead, because they had been so terribly beaten along the way. All the people from Babeltzap were there. Since the ten presumed guerrillas were all from Babeltzap too, the lieutenant wanted everyone to witness the events. One by one they shot the alleged guerrillas. In each case the lieutenant counted one, two, three, and then everyone had to shoot until it was their turn in the earth. One of the presumed guerrillas, while waiting his turn, let himself fall on his knees and crying he started to pray, saying: "Who knows why I have to die now. I am innocent." Then the lieutenant got really angry and said: "Because this fucker is contradicting me in his heart, let's finish now with the fucker" and gave the order to put a gun in his mouth. That is how they killed him.[66]

3557. A description of the event gives a sense of how it triggered total destruction of the group, with mutilations of corpses and the obstruction of their burial.

> After having shot all of them, the lieutenant said: "Now we are tired. It is their fault that you have to patrol to be able to kill so many fuckers, and these fuckers don't want to die." It seemed that not all were dead yet, so some soldiers had to put their arms against the breasts of the three who were still alive and shoot more bullets. That

is how the lives of those ten ended. 'To finish, now we will mutilate the fuckers. You need to do it because I am already tired of killing so many fuckers." That is how the lieutenant talked to motivate all of us who were present, to give us the courage to participate in the mass killing. Then soldiers, patrolmen, and military commissioners began to chop the corpses with machetes until there were only small pieces left.[67]

3558. Finally, at the end of the event, the under-lieutenant summarized the intended social lesson of this violence:

And what do you feel, asked the lieutenant. Now you have acquired courage for the future, to kill fuckers. It's progress. Now you know that you too can be like soldiers.[68]

3559. A similar process was used in Yalambojoch, where the soldiers stayed four days, exploding bombs in a ditch to terrorize people. They threatened them every moment. During the four days they forced people to gather together several times, keeping them in a state of permanent terror. In the end, 17 women with some children fled the community and were raped and executed not far away.[69]

3560. In the community of Campamento, North of Nentón, in July of 1980-1981 [sic], 20 soldiers from the Army arrived. They captured 11 men whose feet they wounded. They then tortured the men by forcing them to walk [on their wounds], eventually killing the men.

They arrived in the community, cut the soles of the feet of eleven men, and forced them to walk, then burned all the houses and left.[70]

3561. In the area north of Barillas, on the road from the Mexican border to Sacchén, the Army left 80 corpses in its wake, most of whom were executed with knives. In most cases it was prohibited to bury the victims. The Army used time and material resources to ban the burials.

They left two guards behind so that we could not bury them, and that is how they were eaten by animals.[71]

3562. In Yalambojoch, the administrator of the plantation of San Francisco was tortured at different times in front of the community. Soldiers tried to force him to accuse the neighbors of Yalambojoch, but he refused several times.

3563. In Jom, San Miguel Acatán, soldiers stripped 18 people completely naked, took their shoes and put hoods on them, then brought them on the road to San Miguel Acatán. In La Cruz they halted, made a fire and burned their victims' mouths, the soles of their feet, their hands and their heads. On the path they gathered others, until they had 25. In Nubilá they forced them to dig a ditch and shot them, burying them there.[72]

3564. The vast majority of testimonies referring to selective executions mention that victims were tortured prior to their assassination. Torture was not carried out solely to obtain information, since most of the victims did not have any important information or information of significance for the Army's operations.

Sexual Violence

3565. Acts of sexual violence were repeated in cases where women, especially young women, were present. Cases were also registered in which soldiers specifically went to look for women from communities to rape them.

3566. The CEH recorded two cases in which the very act of repeated rapes led to the death of the victims. Attacks on the group were constantly repeated through serious physical and psychosocial attacks. For example, a case was recorded on the plantation of San Ramón Barillas, where multiple rapes caused a victim's death:

> The Army entered into the community and registered everything. Afterwards she was raped by many soldiers on multiple occasions. We brought her to the hospital but she did not recover and died.[73]

3567. During the efforts to escape the bombardment of the village Coyá, a couple with their child fled, looking for the path to Chimbam. In the path they met thirty soldiers who raped the woman until she died. Apparently the husband stayed paralyzed, so they did not do anything to him. He was able to escape with the child and to reach San Miguel Acatán.[74]

3568. Collective rapes took place in most massacres. Generally the young women or all women were caught and repeatedly raped. That is what happened in San Francisco, where some women, who were trying to escape, were raped and burned alive in their homes; and in Puente Alto where women under 17 were selected and then raped and executed. In Yalambojoch the women who were fleeing were raped and executed.[75] Collective rapes became one more stage in the violence that preceded execution.

3569. Sexual violence caused serious wounds to the physical and mental integrity of the members of the group. The physical wounds sometimes irreversibly damaged women's reproductive organs, especially in the case of girls and adolescents. Socially, the psychological wounds broke the women's vital connections to the group by stigmatizing them and barring them from forming families.

Destruction of Material and Spiritual Aspects of Culture

3570. During the scorched earth phase, many houses were destroyed, as were plots with or without corn. They were destroyed for their nutritional value but also because of their significance. Maya and Catholic beliefs were particularly attacked. Chimban had been the center of Chuj culture:

> There is a place called Chimban, which is the center of Maya culture in Huehuetenango, and so there is a village that is called Chimban, which is just a few kilometers from San Miguel Acatán.[76]

3571. According to some witnesses there is a ceremonial center in this place:

> It is a little house, like any other small house. Probably that is where they had gatherings at certain times of year, in which the older leaders, the *mamines*,[77] organized ceremonies according to custom.[78]

3572. At the beginning of the resurgence of the violence, in 1980, the Chief Priest[79] of Chimban was murdered along with four or five traditional Maya authorities. Later, the population of Chimban was massacred on July 22, with a death toll of 30 victims.[80]

> The Army arrived and decapitated them, there next to the ceremonial center, decapitated them, and stole their heads, there in front of all the people, like an example that the people would stay decapitated. There was a place that stayed without a chief and they did the same thing to the one who followed him.[81]

3573. The women and children of San Francisco and Puente Alto, where two of the most violent massacres took place, were tortured and assassinated in churches. The following testimonies leave no doubt about such acts:

> Afterwards they proceeded to regroup the women and the children in the church, and the men and elders were rounded up in the auxiliary city hall ... then they started to kill them.[82]

> Because I was a boy, I went with my mother into the Church which was where they were gathering the women. After he said "this firewood will serve to turn them into cooked pork rind," all the people screamed. Then he said there is only one minute and they started to machine gun. Then they poured gasoline and lit us on fire.[83]

Conclusion

3574. The CEH finds that most crimes perpetrated by the armed forces against the Q'anjob'al and Chuj Maya populations of the North of Huehuetenango constituted acts of genocide. Among others, these acts included the massacres at Puente Alto, San Francisco, Yalambojoch, Yocultac and Sebep, which affected all members of the communities especially women, children, and elders, because of their belonging to the targeted ethnic group. The attacks were inspired by a strategic determination of a genocidal nature, insofar as its objective was the partial destruction of the [Q'anjob'al and Chuj Maya] ethnic group under investigation. [The Q'anjob'al and Chuj Maya] were identified as an enemy of the State of Guatemala, even though the [declared] motives in doing so were not racist but rather of a military-political character.

3575. The perception of shared or identical identity across the entire Chuj and Q'anjob'al population and the guerrillas led to a campaign aimed at the partial annihilation of the [Q'anjob'al and Chuj Maya] group. The Army believed that the annihilation of this group would translate into the guerrilla movement's defeat.

3576. The repetitive and massive nature of these operations, their logical and coherent execution, the testimonies from various sources to the CEH, and the examination of official documents, all allow us to conclude that these acts were committed with full prior knowledge, participation, and backing of the institutions of National Defense.

3577. This argument is further corroborated by the fact that both air and land forces were combined to perpetrate acts of violence against the civilian population, with reinforcements of troops from other regions.

3578. The massive and brutal nature of acts committed against the Chuj and Q'anjob'al Maya groups reveal a pattern of attack characterized by genocidal acts. In one phase, community leaders became targets, and were publicly tortured and assassinated, which had the effect of making the group more vulnerable as a whole. Then, operations of annihilation and massive destruction that included women, children, and the elderly— which were perpetrated after tortures, massive sexual violence, persecution, displacement, and bombardments—destroyed the foundations of social cohesion between the members of the group. Moreover, perpetrators tried to prevent any possible social reconstruction of the group, by forcing members to commit acts of violence or to witness them [and hence become complicit in them].

3579. The results of the repeated campaigns of violence committed against the group include a death toll of 2,328. 99.3% of the dead were Chuj or Q'anjob'al, including men, women, and children. Eighty percent of the population [of the region under analysis here] was displaced, and submitted to conditions conducive to death by starvation, cold, or sickness.

3580. The objective of the military counterinsurgency campaign carried out by the Army of Guatemala in the North of Huehuetenango was the partial annihilation of the Chuj and Q'anjob'al group. This was considered the only possible way to defeat the enemy. 3.6% of the total population was annihilated.[84]

Notes

1. The studied area does not correspond to the area of all the districts, but to an area defined according to criteria that the CEH specified in paragraph 4 of its report.
2. This calculation was made by the National Statistics Institute (Instituto Nacional de Estadística,) 1973 and 1981 population censuses, by a linear projection of the data.
3. Beatriz Manz, *Guatemala: cambios en la comunidad, desplazamientos y repatriación.* México, Iglesia Guatemalteca en el Exilio. (México, D.F.: Editorial Praxis 1986), pp. 108-146. [Guatemala, Changes in the Community, Displacement and Repatriation]
4. David McCreery, "Land, Labor, and Violence in Highland Guatemala: San Juan Ixcoy (Huehuetenango), 1890-1940," *The Americas,* (October, 1988), 237-249 and "Tierra Trabajo y Conflicto en San Juan Ixcoy, Huehuetenango, 1890-1940," in *Revista de Historia* (Costa Rica) 19 (Enero-Junio, 1989), 19-35 and *Anales de la Academia de Geografía e Historia de Guatemala* año LXV (1992), pp. 101-112.
5. Ibid.
6. Beatriz Manz, *Guatemala,* pp. 108-146.
7. Ibid.
8. CEH collective testimony by members of the municipal corporation of San Miguel Acatán, Huehuetenango. (T.C. 352). In the region are included the village of Coyá, of San Miguel Acatán because Coyá and Chimbam are centers of Maya culture in Huehuetenango. In this sense, witness (member of the EGP) CEH. (T.C. 154).
9. CEH collective testimony by members of the municipal corporation of San Miguel Acatán, Huehuetenango. (T.C. 352).
10. Beatriz Manz, *Guatemala,* pp. 108-146.
11. César Castañeda Salguero, *Lucha por la tierra, retornados y medio ambiente en Huehuetenango* (Guatemala: FLACSO, 1998), pp. 106. [Struggle for land, returnees, and the environment]

12.   Ibid., pp. 107.
13.   Ejército de Guatemala, Resumen de Inteligencia al plan de operaciones, Gran Ofensiva del área militar de Huehuetenango, Anexo B, 1981. [Armed Forces of Guatemala, Summary of Intelligence on the Operations Plan, Great Offensive in the military area of Huehuetenango].
14.   Ibid.
15.   Ibid. The same Intelligence Plan noted that "our units have encountered great difficulties in penetrating."
16.   According to Carlos Cabarruz's concept of an innate platform of ethnicity, the ethnic group is constituted by three elements: language, race, and history. Language is a facilitating condition of the ethnic group: the language community constitutes in some form the ethnic unit. Race is not taken into account in the strict sense of physical anthropology, but rather as the auto-expression of the indigenous person, permitting the inference of a relationship almost of parentage between "ours," "our people" between the members of a district, identifying themselves by postures that constitute an endogenous whole more than by physical features. Thus, the spontaneous mode of the idea of race or of blood constitutes a base for the substantive construction of an ethnic group. Ultimately, in the Guatemalan case, history responds to indigenous culture which has been attacked and often truncated but which is configured as part of an identity. Carlos Cabarruz, *Q'eqchi' Cosmovision* (San Salvador: Universidad Centro-Americana, 1979), pp. 57.
17.   Ejército de Guatemala, Resumen de Inteligencia, 1981 [Summary of Intelligence]
18.   Ibid.
19.   CI 84. Julio 1981. Coyá, San Miguel Acatán, Huehuetenango.
20.   Ejército de Guatemala, Resumen de Inteligencia, 1981. [Summary of Intelligence]
21.   Ibid.
22.   Collective Interview by the CEH with the EGP.
23.   Instituto Internacional de Derecho Humanitario, "Declaración sobre las normas del Derecho Internacional Humanitario relativas a la conducción de hostilidades en los conflictos armados no internacionales," *Revista Internacional de la Cruz Roja*, Septiembre de 1990, No. 101, pp. 434. [International Institute of Human Rights, "Declaration on the Norms of International Humanitarian Law Relative to the Carrying out of Hostilities in Non-International Armed Conflicts," *International Review of the Red Cross*, September 1990, No. 101].
24.   According to the criteria of the Genocide Convention.
25.   The calculation is the result of the average of the population density of the two districts, applied to the number of square kilometers in the area, which gives an average density of inhabitants in the region, although this is not precise relative to locale.
26.   According to Article 14 of the II Additional Protocol of 1977 to the Geneva Conventions of August 12, 1949 relative to victims of armed conflicts of a non-international character, June 8, 1977.
27.   Witness (retired military) CEH. (T.C. 92).
28.   C 5733. Nov. 1980. Nentón, Huehuetenango.
29.   C 5033. Aug. 1982. Nentón, Huehuetenango.
30.   Consult the box of killings of leaders.
31.   C 5717. July 1982. Nentón, Huehuetenango.
32.   According to Anthony Giddens, social stratification is "the existence between groups of a society of Inequalities structured in terms of access to material or symbolic rewards or any other privilege that affects its possibilities of surviving,

either material or symbolic." Anthony Giddens (*Sociologia*, Alianza Editorial S.A.,1991), p. 780.

33. REMHI Witness 153, former soldier participating in the scorched earth policy.
34. Ejército de Guatemala, Resumen de Inteligencia, Anexo B, 1981 [Summary of Intelligence].
35. C 6096. July 1981. San Miguel Acatán, Huehuetenango.
36. C 5246. February 1981. Nentón, Huehuetenango.
37. CEH database.
38. C 5461. June 1981. Barillas, Huehuetenango.
39. C 6031. July 1982. Barillas, Huehuetenango.
40. CEH database.
41. C 6022. July 1982. San Mateo Ixtatán, Huehuetenango.
42. C 6022. July 1982. San Mateo Ixtatán, Huehuetenango.
43. CI 83. Massacre of the Maya inhabitants of Babeltzap in San Carlos las Brisas, June 1982.
44. CI 84. Bombardment and Massacre in Coyá, San Miguel Acatán July 1981.
45. REMHI *Report on the Massacres in Huehuetenango*, p. 12.
46. C 6187. June 1982. Barillas, Huehuetenango.
47. C 6031. July 1982. Barillas, Huehuetenango.
48. C 6075. July 1982. San Mateo Ixtatán, Huehuetenango.
49. CI 18. July 1982. Nentón, Huehuetenango.
50. Ibid.
51. C 6085, Yaltoyat, Huehuetenango, July 1982.
52. C 6074. July 1982. San Mateo Ixtatán, Huehuetenango.
53. C 6023. May 1981. San Mateo Ixtatán, Huehuetenango.
54. C 6126. June 1982. Barillas, Huehuetenango.
55. Witness (catechist and activist in the Q'anjob'al faith) CEH. (T.C. 6017).
56. C 6274. July 1981. Barrillas, Huehuetenango.
57. Witness (testimony of a Q'anjob'al witness from Xoxlac, displaced community of Huehuetenango). CEH. (T.C. 6017-16).
58. Ibid., continuation of the testimonies on displacement, Q'anjob'al witness from Xoxlac, Huehuetenango.
59. Witness (Quiché thinker) CEH. (T.C. 130).
60. REMHI Testimony, C 0839.
61. CI 18. July 1982. Chuj, Huehuetenango.
62. C 6020. May 1982. Barillas, Huehuetenango.
63. C 6080. July 1981. Barillas, Huehuetenango.
64. C 6080. July 1981. Barillas, Huehuetenango.
65. Ibid.
66. CI 83. June 1982. Babeltzap, Huehuetenango.
67. Ibid.
68. Ibid.
69. C 6085. July 1982. Yalambojoch, Huhuetenango.
70. C 5021. July 1980. Nentón, Huehuetenango.
71. C 5812. May 1980. Nentón, Huehuetenango.
72. C 6009. June 1982. San Miguel Acatán, Huehuetenango.
73. C 6050. 1981. Barillas, Huehuetenango.
74. C 6201. July 1981. San Miguel Acatán, Huehuetenango.
75. C 6085. July 1982. Yalambojoch, Huehuetenango.
76. Witness (member of the EGP) CEH. (T.C. 154).
77. [Ed.: *Mamines* are the village's spiritual fathers or grandfathers. The principle leader is the *alcalde rezador* or mayor and leader of prayers.]

78.   Ibid.
79.   [Ed:. The Chief Priest is the spiritual fountainhead of the community.]
80.   1304 REMHI Report on the Massacres in Huehuetenango, p. 16.
81.   1305 Ibid.
82.   1306 CI 18. July 1982. Nentón, Huehuetenango. C 6031. July 1982. Barillas, Huehuetenango.
83.   1307 C 6031. July 1982. Barillas, Huehuetenango.
84.   Asociación Americana para el Avance de la Ciencia. Estudio sobre Genocidio realizado para la CEH. [American Association for the Advance of Science. Study of Genocide for the CEH.]

Final Conclusions to the Genocide Section

Final Conclusions

3581. In the four regions that the CEH studied to address the issue of genocide, the CEH found that the violence was massive and overwhelmingly impacted Maya people. In the Ixil and Rabinal areas, 14.5% and 14.6% of the population were killed, while in the North of Huehuetenango and Zacualpa 3.6% and 8.6% of the population were killed. Also, the majority of victims of massacres and other human rights violations were members of the Maya people. The proportion of Maya victims was much greater than the proportion of Maya in the general population, relative to *ladinos*. In the Ixil area, 97.8% of the victims were Maya. In the North of Huehuetanango, the proportion of Maya victims was 99.3%, while in Rabinal it was 99.8% and in Zacualpa 98.4%.

3582. These overwhelming percentages indicate that human rights violations were directed in a purposefully discriminatory manner against the Maya population in these regions. Generalized discrimination against the Maya people can also be seen in the manner in which the Army systematically executed those identified as leaders of the Maya community. In the four regions analyzed, during 1981 and 1982, the Army executed the majority of community leaders including: religious leaders such as catechists, Mayan priests, representatives of *cofradías* and members of Catholic Action; development workers; members of community-based organizations such as the CUC [Comité de Unidad Campesina, or Peasant Unity Committee]; members of cooperatives; and political leaders such as deputy mayors. Based on the data collected by the CEH, 198 such leaders were assassinated during the period investigated.

3583. Alongside the generalized discrimination in selecting victims largely from the Maya population, those responsible for killings did not distinguish among victims by age, gender or general condition. For ex-

127

ample, from February to October 1982 in the four regions studied, there were mass killings of men, women, children, and the elderly. The Army targeted entire communities, rather than targeting individuals based on specific accusations.

3584. After analyzing the facts in four selected geographic regions, the CEH was able to confirm that during a specific stage of the internal armed conflict—during the years 1981 and 1982—the Army identified the Maya people as an internal enemy. It did so because it believed that they constituted or could constitute a base of support for the guerrillas, whether through material support, as a source of recruits, or as a population where guerillas could hide. Thus, inspired by the National Security Doctrine (NSD), the Army expanded the concept of internal enemy beyond guerrilla combatants, militants, or sympathizers, to include membership in certain ethnic groups.

First Conclusion

3585. The CEH considered the criminal acts and human rights violations that occurred in these regions during the periods discussed above, and analyzed them in order to determine if they constituted the crime of genocide. The CEH concluded that taken together, these reiterated destructive acts were directed in a systematic manner against groups of the Maya population. Among these acts, the elimination of leaders and criminal acts against minors that could not be understood to serve a military objective make manifest that the only common factor among all the victims was their membership in an ethnic group. These acts were committed "with the intent to destroy in whole or in part" the [Maya] groups (Article II, first paragraph, of the Convention).

3586. Among those acts directed towards the destruction of the Maya groups identified by the Army as the enemy, the most significant include "killing" (Article II, subsection "a" of the Convention), which is most powerfully seen in massacres. In the four regions examined between 1981 and 1982, the CEH found that agents of the State perpetrated killings, which became the most serious elements in a sequence of military operations directed against non-combatant civilian populations. For example, in the beginning of February 1982, the military instituted in the Ixil area one of the bloodiest campaigns documented by the CEH in the entire armed conflict. In addition, between July and August 1982, the military carried out three campaigns that included mass killings.

Similarly, in Zacualpa, the massacre of San Antonio Sinaché was both preceded and followed by massacres in neighboring communities; and the large massacre in Rabinal on September 15, 1981 was followed by other massacres in nearby communities.

3587. In line with testimonies and other important elements of proof, the CEH established that these mass killings, which can be characterized as massacres, involved the participation of regular and special forces of the Army, civil defense patrols, and military commissioners. In many cases, survivors identified the perpetrators, such as the officers who commanded the operation, as being from the closest military base.

Second Conclusion

3588. Close analysis has permitted the CEH to conclude that in almost all of these cases, the perpetrators' objective was to kill the maximum possible number of members of the [aforementioned Maya] groups.

3589. Generally, in all mass killings the Army prepared by: carefully gathering the population before killing them; surrounding the community; or taking advantage of situations when the whole community was gathered together (such as celebrations or market days) in order to commit mass killings.

3590. In studying what happened in the four regions, the CEH established that alongside the mass killings—which were enough on their own to guarantee the elimination of the groups defined as enemies—Army units or civil patrolmen systematically committed acts of extreme cruelty, including torture and other cruel, inhuman and degrading acts. The effect of these acts was to terrorize the population and destroy the basic elements of social cohesion between members, particularly when they were forced to witness or commit these acts themselves.

3591. Army units or civil patrolmen engaged in collective sexual violations against women, often committed in public and designed to leave a mark that would harm the social reproduction of the group over time.

Third Conclusion

3592. The CEH concluded that, among acts perpetrated with the intent to destroy many Maya groups in whole or in part, perpetrators also committed numerous acts "causing serious bodily or mental harm to members of the group" of the affected Maya populations (Article II, subsection "b" of the Convention). The effect was the destruction of the social cohesion of the groups. These acts corresponded with the intention to physically and spiritually annihilate the groups.

3593. The CEH's investigations proved that mass killings, especially indiscriminate massacres, were accompanied by the devastation of communities. The most notable case was that of the Ixil region where between 70% and 90% of rural communities were destroyed. Also, in the north of Huehuetenango, Rabinal, and Zacualpa, perpetrators razed entire communities, destroyed their property and burned communal fields during planting and harvesting, leaving people without food.

3594. In addition, in the four regions that are the subject of this study, populations were persecuted during their forced displacement. The CEH established that in the Ixil area, displaced people were bombed. Similarly, people who were captured or who voluntarily turned themselves in were subjected to human rights violations although they lived under the complete control of the Army.

Fourth Conclusion

3595. The CEH concluded that among the acts previously described, perpetrated with the intention to destroy many Maya groups in whole or in part, some were "deliberately inflicting upon the group conditions of life calculated to bring about its physical destruction in whole or in part" (Article II, subsection "c" of the Convention).

3596. As described in this chapter, the aforementioned acts were committed in the four regions and followed a common pattern. They occurred at a similar time and involved similar acts, operations, and, subsequently, a related mode of controlling the population.

3597. The CEH's analysis shows that committing these acts required coordination of the military system at a national level, which enabled the "efficient" actions of soldiers and civil patrolmen in the four regions studied. One example of this is seen in those operations that relied on aerial support which required the intervention of a superior command that authorized and coordinated this reinforcement with actions in the field.

3598. The Army's campaign plans were provided to the CEH. They included supporting claims, regarding the goals and objectives of acts of violence described above. For example, the plan "Victory 82" claimed that "the mission is the annihilation of the guerrilla and parallel organizations." The plan for the campaign "Strength 83-1" claimed that the army should support "these operations with the maximum number of PAC in order to destroy all communal planting projects subversives have in an area, where there is clear proof of active participation and collaboration by rural communities, which sympathize with and are organized by the insurgency."

3599. All of these issues have convinced the CEH that these acts were perpetrated with the intent of destroying many groups of Maya in whole or in part. They were not isolated acts or excesses committed by out of control troops, nor were they the result of improvised actions by mid-level army officers. With great dismay, the CEH concludes that many of the massacres and other violations of human rights committed against these groups reflected a higher-level policy. They were strategically planned, as is manifested by actions expressing a coherent and logical plan.

3600. In addition, the CEH has information that similar acts of violence took place repeatedly in other regions inhabited by Maya people. In considering all options to combat the insurgency, the State chose the one with the highest cost in terms of lives of non-combatant civilians. The State decided against other options, such as a political negotiation with civilian non-combatants living in conflict zones, or such as the arrest of insurgents, and chose instead to annihilate those the State identified as its enemies. The State made this decision despite the fact that they had adequate sources of information to identify insurgent combatants, analyze their military capacity, and distinguish them from civilian non-combatants.

Fifth Conclusion

3601. As a result, the CEH concluded that agents of the Guatemalan State committed acts of genocide against the Maya people that live in the Ixil region, Zacualpa, northern Huehuetenango and Rabinal during the counterinsurgency operations conducted in 1981 and 1982. This conclusion is based on evidence, and on Article II of the Convention for the Prevention and Punishment of Genocide. There were mass killings of members of Maya groups (Article II, subsection "a"), serious bodily or mental harm to members of Maya groups (Article II, subsection "b"), and perpetrators deliberately inflicted on [Maya] groups conditions of life calculated to bring about their physical destruction in whole or in part (Article II, subsection "c"). This conclusion is also based on evidence that all those acts were perpetrated "with the intention to destroy in whole or in part" a group identified by their common ethnicity, as such, independently of what might have been the cause, motive, and ultimate objective of those acts (Article II, first paragraph).

Sixth Conclusion

3602. Based on the fundamental conclusion that genocide was committed, the CEH is following its mandate in offering objective elements of its judgment regarding what occurred during the internal armed conflict. Thus, the CEH affirms: there is no question that the perpetrators are the intellectual and material authors of the crimes. The genocidal acts committed in Guatemala were also the responsibility of the State. This is because most such acts were the product of a policy established by higher level commanders, rather than the material authors of these acts.

3603. The preceding conclusion has been confirmed by establishing that the military authorities knew about the massacres committed by their agents. These acts were never investigated or sanctioned to ensure that they would not occur again.

3604. The failure to investigate these acts is the responsibility of the military authorities, the competent judicial bodies, and the political authorities.

3605. The State of Guatemala never took any action to investigate or sanction those responsible for these acts, despite the fact that many of them were well known publicly. This is evidenced by the multiple petitions presented before international bodies such as the Inter-American Commission on Human Rights, which required that the Government investigate serious violations to the right to life in their visit to the country in 1982.

Seventh Conclusion

3606. Finally, in relation to the crimes of genocide, the CEH concluded that the State of Guatemala failed to honor its obligation to investigate and sanction acts of genocide committed in its territory. Thus, it has violated

Articles IV and VI of the Convention for the Prevention and Punishment of the Crime of Genocide. The Convention requires that those persons who have committed genocide—whether they are government leaders, functionaries or private citizens—should be tried by a competent court of the State in whose territory the acts were committed or before a competent international criminal court, where the contracting parties have recognized its jurisdiction.

3607. The international legal framework applicable with respect to the violence committed by insurgent groups or guerillas is found in international humanitarian law or the law of armed conflict, specifically the Geneva Conventions of 1949, ratified in 1952. Common Article 3 of the Geneva Conventions prohibits attacks against those who do not participate directly in hostilities—that is, against the civilian population—in any time or place. It prohibits "attacks against life and bodily integrity, especially homicide in all its forms."

3608. In addition, the Second Additional Protocol of the Convention of 1949, ratified by Guatemala on October 19, 1987 (which complements and expands upon common Article 3) establishes in its Article 4 that killing of this type is prohibited at all times and in all places. This is more clearly expressed in Article 13 of the Second Protocol, which established norms of protection for non-combatants. It prohibits anyone from singling out non-combatants as the object of attacks, or acts or threats of violence whose goal is to terrorize the civilian population.

3609. Without questioning the above argument, and recognizing its general principles and their universal application within the civilized world, it is also useful to mention Article 3 of the Universal Declaration of Human Rights of 1948. Article 3 establishes that "Everyone has the right to life, liberty and security of person." This concept is an element of international customary law, and thus must be respected not only by state authorities but also by armed forces organized in opposition to state security forces.

Criminal Prosecutions for Genocide in Guatemala: Advances and Obstacles in Transnational and Domestic Cases

*Naomi Roht-Arriaza**

In November 2006, a local trial court in Guatemala's capital ordered the arrest of the country's ex-President, Oscar Mejía Víctores, along with ex-Defense Minister Aníbal Guevara, ex-Police Chief Germán Chupina, and ex-head of the Secret Police Pedro Arredondo on charges of genocide, torture, enforced disappearances, arbitrary detention, and terrorism.[1] The defendants, along with two others—former president and military strongman Efraín Ríos Montt and former army chief of staff Benedicto Lucas—whose arrest warrants were not executed, were deeply implicated in the conceptualization and execution of the repressive state strategy that resulted in the deaths of 200,000 Guatemalans and the destruction of over 400 villages detailed in the CEH report. Although the arrest order was carried out through a Guatemalan court, it was issued by a Spanish judge,[2] Santiago Pedraz. Judge Pedraz of

---

*   Professor of Law, University of California, Hastings College of the Law. The author is a member of the Legal Advisory Council of the Center for Justice and Accountability and has been a member of the legal team involved in the Spanish Genocide case litigation since 2006. Many thanks to Almudena Bernabeu, International Attorney at CJA and the heart of the legal team, for comments and inspiration. And thanks to our partners in Guatemala and elsewhere, without whom these cases would not have happened. Portions of this Essay appeared in the Summer 2008 Chicago Journal of International Law.

1.   José Elías, *Tres Militares y un Civil Guatemaltecos, en el Banquillo*, El País (Spain) (Nov 14, 2006), available online at <http://www.elpais.com/articulo/internacional/militares/civil/guatemaltecos /banquillo/elpporint/20061114elpepuint_4/Tes/> (visited Apr 5, 2008).
2.   Ministerio de Judicia, Juzgado Central de Instrucción No. 1, Audiencia Nacional, Diligencias Previas 331/1999-10, Spain (July 7, 2006), available online at <http://www.i-dem.org/docs/ OrdendecapturaRiosMontt.doc> (visited Apr 5, 2008).

Spain's Audiencia Nacional[3] issued the warrants in July 2006, followed by formal extradition requests. He based Spanish jurisdiction over crimes committed by Guatemalans in Guatemala on a Spanish law that allows universal jurisdiction over certain international crimes.

Mejía holed up in his house and the secret police chief fled, while the ex-Defense minister and the ex-Police Chief were held in a military hospital under guard. This case represents the first time members of the military high command were affected by any legal action against them, and one of a handful of cases where any Guatemalan military officer has been subject to judicial proceedings.[4] After over a year in detention, the defendants were freed when Guatemala's Constitutional Court ("GCC") decided on December 12, 2007 that it would not honor Spanish arrest warrants or extradition requests.[5] The court held that Spanish courts did not constitute a "competent authority" because Spain did not have jurisdiction over events that took place in Guatemala; the effort to exercise universal jurisdiction was unacceptable and an affront to Guatemala's sovereignty. The court added that the charges were related to political

---

3.   The Audiencia Nacional hears cases involving drug smuggling, terrorism, state corruption, and international crimes that cannot adequately be dealt with at the level of provinces and autonomous communities. Although divided into chambers, it is roughly equivalent to a U.S. district court.

4.   There have been two high-profile trials of military officers in the killings of Bishop Juan Gerardi and anthropologist Myrna Mack. The Mack case, after over a dozen years, resulted in the convictions of three officers, one of whom promptly went into hiding. The sentence is at Recurso de Casación Conexados 109-2003 y 110-2003 (Corte Suprema de Justicia, Jan 14, 2004), available online at <http://www.derechos.org/nizkor/guatemala/myrna/myrnacs.html> (visited Apr 5, 2008). In the Gerardi case, the Supreme Court upheld the convictions of two officers in January 2006. See Conie Reynoso, *Confirman Sentencia: Continúa Pena de 20 Años de Cárcel para Sindicados*, Prensa Libre (Jan 14, 2006), available online at <http://www.prensalibre.com.gt/ pl/2006/enero/14/132159.html> (visited Apr 5, 2008). For an excellent description of the Gerardi case, see Francisco Goldman, *The Art of Political Murder: Who Killed the Bishop?* (Grove 2007). A handful of civil patrollers, members of paramilitary groups created and controlled by the army, have also been convicted of murder in Guatemalan courts. But as detailed in this Article, by and large the prosecutors' office has not pursued cases arising out of the armed conflict, and judges have been intimidated, threatened, or bought off.

5.   Sentencia del 12 de Diciembre de 2007, Corte de Constitucionalidad (Guatemala), Expediente 3380-2007, Audiencia Nacional de Espana, available online at <http://www.cc.gob.gt/index-2.html>, click "Ultimas Resoluciones" at the top of the page for access to the decision. (visited Apr 5, 2008) ("GCC decision").

crimes and thus not extraditable, and that Spain's participation in the 1980s Central American peace process meant that it was bound by the commitments made by the government and the insurgents that an official truth commission would have no judicial effects. Given that commitment, the GCC concluded, it would be inconsistent for Spain to now seek to prosecute crimes arising out of the region's civil conflicts.

The Guatemala Genocide case in Spain is one of three cases now before the courts that attempt to prove, in a court of law, charges of genocide against individual defendants. The second, filed with the Guatemalan Prosecutor's office in 2000 and 2001 by the Center for Legal Action on Human Rights (CALDH), has been stalled by the refusal of the Prosecutor's office to proceed despite overwhelming evidence of crimes. Nonetheless, the domestic genocide case has also provoked interesting developments, especially in the area of access to information. The third involves an ongoing investigation in Belgium of the killing and disappearance of Belgian priests during the same period.[6] This essay summarizes the development of the Spanish and domestic cases and the prospects for holding criminally responsible those who committed the acts detailed in this book.

The Genocide Convention, to which Guatemala has long been a party, requires that states criminalize and prosecute allegations of genocide committed in their territory. It specifically states that official position is not a bar to prosecution. Treaties on torture and forced disappearance similarly require investigation and prosecution of allegations that these crimes have taken place. Nonetheless, getting from the letter of the law to actual practice has been difficult. Victims' groups in Guatemala have pursued a combined inside and outside legal strategy, pushing for domestic prosecutions for genocide while also focusing on transnational prosecution based on universal jurisdiction in other states' national courts. Although not always coordinated, these parallel efforts have the best chance of breaking through the wall of impunity that continues to impede

---

6.   The Belgian cases involve the deaths of two Belgian priests—Serge Berten and Walter Voordeckers—during the early 1980s, presumably at the hands of security forces. Family members of the victims brought a case in Belgian courts in January 2001 under Belgium's then-expansive universal jurisdiction law. The case remained open after the law was amended in 2003. See Naomi Roht-Arriaza, *The Pinochet Effect: Transnational Justice in the Age of Human Rights* ch 7 (Penn 2005).

accountability for genocide and its aftermath.[7] In Guatemala, that wall of impunity has been *de facto* but not *de jure:* the 1996 Law of National Reconciliation, which provides an amnesty for certain crimes committed in the context of the "internal armed conflict," specifically exempts the crime of genocide and other international crimes from its coverage.[8]

I. The Proceedings

In December 1999, Nobel Peace Prize winner Rigoberta Menchú and others brought a complaint in the Spanish Audiencia Nacional[9] alleging genocide, torture, terrorism, summary execution, and unlawful detention perpetrated against Guatemala's Mayan indigenous people and their supporters during the 1970s and 1980s. The complainants' rationale for the genocide charges included the targeting of Mayans as an ethnic group. It was also based, following a gloss on the definition of genocide that the Audiencia had accepted in earlier cases involving Chilean and Argentine defendants, on the intended elimination of a part of the Guatemalan "national" group due to its perceived ideology.[10] Among the events underlying the complaint was the massacre of Menchú's father and thirty-five other people in the 1980 firebombing of the Spanish embassy, the killing or disappearance of four Spanish priests, and a large number of rural massacres, rapes, cases of torture, and enforced disappearance.

---

7. An additional strategy involves the use of the Inter-american Commission and Court to push the state to combat impunity. In a series of important cases and in numerous friendly settlements of cases, the Inter-American system has provided money and symbolic reparations for some victims. Although the state has complied with some of the orders of the Court, it has not responded adequately to continuing orders to investigate and prosecute the violations.

    Other possible accountability strategies are not available for these crimes. The International Criminal Court only deals with cases occurring after 2002, and in any case Guatemala is not a party to the Rome Statute establishing the court. The International Court of Justice could hear a case against the state of Guatemala involving genocide, as it did in the Bosnia v. Serbia case, but only if brought by another state. So far, no state has been interested in bringing the issue before the Court.

8. Ley de Reconciliación Nacional, Decreto Numero 145-1996, art 8 (Dec 27, 1996), available online at <www.acnur.org/biblioteca/pdf/0148.pdf> (visited Apr 5, 2008).

9. See explanation in note 3.

10. See *Auto de la Sala de lo Penal de la Audiencia Nacional confirmando la jurisdicción de España para Conocer de los Crímenes de Genocidio y Terrorismo Cometido Durante la Dictadura Argentina (Decision (Auto) of the Full Penal Chamber Confirming Spanish Jurisdiction Over the Crimes of Genocide and Terrorism Committed During the Argentine Dictatorship)*, Appeal No 84-98, 3rd Section, File 19/97 from Judicial Chamber 5, Autos (Audiencia Nacional, Nov 4,

The complainants grounded Spanish jurisdiction on Article 23.4 of the Organic Law of the Judicial Branch ("LOPJ").[11] That provision allows for prosecution of certain crimes committed by non-Spaniards outside Spain, including genocide, terrorism, and other crimes recognized in international treaties ratified by Spain. On March 27, 2000, Investigating Judge Guillermo Ruíz Polanco of the Audiencia Nacional accepted the Guatemalan complaint and agreed to open an investigation.[12] In reaching that decision, the judge noted that several of the victims were Spanish and that the Guatemalan courts had failed to investigate the crimes.[13]

The Spanish Public Prosecutors' Office, at the time in the hands of the conservative Popular Party, appealed the judge's jurisdiction.[14] An appeals panel of the Audiencia Nacional, and then the Spanish Supreme Court, found that the Spanish courts had no jurisdiction. The Supreme Court held, by a vote of 8-7, that customary international law required a link to the forum state when universal jurisdiction was not grounded in specific treaty provisions or authorized by the United Nations.[15] Thus, only those

1998) (Spain), available online at <http://www.derechos.org/nizkor/arg/espana/audi.html> (visited Apr 5, 2008) (author translation); *Auto de la Sala de lo Penal de la Audiencia Nacional Confirmando la Jurisdicción de España para Conocer de los Crímenes de Genocidio y Terrorismo Cometido Durante la Dictadura Chilena (Decision (Auto) of the Full Penal Chamber Confirming Spanish Jurisdiction To Investigate Genocide in Chile)*, Appeal No 173/98, 1st Section, File 1/98 from Judicial Chamber 6 (Audiencia Nacional, Nov 5, 1998) (Spain), available online at <http://www.derechos.org/nizkor/chile/juicio/audi.html> (visited Apr 5, 2008) (author translation). See also the English translation of the decision regarding Chile in Reed Brody and Michael Ratner, eds, *The Pinochet Papers: The Case of Augusto Pinochet in Spain and Britain* (Kluwer 2000).

11.   Ley Orgánica 6/1985, BOE 1985, 157, available online at <http://noticias.juridicas.com/base_datos/Admin/lo6-1985.l1t1.html> (visited Apr 5, 2008).

12.   Juzgado Central de Instrucción No 1, Audiencia Nacional, Madrid, Dil Previas 331/99, Auto de 27 de Marzo de 2000 (on file with author).

13.   Id.

14.   See Roht-Arriaza, *The Pinochet Effect* at ch 1 (cited in note 6). The Public Prosecutors' Office dropped its opposition to this and other universal jurisdiction cases when the Socialist Party assumed office. See Amnistia Internacional, *La Audiencia Nacional condena a el ex militar argentino Adolfo Scilingo por Crímenes de Lesa Humanidad* (Apr 19, 2005), available online at <http://ania.urcm.net/ noticia.php3?id=13324&idcat=1&idamb=3> (visited Apr 5, 2008).

15.   *Sentencia del Tribunal Supremo sobre el caso Guatemala por Genocidio*, Sentencia No 327/2003, Appeal Roll 115/2000, Case 331/99, File 162/2000 (Tribunal Supremo, Second Penal Chamber Feb 25, 2003) (Spain), available online at <http://www.derechos.org/nizkor/guatemala/doc/gtmsent.html> (visited Apr 5, 2008).

cases that involved Spanish citizens could proceed. In September 2005, Spain's highest tribunal, the Constitutional Tribunal, reversed.[16] The Tribunal began with the plain language and legislative intent of Article 23.4 of the LOPJ. As the Constitutional Tribunal pointed out, the law itself establishes only a single limitation: the suspect cannot have been convicted, found innocent, or pardoned abroad. It contains no implicit or explicit hierarchy of potential jurisdictions and focuses only on the nature of the crime, not on any ties to the forum; it establishes concurrent jurisdiction. Given the absence of textual support for a restrictive interpretation of the law, such a construction would be overly strict and unwarranted given the grave nature of the crimes. The Tribunal re-opened the case for all complainants, including large numbers of Guatemalans who were survivors or family members of massacre victims.[17] The full case, focusing on genocide, could then go forward.

The next step in the re-opened case, which was assigned to Judge Santiago Pedraz, was to take the statements of the suspects, a procedure designed to allow defendants to tell their side of the story before any arrest warrants issued. Judge Pedraz, following long-established rules for taking statements in another state through a rogatory commission, worked through a Guatemalan judge to set up the dates, and the Spanish judge, along with the Spanish prosecutor, traveled to Guatemala. The defendants apparently did not see much advantage to telling their side of the story; they filed extraordinary writs of *amparo* before the local courts claiming their appearance would violate their constitutional rights. In most Latin American countries, the ability to challenge government action in violation of constitutional rights, known as *amparo*, is a cornerstone of individual rights, and the defendants made constant use of the procedure from this point on.[18] At this time as well, the Center for Justice and Accountability ("CJA"), a US-based NGO that had experience litigating transnational cases through its work using the

---

16. Naomi Roht-Arriaza, *Guatemala Genocide Case*, 100 Am J Intl L 207, 207 (2006).
17. Id at 211.
18. See Allan R. Brewer-Carías, *Some Aspects of the "Amparo" Proceeding in Latin America as a Constitutional Judicial Mean Specifically Established for the Protection of Human Rights*, Colloquium in International and Comparative Law, U Maryland School of Law (Oct 2007), available online at <http://digitalcommons.law.umaryland.edu/cgi/viewcontent.cgi?article=1001&context=iclc_papers> (visited Apr 5, 2008).

US Alien Tort Statute,[19] came into the case representing several families of victims.

Meanwhile, in Guatemala victims' groups had been preparing a case for the domestic courts. An association of survivors from over twenty villages covering the worst-hit areas of the country (including those listed in the CEH Report), known as the Association for Justice and Reconciliation ("AJR"), worked with the Center for Legal Action on Human Rights to file complaints in 2000 against the highest officials in the Lucas García (1978-82) regime, followed a year later by complaints against high officials in the Ríos Montt (1982-83) period.[20] The named defendants overlappèd substantially, but not completely, with those named in the case in Spain. Guatemala, like most countries in Latin America, changed its criminal procedure during the 1990s to make it more prosecutor-driven; only the prosecutor's office (*Ministerio Público*) rather than victims or judges could press forward with an investigation. And despite millions in international aid, training, and support,[21] the prosecutors' office remained ineffective, disrespectful to victims, and vulnerable to threats and corruption, and was reportedly infiltrated by military intelligence and criminal networks of various sorts.[22] Early on, the prosecutor called on those named in the complaint

19.   28 USC § 1350 (2006). The statute allows for civil suits in US federal court by aliens for torts in violation of the law of nations or a treaty of the United States.

20.   Case No. 3920-2000, Ministerio Público, Guatemala (on file with author). Although the complaints are unpublished, information (in Spanish) on them is available online at <http://www.caldh.org> (visited Apr 5, 2008).

21.   See, for example, UNDP, *Proyecto de Fortalecimiento del MP (Project for Strengthening the Public Prosecutor)*, avaiable online at <http://www.pnudgua-temala.org/seguridadjusticia/gua00008.html> (visited Apr 5, 2008); World Bank Group, *Guatemala Judicial Reform Project*, available online at <http://lnweb18.worldbank.org/External/lac/lac.nsf/45b1a64b68f7a2d3852 567d6006c364a/8eb97ef168cccbe4852567e8007bb8be?OpenDocument> (visited Apr 5, 2008).

22.   Susan Peacock and Adriana Beltrán, *Hidden Powers in Post-Conflict Guatemala: Illegal Armed Groups and the Forces behind Them* 43, 44 (Washington Office on Latin America, Sept 2003), available online at <http://cgrs.uchastings.edu/pdfs/HiddenPowersFull.pdf> (visited Apr 5, 2008). According to the U.S. State Department Country Report for 2006, "[w]hile the constitution and the law provide for an independent judiciary, the judicial system often failed to provide fair or timely trials due to inefficiency, corruption, insufficient personnel and funds, and intimidation of judges, prosecutors, and witnesses. The majority of serious crimes were not investigated or punished. Many high-profile criminal cases remained pending in the courts for long periods as defense attorneys employed successive appeals and motions." US Department of State, *Country Reports on Human Rights Practices: Guatemala 2006*, Section 1.e (2007), available online at <http://www.state.gov/ g/drl/rls/hrrpt/2006/78893.htm> (visited Apr 5, 2008).

to testify, and a number of former generals did so voluntarily, denying any participation in crimes. Since then, however, the prosecutor's office refused to take any action to move the cases forward, and they have languished for several years.

Fortunately, despite the inability to take formal statements, Judge Pedraz did not leave Guatemala entirely empty-handed. He met informally with several representatives of the AJR, who told him about their long struggle for justice in Guatemala. Judge Pedraz returned to Spain, and a month later, on July 7, 2006 issued charges and international arrest warrants for the defendants on charges of genocide, state terrorism, torture, and related crimes.[23] In early November, Guatemala's Fifth Tribunal for Crime, Drug Trafficking and Environmental Offenses (the local trial court) executed four of the six arrest warrants. Two others were rejected for technical reasons.[24] Although the technical problems were cleared up soon after, those warrants have never been executed.[25] One of them was for General Ríos Montt, the former head of state from 1982–83, who by that time was running for Congress, and the other for General Benedicto Lucas, former army chief of staff from 1978–80. The four defendants reacted differently: one fled, one holed up in his house, one was in a military hospital and was put under guard, and the other turned himself in and also ended up in a military hospital. They all, however, hired lawyers in Guatemala to contest the extraditions.

On November 22, Judge Pedraz followed up with formal extradition requests.[26] He cited an 1895 Extradition Treaty between Guatemala and

23.   See note 2.
24.   Guatemala does not typically publish lower court pretrial decisions, hence no published record of these rejections is available. (Reference documents on file with author.)
25.   The warrants were initially rejected because of a clerical error; the ones that reached Guatemala included only the allegations surrounding the 1980 Spanish Embassy massacre, not the genocide charges stemming from the entire 1979–85 period. New, corrected arrest orders were sent immediately, but by that time the case was suspended due to the first of many *amparos*. The lower court judges then left them pending until the legal issues around the executed warrants could be settled, which is why they were never executed. See Edgar Calderon, "Capturan a Ex Militares," in *La Prensa* (9 November 2006) available online at <http://www.laprensa.com.ni/archivo/2006/ noviembre/09/noticias/internacionales/155170. shtml> (visited Feb 6, 2009)
26.   Juzgado Central de Instrucción No. 1, Dil Previas 331/99, Auto de 22 Noviembre 2006 (on file with author).

Spain and explained in detail why each article of the Treaty applied in this case. He also discussed the crime of genocide and attached a copy of the 2005 Spanish Constitutional Court decision to show that he had jurisdiction under Spanish law.[27]

Rigoberta Menchú had been initially represented in Spain by labor and criminal lawyers who focused on the validity of Spain's jurisdiction. Once the genocide case was re-opened, and after the judge's visit to Guatemala in June 2006, a new legal team led by the CJA began working with lawyers in Menchú's local foundation offices in Guatemala to develop the evidence for the Spanish case. At the same time, the team began dealing with the extradition and rogatory commission cases in the Guatemalan courts. Eventually the legal team grew to include local counsel in Spain with experience litigating universal jurisdiction cases, lawyers in the Hague and San Francisco with knowledge of both international and national criminal law, law students at the University of California-Hastings and Harvard human rights legal clinics, and the Menchú Foundation lawyers in Guatemala (who were coordinating with other legal human rights groups there).

This team had to contend with the intense judicial activity surrounding Judge Pedraz's 2006 arrest orders and extradition requests. These orders and requests set off a furious battle in the Guatemalan courts. The local courts had to decide whether to execute the arrest warrants, whether to grant extradition,[28] and how to deal with requests for judicial cooperation involving witnesses, defendants, documents, and assets. Along the way, the local courts had to grapple with complex arguments about the propriety of universal jurisdiction, the nature of international crimes, and the role of international law in Guatemala's constitutional order. Each of these involved a combination of local and international law.

In general, the rules on extradition are designed to deal with common crimes, not international crimes like genocide. Most extradition

---

27. Id.
28. Even if the courts allowed the extraditions to proceed, the Executive Branch would still have a chance to stop them at a later point. Ministerio de Relaciones Exteriores de Guatemala, *El Procedimiento de Extradición en Guatemala* 6–7, available online at <http://www.oas.org/juridico/MLA/sp/gtm/sp_gtm-ext-gen-procedure.pdf> (visited Apr 5, 2008).

treaties, including the Spain-Guatemala Treaty,[29] have a similar set of rules. The alleged acts must be criminalized in both legal systems, and the requested state must only satisfy itself that the requesting state has jurisdiction under its own laws and has made out the rough equivalent of probable cause; a full evidentiary showing is not required. Political crimes, and common crimes connected to them, are not subject to extradition; however, the treaty does not define what constitutes a political crime. Also like many extradition treaties, the Spain-Guatemalan Treaty does not require (but does allow) the extradition of nationals.[30] Guatemala's Constitution also contains a prohibition on the extradition of nationals, but its Article 27 has an exception that seems tailor-made for this case: it excludes alleged crimes contained in "treaties and conventions with respect to crimes against humanity or against international law."[31]

Even though the arrest orders came from a Spanish court, they would have to be enforced through Guatemalan courts ordering the police to execute the warrants. Extradition proceedings had the immense advantage of bypassing the public prosecutors' office, which had long held up domestic proceedings and was not considered particularly eager to move any of the armed conflict or genocide cases along given their political sensitivity and complexity. If the courts moved towards extradition, at the very least, that might embarrass the prosecutors' office into action. Indeed, in July 2007 the prosecutors' office began threatening to call witnesses in the Spanish Embassy massacre case of 1980, in what seemed to be a feeble attempt to preempt the Spanish proceedings by showing they were prosecuting the case at home. This response vindicated the complainants' legal strategy: by pushing for prosecution abroad, they could prod the courts into acting at home, even if the prosecutor's actual motivation was to undermine the foreign proceedings.[32]

---

29.   Tratado de Extradición entre España y Guatemala, (Nov 7, 1895) and Protocolo Adicional aclarando su articulo VII (Feb 23, 1897).

30.   Id, art IV.

31.   Guatemala Const, art 27 (1985, amend 1993), available online at <http://pdba. georgetown.edu/ Constitutions/Guate/guate93.html> (visited Apr 5, 2008) (author translation).

32.   For a fuller explanation of how this insider/outsider theory has worked in the case of Spanish investigations into military dictatorships in the Southern Cone, see Roht-Arriaza, *The Pinochet Effect* at ch 7, 8 (cited in note 6).

The defendants immediately filed writs of *amparo* complaining that their constitutional rights had been violated by the local court's execution of the arrest warrants.[33] The defendants argued, among other things, that the Spanish courts were not a "competent authority" to issue an arrest warrant and could not exercise extraterritorial jurisdiction because Guatemalan sovereignty forbade it. They further argued that the language of the extradition treaty referred to those who had "taken refuge" in Guatemala, and that as Guatemalan citizens therefore they were not covered by the treaty, that the alleged crimes were not covered by the treaty, and that the treaty was too old and outdated to be effective. The trial court rejected these arguments and found that Spanish jurisdiction was proper.[34] That decision was appealed, but the appeals court sent the case back to the lower court.[35] The trial court again found jurisdiction, and the appeals court, in October 2007, agreed.[36] The court recognized that the extradition treaty was binding, that Spanish jurisdiction was proper, and that the crimes at issue were of "grave importance" under international law and thus subject to extradition even though they were not—and could not have been in 1897—listed as extraditable crimes in the treaty. The trial court also fined the defendants' lawyers for filing frivolous appeals.[37]

The defendants, throughout the process, filed challenge after challenge, some of them almost exact repetitions of earlier ones. The defendants' repeated challenges suspended the proceedings over and over again, to the immense frustration of the complainants. No one begrudged the defendants a legitimate right to defense, but as their lawyers refiled arguments that had already been rejected over and over, it became clear that here, as in other criminal cases involving powerful defendants,[38] the writ of *amparo* had become a mechanism for delay and abuse.

---

33. For a description of *amparo,* see text accompanying note 18.
34. Resolución, Tribunal Quinto, No 2-2006 (Mar 28, 2007) (on file with author).
35. Resolución, Sala Primera de Apelaciones, No 2-2006 (June 1, 2007) (on file with author).
36. The trial court found jurisdiction for a second time on July 31, 2007, and the appeals court agreed on October 26, 2007. Sala Primera de la Corte de Apelaciones, Amparo 87-2006/543-2006, Sentencia Oct 26, 2007 (on file with author).
37. Id.
38. The use of abusive *amparos* was documented, for example, in the Myrna Mack case, one of the few cases in which the Guatemalan courts convicted military officers of killing. See Fundación Myrna Mack, *Caso Myrna Mack, Resumen de las Audiencias' ante el Tribunal Tercero de Sentencia del 3 de Septiembre al 3 de Octubre de 2002*, available online at <http://www.myrnamack.org.gt/main.

As soon as the arrest warrants were announced, three complainants in the Spanish case—Rigoberta Menchú, Jesús Tecú, and Juan Manuel Gerónimo—asked for and were admitted to the case as intervenors (*terceros interesados*). Yet despite their intervenor status, they were continually denied access to the file, notification of hearings, and copies of relevant documents. By August 2007, they were frustrated and decided to file their own *amparo* alleging violations of their rights as victims of human rights violations. Advised by the international legal team, they cited the jurisprudence of the Inter-American Commission and Court on the right to the truth, the right to information, the right to prompt and effective justice without excessive delay, and the right to an independent tribunal.[39] Shortly thereafter, the trial court agreed with them and ordered the case file released. The release was suspended when the defendants filed—yet another—writ of *amparo*. Nonetheless, the offensive (rather than defensive) use of the *amparo* proceeding to claim rights as victims under international law to limit the abusive use of dilatory motions is an innovation in Guatemala. While the use of dilatory writs will, in the end, be curbed only by either legislation or a change in attitude of the higher courts, at least it established a precedent that victims do indeed have internationally recognized rights that must be given effect in local courts.

Through this complicated set of domestic proceedings, triggered by an international warrant, trial-level Guatemalan courts had to grapple with international law and to compare their procedures and ways of thinking with the jurisprudence generated by international courts as well as other Latin American courts facing similar issues. Through the offensive use of the *amparo* writ, international law—in this instance concerning the

---

php?id_area =33> (visited Apr 5, 2008). Guatemala does not typically publish lower court pretrial decisions, hence there is no public record of these *amparos*. A bill has been pending in the Guatemalan Congress to reform the *amparo* procedure, but it has apparently not progressed very far.

39.   See, for example, Consultative Opinion OC 9-87 of Oct. 6, 1987 on Judicial Guarantees in States of Emergency, art 27(2), 25 and 8, ¶ 24, available online at <http://www1.umn.edu/humanrts/iachr/b_11_4i.htm> (visited Apr 5, 2008). See also Blake case, Reparations Judgment (Jan. 22, 1999) Ser C; Resolutions and Sentences, ¶¶ 61, 63, available online at <http://www1.umn.edu/humanrts/iachr/C/48-ing.html> (visited Apr 5, 2008). The complainants also cited, as persuasive authority, cases of the Colombian Supreme Court that balanced defendants' due process rights against victims' rights to truth and access to justice. Corte Constitucional de Colombia, Sentencia C-004/03, Demanda de Inconstitucionalidad (Jan 20, 2003), available online at <http://www.cajpe.org.pe/rij/bases/juris-nac/c-004.PDF> (visited Apr 5, 2008).

rights of victims—was brought into an area of domestic law where international law had not previously been applied. In this way, transnational prosecutions allow local courts to become familiar with international law and to modernize and innovate, while remaining grounded in local legal culture and practice.

II. Limits to Effectiveness: The Constitutional Court Decision of December 2007 and the Spanish Judge's Response

On December 12, 2007, the GCC ruled that the Spanish arrest warrants were invalid and that defendants could not be extradited.[40] The sixty-plus page ruling responded to yet another *amparo*, lodged by Guevara and Arredondo, against the constitutionality of the arrest warrants issued in November 2006. The *amparo* questions only the validity of the arrest warrants, yet the GCC looked beyond that question to consider the validity of the entire extradition proceeding. The ruling began by accepting that the 1895 extradition treaty between Spain and Guatemala is still valid, but found that it must be interpreted in light of the drafters' intentions. Nothing in the treaty explicitly refers to extraterritorial jurisdiction, they noted, and the fact that the treaty speaks of those seeking asylum or refuge in another state indicates that the drafters were thinking about nationals of another state hiding in the requested state.[41] The treaty, they argued, must be read in light of the territorial principle of the criminal law. Therefore, they concluded, the treaty does not apply to crimes committed within Guatemala.

The GCC added that it can look into Spanish law because it needed to convince itself that the courts of the requesting country are a "competent authority" under the Extradition Treaty.[42] Although from 2005 on Spain clearly had jurisdiction under Spanish law, the GCC asks whether the 2005 Spanish Constitutional Court decision that allowed re-opening of the full investigation, comports with international law.

---

40.   See GCC decision (cited in note 5).
41.   See id at 15–17 (cited in note 5). This method of interpreting the treaty is at odds with the method of treaty interpretation set out in the Vienna Convention on the Law of Treaties (1980), 1155 UNTS 331, art 31, available online at <http://www.oas.org/DIL/Vienna_Convention_ on_the_ Law_of_Treaties.pdf> (visited Apr 5, 2008).
42.   See Tratado de Extradición and Protocolo Adicional aclarando su articulo VII (cited in note 29).

It concludes that universal jurisdiction cannot be maintained because it affronts Guatemalan sovereignty. While Guatemala might recognize an international tribunal, the GCC stated, it will not recognize the extraterritorial jurisdiction of another national court. Otherwise, it argued, one state would be judging another state's ability or willingness to prosecute without either Security Council or General Assembly approval. This line of reasoning is highly problematic, as it is in practice an action of judicial review of the decisions of foreign courts. In effect, the Guatemalan court disagrees with the Spanish court's interpretation of Spanish law. In addition, the GCC finds that extradition is improper for other reasons: both Spain and Guatemala prohibit the extradition of nationals. However, this is not strictly speaking true: Article 27 of Guatemala's constitution allows the extradition of nationals where the crimes are based on treaties and conventions with respect to crimes against humanity or against international law.[43] The GCC reads this reference, though, as limited to surrender to international courts like the ICC, the ad hoc international criminal tribunals, or even the Inter-American Court of Human Rights (which has no criminal jurisdiction).

Although not necessary to its decision, the GCC finds that the crimes alleged are common crimes connected to political crimes because they are connected to the armed conflict, and that the Constitution holds that citizens cannot be extradited for political crimes.[44] This is legally incorrect: the Genocide Convention's Article VII specifically states that "genocide and the other acts enumerated in Article III shall not be considered as political crimes for the purpose of extradition."[45] The GCC may

---

43.   Guatemala Const, art 27 (cited in note 31). The Court adds that extradition of nationals is also improper because there is no reciprocity, but this is also not strictly speaking true: where a treaty requires it, Spain will extradite its nationals. Art 1, Ley 4/1985, de 21 de Marzo, de Extradición Pasiva, available online at <http://noticias.juridicas.com/base_datos/Penal/l4-1985.html> (visited Apr 5, 2008).

44.   GCC decision at 22–23, 54 (cited in note 5).

45.   Convention on the Prevention and Punishment of the Crime of Genocide, art VII (9 Dec. 1948). Available online at http://www.unhchr.ch/html/menu3/b/p_genoci.htm (visited Feb 6, 2009). See also Inter-American Convention on Forced Disappearance of Persons (1994), art V, 33 ILM 1529 ("The forced disappearance of persons shall not be considered a political offense for purposes of extradition."). The UN and Inter-American Torture Conventions also require that torture be considered an extraditable offense. Convention against Torture and Other Cruel, Inhuman or Degrading Treatment or Punishment (1984), General Assembly Res No 39/46, UN Doc A/39/51, art 8(1) (1987) (torture must be extraditable offense). See also Inter-American Convention to Prevent and Punish Torture (1985), OAS Treaty Ser No 67, art 13 (1987).

have been signaling that it would consider these crimes in any domestic prosecution as subject to the Guatemalan Law of National Reconciliation, which grants limited amnesty to persons who have committed political crimes and common crimes connected to them.[46] But as mentioned, Articles 4 and 8 of that law specifically exclude the type of crime alleged in the Spanish request.[47] Along the same lines, the Court characterizes the context of the case as a region-wide civil conflict over political and economic models, with external support on both sides and which pitted ethnic and indigenous people against each other. By so labeling the conflict, the Court implicitly rejects the charge of genocide.[48]

Finally, the Court recognizes the obligation of the Guatemalan courts to investigate and prosecute under the principle of *aut dedere aut judicare* (extradite or prosecute) if extradition is denied and invites the complainants to submit their evidence to the Public Prosecutor. This is a bit disingenuous, since the judges know perfectly well that charges on these crimes have long been filed with the prosecutor and have gone nowhere. However, the GCC's recognition that the domestic system needs to prosecute is important. Now they need to follow through.

As a result, the Court finds that the suspects' constitutional rights have been violated and orders the arrest warrants quashed. While technically the judgment should only apply to the two defendants who appealed, they make it extensive to all the other suspects as third-party intervenors. There can be no appeal from the decision.

The GCC's decision is clearly a setback for the complainants and for international law. It exemplifies some of the limits of a transnational litigation strategy. In a climate of intimidation where judges are routinely bribed or threatened into submission, where the legal system has been repeatedly criticized for its ineffectiveness and for allowing rampant impunity, and where some (but not all) of the defendants still hold power,[49] the defensive tone and negative outcome of the case may have been inevitable. The willingness of the lower courts to go forward,

---

46.   Ley de Reconciliación Nacional (cited in note 8).
47.   Id, arts 4, 8.
48.   GCC at 50 (cited in note 5).
49.   Efraín Ríos Montt, for example, was elected to Congress in 2007, in part as a stated attempt to gain immunity from prosecution. As a Congressman, he has immunity for criminal acts committed while in office, but that immunity does not preclude investigation by the Spanish courts. See *Ex-Dictador Ríos Montt Vuelve al Congreso*, La Prensa (Sept 11, 2007), available online at <http://la

the obvious errors and omissions of the GCC's judgment, and even the length of time it took for the GCC to rule on the arrest warrants despite several earlier opportunities to do so, are reasons for hope that there are some cracks in the façade of impunity. After all, early cases in the Chilean and Argentine courts also featured more open lower courts, followed by conservative decisions rejecting international human rights law obligations at the highest levels.[50] Both the Chilean Supreme Court and the Argentine Supreme Court have now invalidated or limited amnesty laws and approved prosecutions for past crimes based in part on international law obligations.

The Achilles heel of all international justice efforts, whether at the ICC, through hybrid courts, or through transnational prosecutions, is the inability to execute arrest warrants against powerful defendants. The ICC, for example, has been hamstrung by the inability to apprehend indicted Sudanese officials accused of crimes against humanity in Darfur, despite the existence of a Security Council referral and numerous resolutions condemning those crimes.[51] The International Criminal Tribunal for the Former Yugoslavia became effective only when NATO troops began to seek out and arrest suspects.[52] Hybrid tribunals, although theoretically less exposed to this problem because they have the cooperation of the territorial government, have still experienced difficulties: Charles Taylor for many years could not be extradited from Nigeria to the Sierra Leone Special Court.[53] The Special Panels on Serious Crimes in East

---

prensa.aplyca.com/ediciones/2007/09/11/ex_dictador_rios_montt_vuelve_al_congreso> (visited Apr 5 2008); Inés Benítez, *Ex-Dictator on Rocky Road to Congress—and Immunity*, IPS (May 23, 2007), available online at <http://ipsnews.net/news.asp?idnews=37871> (visited Apr 5, 2008). As to the other defendants, one strategic consideration here is that they may have less current ability to influence outcomes or to threaten participants than other, lower-ranked former officers who may be more active in current criminal and intelligence networks.

50.   For description and analysis, see Naomi Roht-Arriaza and Lauren Gibson, *The Developing Jurisprudence on Amnesty*, 20 Hum Rts Q 843 (1998).

51.   UN News Centre, *UN War Crimes Prosecutor Calls for Arrest of First Darfur Suspects* (June 7, 2007), available online at <http://www.un.org/apps/news/story.asp?NewsID=22826&Cr=sudan& Cr1=> (visited Apr 5, 2008); Security Council Res No 1593, S/Res/1593/2005 (Mar 31, 2005).

52.   The two most wanted suspects at the ICTY are still at large, and NATO has been criticized for its inaction. See, for example, Human Rights Watch, *Balkans: Srebenica's Most Wanted Remain Free* (June 29, 2005), available online at <http://hrw.org/english/docs/2005/06/29/bosher11228_ txt.htm> (visited Apr 5, 2008).

53.   *Liberia Seeks End to Taylor Exile*, BBC News (Mar 17, 2006), available online at <http://news.bbc.co.uk/1/hi/world/africa/4817106.stm> (visited Mar 2, 2008).

Timor were similarly unable to prosecute members of Indonesia's high command for atrocities in East Timor because Indonesia refused to extradite them.[54] Transnational prosecutions will suffer from the same weakness when the defendant's presence is sought through extradition: unless he leaves his country and travels to a third state willing to execute the arrest warrants, the defendant will be beyond the reach of the foreign court.

III. Aftermath and Current Prospects

Reaction to the GCC decision was not long in coming. International human rights groups uniformly criticized the holding and the reasoning. Above all, human rights and humanitarian lawyers pointed out that if Guatemala was not going to extradite the suspects, it had an international legal obligation to try them at home. That obligation was explicit under the UN and Inter-American Conventions against Torture and Enforced Disappearances as well as the Genocide Convention.[55] It was also, quite obviously, not being fulfilled.

Most spectacularly, Spanish Judge Pedraz also responded to the GCC decision. On January 9, 2008, he issued his own ruling condemning Guatemala's lack of cooperation and abandonment of its responsibilities under international law.[56] In strong language, the judge complained about the complete lack of collaboration on his requests for rogatory commissions and lambasted the GCC decision as ignoring Guatemala's conventional and customary law obligations to extradite or to prosecute, which the judge traced back as far as Grotius, as well as the extradition treaty.[57]

Judge Pedraz also recalled that genocide is a crime in international law that cannot be labeled a political offense and found that Guatemala was also violating an international treaty and customary law obligation

---

54. David Cohen, *Seeking Justice on the Cheap: Is the East Timor Tribunal Really a Model for the Future?* 61 Asia Pacific Issues 1 (East-West Center, Aug 2002), available online at <http://www.eastwestcenter.org/fileadmin/stored/pdfs/api061.pdf > (visited Apr 5, 2008).
55. Ley de Reconciliación Nacional, art 4, 8 (cited in note 8).
56. Auto dejando sin efecto las comisiones rogatorias a la Republica de Guatemala (Jan 16, 2008), Juzgado Central de Instrucción No. 1, Audiencia Nacional, Diligencias Previas 331/1999-10, available online at <http://www.derechos.org/nizkor/espana/doc/pedraz1.html> (visited Apr 5, 2008) (in Spanish).
57. Id.

to prevent and to punish the crime of genocide against the Mayan people. He concluded:

> This resolution of the Constitutional Court, issued by the maximal judicial authority, in light of the above-referenced facts and of the advanced age of the accused, together with the well-known fact that the level of impunity for lesser crimes in Guatemala is among the world's highest, confirms the State's intention not to investigate these crimes and bring those responsible before the courts. This gives clear backing to impunity, ignoring the above-referenced international law and, therefore, placing Guatemala in the sphere of countries that violate their international obligations and disdain the defense of human rights.[58]

Nonetheless, the judge wrote, the GCC decision showed the continued need for Spanish judicial authorities to investigate the alleged crimes. However, he would no longer rely on the Guatemalan courts but would bring witnesses to Spain to testify.[59] In addition, he called on anyone—victims, witnesses, or others—having information about the case to bring it directly to him through the proper channels.[60] He thus opened up new possibilities for evidence gathering by victims' groups, complainants' lawyers and others around the world.

In February 2008, witnesses began arriving at the Spanish court. They included experts, journalists, and eyewitnesses from some of the areas of the country where, according to the CEH Report, acts of genocide were committed. The eyewitnesses detailed massacres, rape, torture, bombings and persecution of massacre survivors, destruction of crops and livestock, and targeting of Mayan religious practices and community authorities. They also named specific military officials, including the defendants, and specified their role in these crimes.[61] The witnesses spent a full week in February, followed by a second week in May, telling the judge their story. This in itself can have reparatory effects.[62]

---

58.   Id at sec 6 (translation by author).
59.   In another innovation, the Spanish Public Prosecutor designated some of the eyewitnesses as witnesses for the Spanish Crown, which allows Spain to pay their travel expenses. Given the modest economic status of almost all the witnesses, this made it possible for them to testify. Unpublished decision of Public Prosecutor, Audiencia Nacional.
60.   Id. The proper channels for submitting additional information or evidence presumably would include Spanish consulates throughout the world.
61.   Gerson Ortíz, *Declaran en Espana por Genocidio*, La Hora (Feb 5, 2008), available online at <http://www.lahora.com.gt/notas.php?key=25579&fch=2008-02-05> (visited Apr 5, 2008).
62.   There is extensive literature on truth-telling and its potential salutary effects for some victims. See, for example, Priscilla B. Hayner, *Unspeakable Truths: Confronting State Terror and Atrocity* (Routledge 2001). On the other hand, there

The May witnesses included a number of academic experts who testified about the history of racism and discrimination in Guatemala that set the stage for military authorities to decide that entire communities of Mayans had to be eliminated. These witnesses included University of California Professor Beatriz Manz, University of Texas Professor Charles Hale, and Autonomous University of Madrid Professor Marta Casaús, as well as well-known Guatemalan anthropologist Father Ricardo Falla. They posited that a combination of seeing Mayans as an undifferentiated, traditional, unthinking and inferior mass, deep-seated fear of this mass rising up and taking revenge for their exploitation, and a desire by the military to mete out exemplary punishment for what it saw as acts of rebellion, underlie the intention to destroy part of the Mayan group "as such."[63] This process included not only the massacres, but the continuing attacks on survivors, internally displaced persons and even refugees who had crossed the Mexican border. Thus, they not only seconded the opinion and analysis of the CEH but in some cases went further.

Another piece of the evidence involves showing that the highest levels of the military had to have been involved in planning and executing a military strategy; this was not a case of a "few bad apples" or of the individual excesses of rogue officers. Part of this evidence comes from declassified U.S. State Department and CIA documents, made available during the Clinton administration, and analyzed by the National Security Archive. Another part comes from analysis of the military's own rules, orders, and communications protocols, showing that this was a tightly-run and tightly-controlled chain of command. A third piece of evidence is the simple comparison of the massacre and post-massacre patterns. Everywhere in the highlands, the pattern was the same, involving gathering as many people as possible, closing off the village, separating men and women and killing them sequentially, and then attacking any survivors using helicopters and aviation. It is difficult to explain this degree of similarity as simply the result of training; rather it seems to correspond to a carefully conceived strategy. The judge will have to consider this evidence as well.

The continuing political pressure and what is expected to be an ongoing parade of witnesses will no doubt keep the issue in the public eye in

---

is a risk that victims will end up frustrated by the continued inability to acquire custody over the defendants and thus to proceed to full trial and sentencing. The witnesses were well aware of that possibility and chose to testify nonetheless.

63.   Summaries of the testimony are posted on the websites of the National Security Archive, http://www.nsa.org, and of CJA, http://www.cja.org.

Guatemala. Whether this translates into effective change in the attitude of Guatemala's prosecutors and judges is, at this point, unknown. It is of course more difficult for such change to happen without at least a modicum of physical security for all those involved.[64] However, the pressure has already apparently had some result: on February 25, 2008, Guatemalan President Álvaro Colom announced that he would order the military to open up its archives from the armed conflict period and turn them over to the Human Rights Ombudsman.[65] Shortly thereafter, the Constitutional Court ruled that specific military plans had to be turned over to the complainants in the domestic genocide case. The courts had initially ordered the documents turned over to CALDH in 2007, and the Defense Ministry had agreed, but lawyers for Ríos Montt alleged that handing over the documents would violate his constitutional rights. In March 2008 the Constitutional Court dismissed that appeal. It remains to be seen however how many documents the military will actually turn over to either the complainants or the government.

In April 2008 the proceedings took yet another turn. Guatemalan trial court judge José Eduardo Cojulún, whose chambers had received Judge Pedraz' repeated requests for a rogatory commission to interview witnesses, decided that he would honor those requests. He reasoned that the GCC's decision had no bearing on his international judicial cooperation obligations, and that, while he could not allow Judge Pedraz to come to Guatemala, he could conduct the interviews himself and forward the results to the Spanish court. He thus set out a demanding schedule of witness interviews, which lasted for some three weeks.[66] He rejected the predictable *amparos* from the defendants. He also took the packet of completed testimonies and turned them over to the public prosecutor's office, noting that he had obtained evidence of a crime. His courage has been met with death threats.[67]

---

64.   On March 5, 2008, unknown assailants shot at the house of the director of the Fundación Nueva Esperanza, Guillermo Chen. The Fundación represents some of the witnesses and complainants involved in the Spanish case. Amnesty International, Urgent Action, Public AI Index 34/006/2008 (Mar 7, 2008).

65.   Antonio Ordonez, *Presidente Colom Ordena Abrir Archivos del Ejército*, Prensa Libre (Feb 25, 2008), available online at <http://www.prensalibre.com/pl/2008/febrero/25/222513.html> (visited Apr 5, 2008).

66.   "Denuncia juez guatemalteco amenazas de muerte por proceso de genocidio," MetroLatino USA, May 22, 2008.

67.   Id.

In any case, along with internal pressure, the Spanish case has already changed the national equation, bringing the issue again to the forefront of national consciousness. Unless the GCC changes its mind or one of the named defendants (or other defendants named in the future) leaves the country, the case may never come to trial; Spain does not allow trial *in absentia*. Nonetheless, the judge will continue taking testimony and eventually, if the evidence is sufficient, is expected to issue individualized indictments (*autos de procesamiento*) against these and, perhaps, other defendants. These indictments would set out the evidence that the charged crimes were committed and that the defendants were responsible, and at a minimum, they would serve as a valuable historical record and a validation of the witness testimony. The indictments would also serve as a powerful tool for lawyers, victims groups and even, if it so chose, the Executive Branch in Guatemala to pursue new avenues of investigation and prosecution.

IV. Conclusion

The CEH's Report played an important role in making the case that Guatemala is one of the world's most under-reported cases of genocide, one that today remains unpunished and unacknowledged by the perpetrators. Impunity remains a core problem of post-armed conflict state building. Early efforts to combat impunity worldwide focused largely on the creation of new global institutions like the ad-hoc international criminal tribunals and the ICC. As the limitations as well as the strengths of those institutions have become clearer, a more diversified and complex set of responses, grounded in the particular realities of each state, have begun to proliferate. In particular, hybrid courts, with explicit goals that include strengthening domestic legal systems and training local lawyers in international criminal law, have emerged. Transnational prosecutions can serve many of the same functions as these hybrid tribunals, although they suffer from the same weaknesses as other international criminal justice mechanisms in being able to apprehend suspects. These prosecutions, together with domestic efforts, can play complementary roles in catalyzing changes in domestic ability and will to investigate and prosecute the powerful. The success of these mechanisms, like that of international prosecutions more generally, should be measured not only (or even principally) by how many convictions they secure, but at how well they succeed in changing the possibilities for justice at home.

Appendix I

Historical Clarification Commission: Mandate and Investigative Procedures

Reproduced from the CEH's Final Report:
Guatemala, Memory of Silence

I. COMPOSITION, ESTABLISHMENT AND GENERAL OPERATION

Establishment of the CEH

1. The Commission for the Historical Clarification of Human Rights Violations and Acts of Violence that Have Caused Suffering to the Guatemalan Population was established during the Guatemalan Peace Process by the Oslo Accord, signed June 23, 1994, in Oslo, Norway. Said Accord establishes the Commission's mandate as well as other elements of its composition and functioning. The Accord's content is as follows:

> *Agreement on the establishment of the Commission*
> *to clarify past human rights violations and acts of violence*
> *that have caused the*
> *Guatemalan population to suffer*

Whereas the present-day history of our country is marked by grave acts of violence, disregard for the fundamental rights of the individual and suffering of the population connected with the armed conflict;

Whereas the people of Guatemala have a right to know the whole truth concerning these events, clarification of which will help avoid a repetition of these sad and painful events and strengthen the process of democratization in Guatemala;

Reiterating its wish to comply fully with the Comprehensive Agreement on Human Rights of 29 March 1994;

Reiterating its wish to open as soon as possible a new chapter in Guatemala's history which, being the culmination of a lengthy process of negotiation, will put an end to the armed conflict and help lay the bases for peaceful coexistence and respect for human rights among Guatemalans;

Whereas, in this context, promotion of a culture of harmony and mutual respect that will eliminate any form of revenge or vengeance is a prerequisite for a firm and lasting peace,

The Government of Guatemala and the Unidad Revolucionaria Nacional Guatemalteca (hereafter referred to as "the Parties") have agreed as follows:

To establish a Commission whose terms of reference shall be as follows:

Purposes

I. To clarify with all objectivity, equity and impartiality the human rights violations and acts of violence that have caused the Guatemalan population to suffer, connected with the armed conflict.

To prepare a report that will contain the findings of the investigations carried out and provide objective information regarding events during this period covering all factors, internal as well as external.

Formulate specific recommendations to encourage peace and national harmony in Guatemala. The Commission shall recommend, in particular, measures to preserve the memory of the victims, to foster a culture of mutual respect and observance of human rights and to strengthen the democratic process.

Period covered

The Commission's investigations shall cover the period from the start of the armed conflict until the signing of the firm and lasting peace agreement.

Operation

The Commission shall receive particulars and information from individuals or institutions that consider themselves to be affected and also from the Parties.

The Commission shall be responsible for clarifying these situations fully and in detail. In particular, it shall analyze the factors and circumstances involved in those cases with complete impartiality. The Commission shall invite those who may be in possession of relevant information to submit their version of the incidents. Failure of those concerned to appear shall not prevent the Commission from reaching a determination on the cases.

The Commission shall not attribute responsibility to any individual in its work, recommendations and report nor shall these have any judicial aim or effect.

The Commission's proceedings shall be confidential so as to guarantee the secrecy of the sources and the safety of witnesses and informants.

Once it is established, the Commission shall publicize the fact that it has been established and the place where it is meeting by all possible means, and shall invite interested parties to present their information and their testimony.

Composition

The Commission shall consist of the following three members:

The present Moderator of the peace negotiations, whom the Secretary-General of the United Nations shall be asked to appoint.

One member, a Guatemalan of irreproachable conduct, appointed by the Moderator with the agreement of the Parties.

One academic selected by the Moderator, with the agreement of the Parties, from a list proposed by the University presidents.

The Commission shall have whatever support staff it deems necessary, with the requisite qualifications, in order to carry out its tasks.

Installation and duration

The Commission shall be set up, installed and shall start to work as of the day the firm and lasting peace agreement is signed. The Commission shall work for a period of six months starting from the date of its installation; this period may be extended for a further six months if the Commission so decides.

Report

The Commission shall prepare a report which shall be handed over to the parties and to the Secretary-General of the United Nations who shall publish it. Inability to investigate all the cases or situations presented to the Commission shall not detract from the report's validity.

Commitment of the Parties

The Parties undertake to collaborate with the Commission in all matters that may be necessary for the fulfillment of its mandate. In particular, they undertake to establish, prior to setting up the Commission and during its operations, the necessary conditions so that the Commission may fulfil the terms of reference established in the present agreement.

International verification

In conformity with the Framework Agreement of 10 January 1994, implementation of this Agreement shall be subject to international verification by the United Nations.

Measures for prompt execution following the signing of this Agreement

The Parties agree to ask the Secretary-General to appoint the Moderator of the negotiations as a member of the Commission as soon as possible. When he is appointed, he shall be authorized to proceed forthwith to make all necessary arrangements to ensure that the Commission functions smoothly once it is established and installed in conformity with the provisions of this Agreement.

Oslo, June 23, 1994

The Government of the Republic of Guatemala

The Guatemalan National Revolutionary Unity

The United Nations

After the Accord was signed, the United Nations Secretary-General took the necessary steps to prepare for the adequate functioning of the Commission, whose creation remained pending until the signing of the Firm and Lasting Peace Accords on December 29, 1996.

Integration

When the Firm and Lasting Peace Accords were signed, the United Nations Secretary-General, in accordance with the request made to him in the Oslo Accord, began the process of designating the CEH's three members by naming the first Commissioner.

According to the Oslo Accord, the first Commissioner was to be "the current moderator of the peace negotiations, whom the Secretary-General of the United Nations shall be asked to appoint." Given that on January 31, 1997, the UN Secretary-General had named the moderator of the peace negotiations, Mr. Jean Arnault, as his Special Representative in Guatemala, on February 7, 1997, with the approval of the parties to the conflict, the Secretary-General appointed Professor Christian Tomuschat as the first member of the CEH. Professor Tomuschat was formerly independent expert on Guatemala for the United Nations Human Rights Commission.

Professor Tomuschat held numerous meetings between February 19 and 21, 1997, with the parties to the conflict and a wide spectrum of civil society representatives. As a result of these meetings, and in common accord with the parties to the conflict, Otilia Lux de Goff and Alfredo Balsells were named as the remaining two Commissioners on February 22, 1997. Alfredo Balsells was selected from a list of people nominated by university rectors.

On February 13, 1997, through the United Nations Department of Political Affairs, the UN Secretary-General appointed Mr. Fernando CastariOn, a UN functionary, to assist the members of the CEH in preparing its operation.

Legal statute

In order to guarantee objectivity, equity and impartiality in its operations, conditions that were absolutely essential, the CEH required a legal statute that would allow it to fulfill its mandate, free from external pressure or actions that could jeopardize its independence.

To this end, the United Nations, in a December 12, 1997 letter from the Secretary-General's Special Representative in Guatemala to the Guatemalan government, proposed that "the immunities established in Section 22 (a), (b), and (c) of the United Nations Convention on Privileges and Immunities, adopted by the Guatemalan government on July 7, 1947, be applied using the classification of experts to the Commission's three members and their support personnel, whose names and functions will be submitted to the government of Guatemala, regardless of their nationality or conditions of residence, and without jeopardizing any other privileges and immunities that, according to their category and designation, they may receive under the cited Convention.

In all cases, the application of the United Nations Convention on Privileges and Immunities to Guatemalan personnel will be limited to that established in Section 22, (a), (b) and (c) of the same."

9. On December 17, 1997, the Guatemalan Foreign Minister responded to the proposal, accepting its terms, and submitted the aforementioned exchange of letters to the Congress of the Republic for legislative approval.

10. The Congress of the Republic issued Decree number 21-98, on March 25, 1998, which stated in article 1 that "the Accord between the United Nations and the Guatemalan government for the establishment of Immunities and Privileges for the Members of the Historical Clarification Commission and Support Personnel, outlined in an exchange of letters, is approved."

11. Article VI, section 22, of the UN Convention on Privileges and Immunities establishes that United Nations experts, among other Privileges and immunities for the independent exercise of their functions,

... shall be accorded: immunity from personal arrest or detention and from seizure of their personal baggage;

in respect of words spoken or written and acts done by them in the course of the performance of their mission, immunity from legal process of every kind. This immunity from legal process shall continue to be accorded notwithstanding that the persons concerned are no longer employed on missions for the United Nations;

inviolability for all papers and documents...

12. Section 23 of the Convention establishes that: "...the Secretary-General shall have the right and the duty to waive the immunity of any expert in any case where, in his opinion, the immunity would impede the course of justice and it can be waived without prejudice to the interests of the United Nations."

Installment

Once appointed, the Commissioners, with UN assistance, completed all necessary preparatory tasks to begin functioning, so that the CEH could formally begin the period of its work. Initially, the CEH had neither the funds nor the adequate logistical infrastructure to fulfill its mandate.

The Commissioners held meetings with the Parties and civil society representatives—especially from human rights, victims and indigenous organizations—which allowed them to listen to suggestions and proposals regarding procedures that would allow them to conduct their work in fulfillment of their mandate. Also taken into account were the procedures used by other commissions and the accumulated experience of the UN.

The best form of organizing support personnel was also studied. To this end, on May 7, 1997, the UN Department of Political Affairs (UNDPA), following the Secretary-General's instructions, established an internal mechanism enabling the UN Office for Project Services (UNOPS) to enter into an agreement with the CEH to execute a project, which would be its Support Office (SO).

In conformance with the mechanism established by the DPA, on May 19, 1997, the CEH signed a memorandum of understanding with UNOPS, which designated the latter as fund manager and responsible for the operations of the Support Office. The SO has functioned as a United Nations project, implemented by the UNOPS Guatemalan Unit, which forms part of the Rehabilitation and Social Sustainability Division. Characterized by high degrees of flexibility and efficiency, UNOPS' management has permitted an adequate handling of this complex operation.

The Commissioners approved the CEH's budget on May 19, 1997. This budget, including later increases due to extensions in the Commission's activities and including expenses for the Report's publication, totaled US$9,796,167.

The preparatory phase prior to the CEH's formal installation included the following essential tasks: selecting national and international Support Office personnel (particularly investigators), providing specialized training for these professionals, designing the methodology, siting and equipping field office and organizing the territorial deployment, which will be discussed later.

The CEH was formally installed and began its mandated work on July 31, 1997.

The Commissioners' work regime and procedures

In 1997 the three Commission members adopted the Internal Rules for the Procedure of the Commissioners, which established their internal work regime, mechanisms for decision-making, meeting schedules and other procedural issues.

Financing

The CEH's expenses budget was approved on May 19, 1997. The following day, the CEH formally appealed to the Guatemalan government and the international community for financial contributions. The response from all was extremely positive, and within a short time, the CEH was able to meet the operation's financial requirements.

The governments of Guatemala, Austria, Belgium, Canada, Denmark, the European Union, Germany, Italy, Japan, the Netherlands, Norway, Sweden, Switzerland, the United Kingdom of Great Britain, and the United States of America all contributed funds that have allowed the CEH to cover its budgetary needs.

The United Nations System contributed materials and experts to complement the Commission's financial needs. Experts were contributed by the United Nations Secretary-General, the UN High Commissioner for Refugees (UNHCR), the UN Children's Fund (UNICEF), UNOPS, the UN Development Program (UNDP), and the International War Crimes Tribunal for the Former Yugoslavia. The United Nations Verification Mission in Guatemala (MINUGUA) provided very significant logistical support for the Commission's work.

Also making material contributions to the CEH were the American Association for the Advancement of Sciences, which contributed an expert, the Ford Foundation, which provided a grant, and the Soros Foundation of Guatemala, which loaned vehicles.

Operational structure and organization

To carry out its activities in compliance with its mandate, the Commission created the Support Office, which functioned as a project.

The CEH Support Office

In February 1997, the UN Department of Political Affairs (UNDPA), responding to a request by the Commission, began to assist the Commission in the search for an adequate operating mechanism.

The Support Office, under the supervision of the Commission's Executive Secretary, established the Central Team, comprised of the Executive Secretary, the Final Report Coordinator, the Director of Investigations and the Chief of Operations. The CEH was assisted by 269 professionals, support personnel and security officials – 142 were Guatemalans, and 127 were foreigners of 31 different nationalities (Argentina, Bosnia Herzegovina, Brazil, Canada, Cape Verde, Chile, Colombia, Costa Rica, Ecuador, El Salvador, France, Germany, Great Britain, Haiti, Honduras, Ireland, Iceland, Italy, Mexico, the Netherlands, Nicaragua, Norway, Peru, Portugal, Puerto Rico, Spain, Switzerland, Ukraine, the United States, Uruguay and Venezuela).

The central office was organized around three key areas of activity, each under the direction of the Final Report Coordinator, the Director of Investigations and the Chief of Operations, respectively.

The Public Information Office, staffed by only one person during the entire operation, was directly supervised by the Executive Secretary. The three Commissioners and the Executive Secretary were the only officials authorized to give public statements to the media, and the CEH Coordinator was designated to be the principal spokesperson.

The second functional unit was the Documentation Center, which was created with the purpose of systematizing written source documentation and other generic documentation produced by the investigators. The Historical Analysis Group was comprised of outstanding Guatemalan investigators and academics, who conducted studies on recent Guatemalan history and the causes and factors underlying the conflict, and created documents used by the Commissioners and Thematic Teams.

The Director of Investigations organized and supervised the work of the investigators, the Special Team, and the Database, whose activities will be discussed later. The Special Team was responsible for compiling and analyzing information provided by the military parties to the conflict, declassified documents from the United States government and other specialized input, as well as for analyzing the military aspects of the armed confrontation, their relationship to International Humanitarian Law and the respect for human rights in those aspects connected to the armed confrontation.

The Chief of Operations directly supervised the Administrative Unit, which was comprised of five people, and the Security Unit, whose function was to provide protection for the Commissioners, maintain control over the security situation of staff in all of the offices and guarantee the security of archives and other confidential information.

Territorial deployment

The Commission decided to organize the Support Office in such a was as to facilitate access for the majority of Guatemalan citizens in presenting their voluntary testimony. To fulfill this goal, the Commission deployed personnel to cover the greatest possible territory. By opening field offices throughout the country, with permanently mobile teams, the Commission's investigators were able to cover the entire national territory. When siting offices, special priority was given to those areas most affected during the armed confrontation by human rights violations and acts of violence, as well as to the most isolated parts of the country. Considering these factors, the greatest number of offices were opened in the western part of the country.

34. On September 1, 1997, the Commission decentralized operations by creating four regional offices in Guatemala City, Coben, Santa Cruz del Quiche and Huehuetenango; and ten liaison offices in Barillas, Cantabal, Escuintla, Nebaj, Poptun, Quetzaltenango, San Marcos, Santa Elena, SoIola and Zacapa. From these offices, investigators expanded their coverage to municipalities and communities in all the country's departments. Distribution is detailed in the following box[1]:

OFFICE	DEPARTMENTS COVERED
Barillas	Northern Huehuetenango
Cantabal	Ixcen (northern Quiche)
Guatemala City	Chimaltenango, Guatemala, Jalapa and Sacatepequez
Coban	Alta Verapaz, Baja Verapaz
Escuintla	Escuintla, Jutiapa, Santa Rosa, Suchitepequez
Huehuetenango	Southern Huehuetenango
Nebaj	Ixil (north-central Quiche)
Poptun	Southern Peten
Quetzaltenango	Quetzaltenango, Retalhuleu, Totonicapen
San Marcos	San Marcos
Santa Cruz	Central and southern Quiche
Santa Elena	Northern Peten
Solole	SoIola
Zacapa	Chiquimula, El Progreso, Izabel, Zacapa

From field offices, investigators visited municipal capitals in order to inform the public about the CEH mandate. Investigators conducted these visits directly, or through local NGOs and local government and traditional authorities. As a result of these visits, the public information campaign and the participation of diverse civil society organizations, thousands of citizens visited the Commission's offices, either requesting community visits to give testimonies or providing their testimonies directly in those offices.

Between September 1997 and April 1998 (and in some cases through May) CEH investigators visited nearly 2,000 communities, many, more than once, and some up to ten times, and compiled more than 500 collective testimonies and 7,338 total testimonies'. More than 20,000 people participated in the CEH project with testimony and other information. More than a thousand were key witnesses: members and ex-members of the Army and other State institutions, ex-members of the Civil Defense Patrols and Military Commissioners, former guerrilla combatants, politicians, union leaders, intellectuals, civil society representatives, etc.

The Commission also collected testimony in Canada, the United States, Mexico, and various European countries. With the exception of Mexico, these testimonies were taken by non-governmental organizations, who generously provided their support.

Investigations of those cases admitted by the Commission were conducted both by the field offices and the Central Office in the capital city. Once the field offices closed on April 15, 1998, any additional investigations were conducted from the Central Office, using mobile teams, which traveled to the country's interior.

Personnel reductions and restructuring

When the 14 field offices finished their work, personnel was concentrated in the Central Office and staff levels reduced once the main testimony-taking period was finished. Nonetheless, the Central Office continued receiving testimonies and information from anyone wishing to contribute within the framework of the mandate, until July 31, 1998.

After that date, the Support Office was restructured to focus on three areas input systematization, thematic analysis, and recommendations —along with an operational section; both the Central Team and the Public Information Office continued with the same functions as in the previous period.

The following teams comprised the Input Systematization Area: Illustrative Case Team, Ordinary Case Team, Data Base, Documentation Center, Historical Context Team, Key Witness Team, Special Team, Administration of Justice Team, a Foreign Governments' Document Team (with a liaison person in Washington) and Legal Advisory Team.

The Thematic Area was made up of three teams, which, respectively, dealt with the causes and origins of the internal armed confrontation, the strategies and mechanisms of the violence, and the consequences and effects of the violence.

The Recommendations Area was comprised of a single recommendations team.

Beginning August 17, 1998, these Central Office teams were gradually reduced as they completed their work.

Beginning November 15, as other teams were being reduced, the Coherence Section was created, consisting of the Coherence Team, the Text Review Team and the Text Edition Team. In the final month, a team was created to organize the public presentation of the Report and another for the printing and publication of the Report. The Support Office continued to operate until the presentation of the Final Report on February 25, 1999,

The Support Office's organizational structure and its evolution througho ut the operation as principal tasks varied.

Informing and Convoking the Public

The Oslo Accord stated that the CEH invite any citizen who might possess pertinent information to present their version of events. It was important that this invitation be preceded and accompanied by a public information campaign announcing that the CEH had begun its period of operations and providing information on the location of those places where any citizen so desiring could go to present their testimony or provide information.

To this end, the CEH developed its public information campaign, beginning with the public event when the Commission was formally installed and initiated its work. This campaign was developed through the press and radio and also made extensive use of alternative forms of communication.

During the 18 months that the CEH operated, 14 press statements were published in newspapers and magazines with a national circulation, regional weekly publications (in the western part of the country), and a

Central American magazine. Each of these statements was published at least twice in each medium. Twelve spots and six micro-programs were produced for radio in nine Mayan languages and Spanish, and transmitted via 142 stations, 112 of which provided national coverage, while the rest provided specific local or municipal coverage. The radio messages covered various topics: convoking citizens to come to the CEH's offices and share their information and testimony, explaining the importance of historical clarification, guaranteeing the confidentiality of witnesses and their sources, and explaining the importance of overcoming fear and breaking the silence. At least one spot and one micro-program were specifically directed to perpetrators.

Alternative means of communication included distribution of posters, fliers, and pamphlets; in addition, a simple brochure was produced with cartoon figures for illiterate citizens or those with very limited reading skills. All materials were colorfully designed, with creative and direct language. During the public information campaign, some 1,470,000 copies of these materials were published and distributed throughout the country, via field offices, NGOs, universities, professional societies, indigenous organizations, diverse associations, cultural organizations and the agencies of the United Nations System with offices in Guatemala.

At the same time, careful attention was paid to developing solid relationships with national and international media, both to respond as well as possible to their requests and as a means of informing the public about the advances of the Commission's work.

The Commission gave UNOPS the responsibility for conducting actions to assure distribution of the Final Report, transfer its assets to national organizations and assure an orderly closing of operations. UNOPS was to conduct these activities during a six month period to begin once the Final Report was presented to the parties to the conflict.

The CEH expresses its gratitude for the respectful and generous support from the media.

Duration

According to the Accord signed by the parties to the conflict, the CEH would function for a six-month period, beginning at its installation, with the possibility of a six-month extension per the Commission's discretion.

Because of the scope of the Commission's mandate — particularly the length of the period to be studied — and the territorial and social complexities of the work—the Commission decided to utilize the maximum 12 month time period. The Commission utilized this 12-month period to complete its investigations and analysis, according to the mandate. When this period closed, the Commission appealed to the Accompaniment Commission for an additional period to finish drafting and printing the Final Report, which would contain the results of the Commission's investigations.

The Accompaniment Commission granted the CEH an additional six-month period to complete the previously mentioned tasks. This was done without altering the terms established by the Commission's mandate.

IV. THE MANDATE

Fundamental aspects

The principal inspiration underlying the mandate is the need to satisfy the Guatemalan people's right to know the truth about what happened during the armed confrontation (Oslo Accord, Preamble, paragraph 2; Agreement on the Basis for the Legal Integration of the Unidad Revolucionaria Nacional Guatemalteca, point 18; Firm and Lasting Peace Accord, point 4).

A second underlying principle of the Accord is the hope that knowing the past would prevent "these sad and painful pages [of Guatemalan history] from being repeated" (Oslo Accord, Preamble, paragraph 2; Accord on the Basis for the Legal Integration of the Unidad Revolucionaria Nacional Guatemalteca, point 18). In other words, the parties to the Accord believed a firm and lasting peace cannot be constructed based on silence, but rather on knowing the truth.

A third fundamental aspect of the Accord is the need to strengthen the democratic process (Preamble, paragraph 2; Firm and Lasting Peace Accord, point 4), as well as the need to "establish the foundations for peaceful coexistence and respect for human rights among Guatemalans" (Preamble, paragraph 4), and "to promote a n new culture of harmony and mutual respect" (Preamble, paragraph 5).

A Systematization of Support Office Experiences

60. A final and extremely important principle that inspired the mandate is the need to eliminate "any form of revenge or vengeance" (Preamble, paragraph 5), which the Commission has considered to be one of the

main criteria guiding its work.

Purposes

The Accord established three purposes for the Commission's work:

To *clarify with all objectivity, equity and impartiality the human rights violations and acts of violence that have caused the Guatemalan population to suffer, connected with the armed conflict.*

To prepare a report that will contain the findings of the investigations carried out and provide objective information regarding events during this period covering all factors, internal as well as external.

Formulate specific recommendations to encourage peace and national harmony in Guatemala. The Commission shall recommend, in particular, measures to preserve the memory of the victims, to foster a culture of mutual respect and observance of human rights and to strengthen the democratic process.

61. In accordance with these objectives, the CEH mandate focused on clarifying these acts, facilitating an understanding of what happened during the period under study, and formulating recommendations oriented towards assuring that these acts would never be repeated.

62. It is important to emphasize that the purpose of the CEH's mandate was not to clarify the armed confrontation, itself, but rather the human rights violations and acts of violence connected to it. Therefore, an investigation of the internal armed confrontation serves as the fundamental reference for establishing the period of investigation, particularly for the question of when the period under investigation should begin.

63. With respect to the recommendations, the Oslo Accord makes no mention of reparations or assistance for victims. However, paragraph 19 of the Accord on the Basis for the Legal Integration of the URNG, in conjunction with Commitment 8 of the Comprehensive Accord on Human Rights, established that the entity responsible for public policy for reparations and victims' assistance "shall take into account the Historical Clarification Commission's recommendations in this regards."

Operation

64. The section of the Oslo Accord entitled "operation" stipulates that theCommission collect " particulars and information from individuals

or institutions that consider themselves to be affected [by the armed confrontation] and also from the Parties to the conflict]." Also, the Commission shall be responsible for "clarifying these situations fully and in detail", analyzing "the factors and circumstances involved in these cases with complete impartiality," and inviting any and all person(s) "who may be in possession of relevant information to submit their version of events." The Accord also states, "the Commission's proceedings shall be confidential so as to guarantee the secrecy of the sources and the safety of witnesses and informants." The interpretation of these aspects of the mandate can be found in the section of this chapter entitled "Case clarification of human rights violations and acts of violence connected to the internal armed confrontation."

The same section of the Oslo Accord states that "the Commission shall not attribute responsibility to any individual in its work, recommendations and Report, nor shall these have judicial aim or effect."

The Commission has understood the phrase "shall not attribute responsibility to any individual" for human rights violations and acts of violence to be a condition that actually derives from its objective, which is not a penal process, but rather one of historical clarification. Given this, as well as a literal, historical, teleological and systematic interpretation of the words, "shall not attribute responsibility to any individual," the CEH concluded that it is not empowered to give the names of individuals responsible for the events to be clarified. As a result, the names of people responsible for the human rights violations and acts of violence, which were investigated, have been omitted from the Final Report, particularly in the case descriptions.

The second limitation on the Commission's work contained in the above mentioned section of the Oslo Accord, which refers to the lack of judicial aim or effect, derives from the previously mentioned condition and from the fact that, in and of themselves, the Commission's work, recommendations and Report have neither a judicial character nor purpose since the CEH is not a judicial body recognized under the Guatemalan Political Constitution or other national legislation.

Although the Accord states that neither the Report nor the Commission's investigation have judicial effect, nothing prevents State institutions, particularly those responsible for the administration of justice, from using elements contained on the Report. This same reasoning applies to citizens who were victims or relatives of victims, who maintain the same rights that they may have, as such, to legally pursue cases discussed in the Report.

Interpretation and application of the CEH mandate's central themes

Legal framework

The *Accord's references to human rights essentially reflect international human rights standards and norms. Only international rules and principles permit objective measurement of the distortions and even perversions of the country's justice* system, at least partially, under various military governments. The fundamental parameter for the Commission's legal framework is the Universal Declaration of Human Rights, adopted on December 10, 1948, by the UN General Assembly via resolution 217 A (III), which formalized member States' commitment to promote and protect human rights. While the resolution, by itself, was not binding on member States, it very soon became accepted that the essential core elements of the Declaration have legal import as part of customary law. This applies especially to the right to life and personal integrity, including the prohibition of torture. The prohibition of genocide also forms part of customary law in this way. These norms were unquestionably in effect at the beginning of the Guatemalan internal armed confrontation.

The Commission also took into account international human rights treaties. Although the majority of these treaties were ratified by Guatemala after the worst horrors of the armed confrontation — with the exception of the Convention on the Prevention and Sanctioning of the Crime of Genocide—they all contain the legal norms that have been established by humanity in the course of the second half of the 20th century, with the purpose of assuring respect for human rights in all countries. Therefore, these treaties provide a precise legal framework for the classification of the acts the Commission was established to investigate.

The Oslo Accord does not mention International Humanitarian Law. However, in the broadest sense, humanitarian law also forms part of the international system to protect human rights. It covers all of the rules that govern the conduct of an armed conflict. Humanitarian law seeks to maintain a minimal level of civilization, even during war. This is the main reason that the Commission has also referred to this body of law as part of the legal framework for its work.

It can be said that humanitarian law is oriented toward adapting a general regime for the protection of human rights to the specific circumstances of an armed conflict, in which life—generally held to be a supreme value — does not enjoy the same degree of preeminence as during normal situations.

International rules applying to internal conflicts are outlined in Common Article 3 of the four 1949 Geneva Conventions, all of which were ratified by Guatemala. Their applicability is based on minimal requirements, such that the party in conflict with government forces be an armed movement, with certain stability seeking political ends, without necessarily controlling a part of national territory.

While the Additional Protocol II adopted in 1977 to enhance international rules regarding internal armed conflicts was ratified by Guatemala on October 18, 1987, that is, very late in the process, and while the government has always denied its applicability to the internal armed confrontation in Guatemala, the CEH has considered it as part of its legal framework given that most of the rules outlined in said Protocol form part international customary law.

As a result, and responding to the distinction made in the Oslo Accord between human rights violations and acts of violence, the CEH has established that during the internal armed confrontation, both parties were obliged to respect the minimum standards outlined in Common Article 3 of the Geneva Conventions. Therefore, this was the general criteria that the CEH applied to both parties and formed the basis for its findings on their respective responsibilities. This was done without detriment to the application of international human rights law to State agents, in order to determine the Guatemalan State's responsibility.

In addition, the Commission applied the common principles of International Human Rights Law and International Humanitarian Law to the acts of violence committed by the guerrilla, so as to provide fair and equal treatment to the parties to the conflict. In doing so, the Commission took into account the current, predominant tendency to consider that human dignity has been equally offended whoever may have been the author of actions that violate or infringe on that dignity.

The Commission also took national law into account, specifically Guatemala's Constitutions, in analyzing the parties' conduct. It is an undeniable fact that certain basic guarantees, such as the obligation of the State to respect and protect the right to life, were never repealed, even during the most difficult periods in the country. Thus, these guarantees were obligatory for all authorities — even the military — not only because of international rules and principles, but also based on the country's Constitutions and complementary laws.

Therefore, when the Report refers to human rights violations, it refers to acts committed by State agents, or to those acts committed by private individuals, with the knowledge or acquiescence of State agents. "Acts of violence" refers to acts committed by members of the URNG, as well as to all other acts of violence committed by private individuals, either taking advantage of or abusing the prevailing conditions created by the armed confrontation, in order to defend or favor individual interests, without the State's consent, collaboration, tolerance or acquiescence.

Period of investigation and connection to the armed confrontation

According to the Oslo Accord, the Commission was to investigate human rights violations and acts of violence "connected to the armed confrontation." Therefore, the period to be investigated starts with the beginning of the internal armed confrontation, which the CEH established as January 1962 and ends with the signing of the Firm and Lasting Peace Accords.

Because the Oslo Accord did not stipulate the type of connection between the acts to be investigated and the armed confrontation, and in an attempt to fulfill its mission of historical clarification, the CEH has given a broad interpretation to this phrase, and does not limit it to those acts committed strictly in the framework of the internal armed confrontation, In order to establish parameters for the "connection" to the armed confrontation, the CEH took into account the fact that the violence which was generated by or related to the armed confrontation greatly transcended those actions materially connected to combat situations and included situations that violated human rights, as well as acts of violence that were facilitated by said confrontation.

Therefore, in the Report, the term "connected to the armed confrontation" is considered applicable to all acts motivated or occasioned by the armed confrontation; or that formed part of the opposing strategies and ideologies; or in which the perpetrators took advantage of belonging to one of the parties to the conflict; or those due to the victim's relationship to the confrontation; or because the victim was considered to have some tie to said ideologies.

Recommendations

In the Report, the CEH has formulated recommendations it believes are necessary in order to consolidate peace and national harmony in Guatemala. The CEH took into account the terms defined in the Oslo

Accord's section on purposes, as well as the requests contained in other Peace Accords that the CEH recommend measures for victim reparation, as mentioned earlier.

As a matter of method, in order to develop these recommendations, the CEH solicited suggestions and opinions from each and every person who gave testimony or provided information, as well as from public political figures and professionals.

But the CEH considered this to be insufficient and went even further to seek suggestions and proposals from civil society, through a progressive process of collective reflection. On May 27, 1998, the Commission held the National Forum for Recommendations, with the participation of more than 400 people and 139 organizations. The Forum was an extremely important source of reflection and proposals for the Commission.

At the same time, the Forum demonstrated that civil society is capable of working together towards common goals — independent of the origin or specific sector of the participants — and is the fundamental guarantee for the Guatemalan peace process.

V. The Parties' collaboration

In conformity with the Oslo Accord, "the Parties [to the conflict] undertake to collaborate with the Commission in all matters that may be necessary for the fulfillment of its mandate." According to Article 10 of the National Reconciliation Law, the CEH is responsible for "designing necessary measures to facilitate knowledge and acknowledgement of the historic truth regarding the internal armed confrontation, in order to prevent such acts from being repeated. To this end, State organisms and entities shall provide the Commission with the support that it may require."

State collaboration in the CEH's installation and functioning

The Commission recognizes the support given by the Legislative and Executive branches of government for the Commission's integration, installation, financing and operations. The Commission particularly acknowledges and expresses its gratitude for the constant collaboration from the Executive branch, via the Secretariat for Peace, a Presidential dependency.

State collaboration in CEH investigations

On various occasions, the CEH requested support from the President of the Republic, from Ministers of State and from the Judiciary system, in providing information relevant to its investigations. The Commission believes it necessary to make public the correspondence on the most important issues, which it maintained with different State entities (see Appendix III to the Final Report).

The CEH characterizes the National Army's collaboration as precarious and unsatisfactory. Although the liaison mechanism established by the National Army with the Commission allowed for the creation of cordial relations, the centralized nature of that mechanism made access to information difficult. The National Army's responses to the Commission's requests for specific information were slow, incomplete and insufficient. The majority of requests for information went unmet or received only a partial response, with up to four months of delay.

As examples, the Army's responses were nil or manifestly insufficient to Commission requests for information regarding territorial deployment of military units during the armed confrontation, as well as for information about URNG prisoners of war and military casualties.

Also, the documents the National Army supplied the CEH were incomplete. For example, CEH requests to be able to review the operational plans of military units was dealt with by providing only some plans for a few military zones; even then, the documents provided turned out to be incomplete, with pages and appendices missing. The Army provided no operational plans for military zones in those regions most affected by the armed confrontation. Nor was the Commission provided with any operational reports prior to 1987, nor given access to any official documents related to the Presidential Chief of Staff *(Estado Mayor Presidencial* in Spanish).

At the same time, the CEH's requests that did receive a partial response from the National Army were handled through slow and complicated mechanisms. With the exception of a few military instruction manuals, none of the documents requested by the CEH were provided in the original or in photocopies. In some cases, documents were made available for review by CEH investigators at the Center for Military Studies, but photographs and photocopies of the documents were prohibited.

During the course of the Commission's work, the Executive branch — through a variety of dependencies, including the National Army and the President's Private Secretariat— gave different justifications for not providing the requested documents. Initially the Executive claimed that the documents were classified under the Constitution. Later, the Executive changed its position and claimed the documents never existed or had been lost or destroyed. Nonetheless, the Commission has verified that documents, whose existence the Executive has consistently and repeatedly denied, in fact do exist and are stored in National Army installations. For example, before the Army centralized its relationship with the CEH through a special liaison group, the Commission had access to various military operational plans and intelligence reports, whose existence was later denied.

The Commission also calls attention to the extreme gravity regarding the supposed "misplacement" of certain documents belonging to different dependencies of the Executive and Judiciary branches. In many cases the misplaced documents contain key information regarding important procedures, including death penalty convictions.

Information provided by the Interior Ministry, the National Police and the Judiciary system regarding the investigations in certain cases has been extremely poor, demonstrating the lack of investigation into grave human rights violations, which should have been prosecuted ex oficio

In compliance with the final paragraph of Article 11 of the National Reconciliation Law, the Appellate Courts of Judiciary system provided certification of the resolutions in cases in which the application of the National Reconciliation Law had been sought, therefore adequately complying with this legal precept.

URNG collaboration with CEH investigations

The URNG established a liaison mechanism with the Commission after a certain delay in November 1997.

Both the joint working dynamics and the methods established by the URNG for providing information to the CEH proved to be effective. The CEH considers that all URNG member organizations had a collaborative attitude. Particularly, members of the FAR and the EGP provided relevant documents and war reports. In many cases, this information actually enabled the Commission to determine the URNG's responsibility for acts of violence under investigation.

Within this generally collaborative context, the Commission calls attention to the fact that one request for information regarding presumed URNG responsibility in certain cases went unanswered. In addition, ORPA failed to submit war reports requested by the Commission, and many ORPA members' responses to Commission questions regarding responsibility for acts of violence acts were evasive or unclear.

Given the above, the Commission considers that URNG collaboration was satisfactory, excepting the previously mentioned problems.

VI. THE INVESTIGATION OF HUMAN RIGHTS VIOLATIONS AND ACTS OF VIOLENCE CONNECTED TO THE INTERNAL ARMED CONFRONTATION

Principal criteria

The principal criteria substantiating the historical clarification of human rights violations and acts of violence connected to the internal armed confrontation is the conviction formed by the Commissioners that each case presented in the Report actually occurred and that each of these was either a human rights violation for which the State was responsible or an act of violence for which the guerrilla was responsible. To meet this first objective, the Commission has primarily used those legal categories belonging to international Human Rights Law and International Humanitarian Law.

The clarification of the specific cases included in the Final Report forms the principal foundation through which the Commission has fulfilled its mandate to provide historical clarification of human rights violations and acts of violence, which includes the analysis of the causes and origins of the violence, its development throughout the armed confrontation, and finally its consequences. This historical clarification makes it possible to formulate conclusions and recommendations aimed at promoting peace and national harmony.

In order to achieve its purposes, in addition to applying legal categories, the Commission also used categories provided by other disciplines, such as history, anthropology, sociology, economics and military science. This has enabled the Commission to reveal complex aspects of the Guatemalan reality, which are different from other countries, even those in Central America.

Types of information compiled by the Commission

Based on the previously mentioned criteria, from the very beginning the Commission encouraged numerous national and international actors to provide information regarding situations that might later be classified as human rights violations or acts of violence connected to the internal armed confrontation. It also sought information at all levels – be it local, national or international – on the historical, political, socio-economic and cultural contexts in which those situations occurred.

Information sources, utilization and value

With regards to both types of information, the Commission utilized an array of sources in compiling information. From each source, the Commission extracted the information that was useful for different aspects of the Final Report.

It is important to emphasize that the Commission worked with absolute independence in deciding the usefulness and value of the different sources; this independence was respected by all actors, both national and international. Neither the parties to the conflict, nor civil society organizations, nor any Guatemalan or foreign individual or institution ever sought preferential treatment for their information or viewpoints.

The following paragraphs refer to the utilization and value assigned to each particular source of information.

Sources of a personal character

The Commission's primary and most relevant information sources were the testimonies of those people who suffered human rights violations or acts of violence. The CEH, using a variety of media, invited all victims and their families, without distinction, to give their testimony describing events that had affected them. Their testimonies, given under the norms established by the Commission, have provided indispensable information for the investigation of every one of the cases presented, and together, they have served as an invaluable source, in both qualitative and statistical terms, for the general analysis of the topics contained in the central chapters [of the Report], and for developing the Report's conclusions.

Collective testimonies formulated by communities affected by human rights violations or acts of violence also had special value. With collective testimonies, the set of testimonies presented by survivors, which together served as confirming versions, enabled the Commission to reconstruct very complex cases, some of which happened more than 15 years ago. These testimonies were also useful in reconstructing local historical contexts, given that relevant documentation and bibliographic materials are very scarce.

Direct witness testimony by non-victims was also a fundamental source of information for the investigation and clarification of cases, as well as for the more comprehensive analysis.

There were also people who gave referential testimony; this was the case with persons who were familiar with victims' or other direct witnesses' versions of events or whose social position allowed them privileged access to knowledge of the context of those events. These sources provided the CEH with information that was important for verifying denunciations, and that contributed to the analysis of specific, local and national phenomena connected to the internal armed confrontation.

At a certain stage in the investigations, the Commission began to receive information regarding the identities of individuals who could have participated directly in human rights violations and acts of violence connected to the armed confrontation, or who, in one way or another, could have been involved in these actions. Given the importance of the testimonies that these people could provide, the Commission established a special procedure to invite said individuals to relate their versions of events and developed specific procedures for preparing and conducting these interviews.

The testimonies given by these persons constituted fundamental elements for the clarification of an important number of individual cases and an invaluable input for the analyses of the strategies and mechanisms that led to said human rights violations and acts of violence. As with all testimony given, the identity of these witnesses was and will be guarded in the strictest of confidentiality, unless they gave expressed consent for their names to be made public. It is important to note that a negative reply to the Commission's request for an interview did not prevent the Commission from clarifying each case, using the other sources at its disposal.

In addition, there were more than 1,000 "key witnesses" who were important sources for the different aspects of historical clarification. People were defined as key witnesses when, due to their characteristics or circumstances, they were privileged witnesses to general or particular situations related to grave human rights violations or acts of violence connected to the armed conflict, or who had knowledge of the structures, organization or strategies of the parties to the conflict, or of groups and institutions that participated in some form in the internal armed confrontation. Key witnesses included, for example, former presidents, State ministers, former and current military officers, former guerrillas and other individuals with the previously mentioned characteristics, either on the local or national level. Key witness testimony contributed both to confirming the occurrence of particularly grave acts and to the development of criteria for understanding specific strategies of the parties or on prevailing policies in the country at a specific moment.

The work by a select group of Guatemalan historians, who for months analyzed the causes, origins and development of the internal armed confrontation, provided the main source of reflection for the historical aspects of the Report.

In the same manner, the Commission highly values the substantive assistance on issues such as the effects of the confrontation on children and the economy, which were provided by consultants from the United Nations system.

The multitude of testimonies provided by all of the sources mentioned in previous paragraphs allowed the CEH to have direct contact with thousands of Guatemalans who placed their trust in the Commission, many talking about their experiences for the first time; these testimonies were the primary foundation for the Commission's Report.

Documentary sources

Many of the people mentioned, be they victims or key witnesses, provided the CEH with private and public documents, whose contents were used both to confirm specific events and in the analyses contained throughout this Report.

Many national institutions, including social organizations, businesses associations, professional societies, Mayan organizations, student associations, retired military associations, and others who had been affected by human rights violations or acts of violence, came voluntarily to the Commission to provide invaluable documentary materials, which in some cases contained denunciations of actions that affected members of their organization. While these denunciations did not meet the [CEH's criteria to open a case], which required personally presented, signed testimony, the information was invaluable for the analysis of different stages of the confrontation and was also used in the clarification of certain illustrative cases.

The Commission also examined and utilized with special attention the information provided by national and international non-governmental human rights organizations, including organizations of victims and family members. Especially helpful were their data bases and victims lists, which were used to check and ratify information compiled during field investigations and to cross with and compare to the Commission's own statistics.

The investigations and analyses were also enriched in many ways by the data bases, case listings and special reports on human rights abuses committed in Guatemala, presented to the Commission by entities that form part of the International and Inter-American human rights systems.

Information provided by the Parties and other official entities

Information, mostly verbal in nature, provided by the guerrilla, through ex-commanders and other representatives, while sometimes fraught with gaps or was otherwise inexact with reference to specific situations, was very useful for the historical reconstruction of the various stages of the internal armed confrontation and of the political contexts in which human rights violations occurred. The information also helped confirm some of the very same acts of violence committed by the guerrilla, which were under investigation by the Commission.

While information, mostly of a documentary nature, provided by the Guatemalan government, and particularly the Army, was precarious and unsatisfactory, it was useful for the systematic analysis of State strategies during the armed confrontation. In some specific cases, government information also constituted an element of certainty that fully ratified the investigation, legal typification and definition of different degrees of responsibility in extremely grave human rights violations.

In a similar way, information provided by national authorities with competence to investigate the acts in question, including official government documents and court files (in those few cases for which legal proceedings were opened and access given to the files), was useful in a number of cases to: substantiate the degree of certainty, strengthen the investigation of illustrative cases or to form objective criteria regarding fulfillment by the State of its obligation to investigate and prosecute human rights violations.

Information provided by foreign governments

Foreign governments also provided the Commission with useful documents; this was especially the case with declassified documents from the United States government. The contents of these documents confirmed the conclusions of the investigations in several illustrative cases and helped clarify responsibility for grave human rights violations.

At the same time, in some cases when the persons who suffered human rights violations or acts of violence were not Guatemalans, the CEH received pertinent information from those States of the victims' nationalities.

Collaboration of foreign government

In order to complement its information regarding the external factors that influenced the internal armed confrontation and to understand them in all of their complexity, the CEH requested the collaboration of several foreign governments, especially those that may have supported or collaborated with the Parties, in different ways and to different degrees, during the internal armed confrontation.

On November 20, 1997, the CEH made a request to the President of the United States for information on the Guatemalan internal armed confrontation contained in US government archives. The information provided by the US government from its files was very useful to the Commission during the course of its work. The CEH gives special recognition to the effort made by the US government to respond to its requests, an effort that required the dedication of numerous government employees.

On the same date, the Commission requested information or comments from the Israeli government regarding its possible collaboration with counterinsurgency operations. The Israeli ambassador responded to the requests on March 19, 1998, in the name of the Israeli government; he stated, "Our investigations reveal that no assistance or training was provided by official Israeli representatives," and the Israeli government "is unable to receive information, nor is it able to investigate initiatives by private Israeli citizens in Guatemala."

The Commission requested any information from the Cuban government on November 21, 1997, regarding Cuba's possible relations with the parties to the conflict. The Cuban government did not reply to the request. On December 19, 1997, the Commission requested similar information from the Argentine and Nicaraguan governments, again, to no avail.

Press and other documentation

Finally, numerous books and written documents on the Guatemalan reality were consulted to corroborate case investigations and to aid in historical clarification; a huge volume of press sources, especially from the Guatemalan press, were also consulted for the same purposes.

Clarification of cases of human rights violations and acts of violence connected to the internal armed confrontation

Registered cases

"Registered cases" as defined by the CEH, are those for which the Commission has decided, in all conscience, that it has sufficient elements to guarantee, with varying degrees of certainty, that the events actually occurred, as well as the identity of the perpetrators. The CEH presents its summaries of these cases in the Appendix of Presented Cases.

The term "case" is applied to the description of an action that occurred in a specific place on a determined date, consisting of one or more human rights violations or acts of violence committed against one or more victims, and connected to the internal armed confrontation.

As can be implied from the previous paragraphs, In order to clarify 7,517 cases, the Commission compiled an enormous amount of information from multiple sources. The main basis for said clarification was the field investigation carried out by the Commission, itself, using as especially relevant sources victims' testimonies, testimonies by direct or referential witnesses, key witness testimony, testimony from current and former State agents, ex-members of the guerrilla, and the results from exhumations.

With respect to exhumations, for the investigation of some particularly grave or noteworthy cases, the Commission required assistance from the Guatemalan Forensic Anthropology Foundation (FAFG) to provide four forensic anthropology reports on victims' remains from four massacres. These exhumations were conducted in Panths, Alta Verapaz; Belen, Suchitepezuez; and Acul and Chel, in El Quiche. CEH investigators were also present at and collaborated with other exhumations conducted by the Center for Human Rights Legal Action (CALDH) and the Guatemalan Archbishop's Human Rights Office (ODAGH), which were conducted during the same period as CEH fieldwork. The results of their reports were given to the CEH and provided important data for the clarification of certain cases.

During the first stage of case investigation, field investigators carried out the Commission's main responsibility for that period– the collection of victims' testimony.

Investigators in every CEH field office traveled throughout the territory covered by their respective offices, whenever the number of those wishing to give testimony was high, distances were great, or other circumstances made travel necessary.

In order to open the investigation of a case, the acts described by testimony needed to meet certain minimal requirements, including the following: the act had to have occurred during and be connected to the armed confrontation; be classified as a human rights violation or as an act of violence in the framework of the CEH's mandate; and be clearly connected to the armed confrontation.

In addition, during this initial stage, the Commission considered that, in order to guarantee the objective and impartial nature of its investigations, it was indispensable to begin with an evaluation of the likelihood and credibility of the testimonies and of the informants, themselves, while at the same time, seeking relevant information from other sources. Therefore, important emphasis was placed on the descriptions of the events. For example, the mere affirmation of an assassination was insufficient to register a case. In order to register a case, the informant had to provide concrete descriptions of the event and its circumstances.

In addition to an insufficient description of the events, a testimony's credibility was also questioned when its content was inconsistent with the patterns of events in the location and corresponding period.

The general rule was that each declaration given to the CEH should be signed by the informant, in order to guarantee the seriousness of the declaration and to convey the solemnity of the process, while maintaining the confidentiality of the source, whenever requested. Informants who could not write, signed their testimony with a fingerprint.

Information in the CEH database, which was used for all statistics contained in the Report, was compiled exclusively from testimonies that fulfilled these requirements.

For this reason, the events presented in documents submitted by some institutions, all of which had been informed of the Commission's procedures, could not be considered "registered cases" by the CEH, unless a witnesses personally signed a statement. Rather, when lacking a signed statement, the information provided was used as input for the analyses in the Report's central chapters and to complement information on other cases that had met said requirement.

To summarize: the information contained in a declaration, which was presented to a CEH representative and which met the requirements mentioned above, served as the basis for opening and investigating a case.

In addition, whenever the Commission was presented with a denunciation, investigators collected further information about the specific circumstances surrounding the events, in order to help with the legal classification and to determine their connection to the armed confrontation. In general, the greatest possible amount of information was collected for each case, which would later be submitted to the Commissioners for their consideration.

In order to be able to submit a case to the Commissioners for their consideration, as a minimum, it was necessary to establish that the acts and the circumstances surrounding them had effectively occurred, especially with reference to the perpetrators, and that they could be classified as a human rights violation or an act of violence connected to the internal armed confrontation.

The long periods of time that had passed since many of the events had occurred was an objective difficulty in the investigation. This was especially so given the fact that when field investigations began, virtually the only source of information was the victims' memories; their testimonies, which were cross-checked and complemented with information from other sources, formed the basis for construction the elements of certainty for a case.

Compiling the information was a complex task, in part, because the vast majority of the victims of the most serious acts were indigenous *campesinos,* many of whom speak a Mayan language, have great difficulty communicating in Spanish, and may not be able to read or write. In addition, the narrative style of their languages makes it difficult to establish detailed events according to the Commission's categories and methodology. To facilitate the testimony collection from indigenous citizens, the CEH contracted translators and interpreters, which enabled people to speak more comfortably in their native language.

Despite these difficulties, the wealth of testimonies collected in the field is the most valuable capital in this Report; it's pages breathe with the living memories of many, many Guatemalans.

For numerous cases, documentation from external sources which had already investigated or learned about these cases, was often important to confirm, complement or modify the information collected by the CEH. Important in this regard were data bases from national and international non-governmental organizations and declassified documents from the US government.

If contradictions among sources on a case persisted, investigators were not to submit the case to the Central Office without first resolving the contradictions or calling clear attention to them.

During this stage, anyone who might possess relevant information – including direct or indirect participants in the acts or those who might have had the obligation to investigate them – was invited to give their version of events. Statements were always collected discreetly and with confidentiality.

Determining responsibilities was one fundamental aspect of clarification the acts being investigated. The Commission did indeed collect reliable information regarding the material or intellectual authors in many cases. However, the Commission gave priority to determining institutional responsibility, not only because of the mandate, which forbid the attribution of individual responsibility, but also with the understanding that historical clarification was the Commission's overriding purpose.

Nevertheless, the Commission highly valued information relating to individual responsibility. Although this information could not be included in the Final Report, it was useful for compiling a list of people to invite to provide their versions of events. It also assisted in the reconstruction of certain complex contexts, made up of several cases, which aided in building greater certainty about the events.

Degrees of certainty

The objective of case investigation was not clarification in a police or judicial sense of the word or to determine penal responsibilities, but rather to establish if human rights violations or acts of violence connected to the internal armed confrontation were committed. The Commission is not a tribunal, with the purpose of collecting material proof of a crime in order to attribute individual responsibility; nor did it have the authority to supoena witnesses or to undertake certain evidentiary proceedings.

The Commission's mission in case investigation was to collect the greatest amount of particulars and information, provided voluntarily from various sources, in order to develop, in all conscience and based on the Commissioners' moral authority and independence, a determination on the occurrence of the events, their legal classification, and those responsible for them, emphasizing institutional responsibility or the responsibility of one of the insurgent groups.

In certain cases, especially with forced disappearances and in arbitrary executions without witnesses, the determination that human rights violations had been committed was based on the accumulation of circumstantial elements of judgement, such as the victims' backgrounds, the *modus operandi,* circumstances at that time or place and the existence of coetaneous cases.

Cases investigated and clarified by the Commission are included in the Commission's statistics and the Appendix of Presented Cases. They are arranged according to degrees of certainty, basically with regards to the occurrence of the act and to its perpetrators(s), and established according to an evaluation of all of the information collected on the case.

In evaluating the information on these two aspects, the Commission considered, among other things, whether the witnesses providing testimony were direct or indirect, their credibility and the existence of additional evidence.

Three different degrees of certainty were defined, which would be applied upon evaluating a case:

A Systematization of Support Office Experiences

Complete certainty[12]: this level is established for cases with direct witnesses whose testimonies left no doubt for the Commission regarding their credibility, in reference to the occurrence of the events and perpetrators; or where documented evidence confirms both the act and its author.

Well-founded probability[13]: this second level of certainty pertained to cases when not every witness was a direct witness of the act or its perpetrator(s), but when the Commission had no doubt regarding their credibility.

Reasonable likelihood[14]: this third level of certainty describes cases lacking direct witnesses of the act or its perpetrator(s). These cases are supported either by referential witnesses whose testimonies corroborate each other, or when there is collective public knowledge of the perpetrators, or when, in all conscience, the Commissioners considered that the information was sufficient to determine the existence of the case.

This third level of certainty was the minimum requirement for cases to be used in the statistical analyses or included in the Appendix of Presented Cases.

Of the total number of cases registered by the CEH, 32.63% were classified as being of complete certainty regarding occurrence and perpetrator(s).

The percentage of cases with well-founded probability of occurrence and perpetrator(s) was 42.54% of all registered cases.

The percentage of cases with reasonable likelihood of occurrence and perpetrator(s) was 24.82% of all registered cases.

It is important to reiterate that, with respect to the cases grouped in any of these three categories, the Commissioners have established and affirmed, with the same authority in all of them, the existence and responsibilities for said cases, even though the determination was based in some cases on complete certainty, in others, on well-founded probability and in others, on reasonable likelihood.

Case validation

in order to be included in the Final Report, each case needed to be validated, first by field investigators, who sent all relevant information to the Central Office. Data Base analysts then analyzed this testimonial and documentary information and classified cases according to type of violation or act of violence and the perpetrator.

Before registering a case, the Data Base cleaned the information, reviewing the victims list, looking for repetitions of dates or locations, errors in the legal classification or possible technical errors.

Once the cases were registered in the Data Base, they were reviewed again, this time by a team of legal experts. These experts drafted the summaries that are included in the Appendix of Presented Cases. Their conclusions were submitted to the Commissioners, who made the final determination regarding their publication and the level of certainty.

Illustrative cases

Almost 100 cases were selected from among all the registered cases to be investigated in greater depth and which served as special input for the comprehensive analysis of the phenomena covered in the Report. Eighty-five of these cases are presented in the Appendix of Illustrated Cases.

Illustrative cases were chosen using the following criteria: they highlighted an important change in the strategies or tactics of one of the parties to the conflict; or they had special impact on the national conscience, due to their severity; or they illustrated patterns of human rights violations or acts of violence connected to the internal armed confrontation in a determined region or period.

In general, the information sources for illustrative cases were similar to those previously outlined in this section. Often as the investigation proceeded, certain sources took on special importance, such as key witness testimony, declassified US government documents and information regarding regional or national contexts.

Each illustrative case was analyzed and reviewed by a special team of professionals at the central office, then submitted for the Commissioners' final approval.

Systematizing and analyzing information and drafting the Final Report

Using the registered cases as a starting point (and including those chosen as illustrative cases), together with all of the available sources and statistical support from the data base, staff began the process to systematize and analyze all of the information that had been collected and to draft the Report.

The degrees of certainty assigned to each case was key for this more comprehensive and general task.

Because of the enormous number of testimonies given, as well as the additional information compiled from other sources and compared to the versions provided by the Parties, the Commission was able to establish firm determinations regarding the nature of human rights violations and acts of violence connected to the armed confrontation, their causes and origins, and their consequences, which then served as the basis for the conclusions and recommendations.

Specialized teams systematized this information, in order to facilitate the work of analysts in charge of drafting the Final Report. These were the "input" teams, which included the Data Base, the Presented Cases Team, the Illustrative Cases Team, the Key Witness Team and the Documentation Center.

All of the inputs used by the teams in charge of drafting the Report's three main chapters were indispensable. However, certain sources, such as testimony given by important actors in the armed confrontation, in particular those who were part of institutions or groups that perpetrated human rights violations or acts of violence, as well as the declassified documents provided by the US government, often took on special importance.

In the stage prior to drafting the Final Report, the Commissioners decided that not only was it necessary to examine human rights violations and acts of violence, but also to study their historical context, particularly the causes and origins of the violence. This task was mainly the responsibility of the Historical Analysis Group, which was comprised of high-level academics from various disciplines. This work was the basis for Chapter One of the Report.

Similarly, the Commissioners decided to analyze the wealth of information at its disposal on a number of the painful consequences of so many years of internal armed confrontation in Guatemala, and which also caused suffering in the population. This decision gave birth to Chapter Three of the Report.

Chapter Two specifically refers to human rights violations and acts of violence connected to the armed confrontation. In developing this chapter, the Commission developed in-depth studies of the strategies of the parties to the conflict and the methods employed by certain State institutions, as well as a rigorous legal analysis of all of the registered cases. These studies allowed the Commission to arrive at conclusions based on the facts and founded in law. The conclusions assign respective responsibilities to the Guatemalan State and to the former guerrilla based on multiple proof of acts: committed by State agents or by private individuals acting with their consent or acquiescence; or by former members of the guerrilla who acted in accordance to policy or upon superior orders; or by State agents and ex-guerrilla members, acting independently of superior orders or policies.

The progressive systematization and analysis of all of the information culminated in the final drafting of the chapters included in the Report, which were reviewed, discussed and approved by the Commissioners, in lengthy work sessions.

The Commissioners developed their final conclusions and formulated their recommendations based on the acts and phenomena described in the three central chapters.

The Data Base

A data base is a center where information is compiled and systematized under previously defined criteria and in accordance with the study's objectives.

The CEH Data Base was created to electronically systematize cases of human rights violations and acts of violence collected by the CEH throughout the country's different regions. The systematization was designed to organize information according to certain previously defined criteria, in order to produce statistics regarding frequencies of acts and their specific characteristics: dates, places, responsible forces, victim characteristics, and types of violation.

CEH investigators used five case documentation forms to record information on each case, according to previously mentioned criteria. These forms refer, respectively, to: general case data; information about the victims; the perpetrators; the violations committed against the victims; and information on the person providing the testimony; in addition, the forms were accompanied by a narrative summary of the events. Case documentation forms were transferred to the Data Base, where they were processed.

Twenty people, including analysts, data entry specialists, programmers, a systems assistant and an information assistant, made up the team that was responsible for systematization this information. All members worked were under the direction of the Data Base director, who also had an assistant for specific support.

Basic structural criteria for the Data Base

The Data Base was the source for the Commission's statistical analyses. It was structured around a set of interrelated, dependent concepts or basic criteria, which can be understood only as a part of the overall structure.

The CEH Data Base registered cases of human rights violations and acts of violence presented by witnesses (known internally as "declarants").

"Witness" refers to an individual or group that give testimony to the CEH.

Individual witnesses were registered under their full names. Group witnesses were registered under the name of the village, community or specific group to which the people belonged.

Individual and collective witnesses could give testimony referring to one or more cases. Or, for single case, there could be one or several different witnesses, who may have given testimony at different places in the country.

In the Data Bases, a "victim" was registered as the person against whom the human rights violation(s) or act(s) of violence was aimed and who suffered it directly.

A person could be a victim of one or numerous human rights violations or acts of violence committed during a single action. Likewise, one human rights violation or act of violence could be committed against a single person or a group of people during the same action. Finally, a person could be the victim of one or more violations or acts of violence committed in different places or times.

Type of information registered in the Data Base

197. Information contained in the CEH Data Base was exclusively comprised of information compiled from individual or group testimonies.

198. The Data Base was constructed exclusively to register said primary information. Information the CEH obtained from other sources was classified and systematized separately by the Documentation Center or by the investigative teams.

199. In addition to the previously mentioned criteria, the following requirements were established to register cases:

the information sources were testimonies given to the CEH, and case information contained at least three of the following elements: date, place, type of violation and victims.

200. Cases provided both quantitative and qualitative information.

Quantitative information

201. Quantitative information refers to concrete data systematically collected in previously designed formats or forms, in order to quantify and obtain a corresponding statistical base. This kind of data referred to: the case (date, place); victims (name, age, sex, type of victim); perpetrators (name, age, sex, group or organization); type of violation or act committed; and finally, those testifying (name, age, sex).

202. Glossaries were developed to classify this information as typologies of human rights violations and acts of violence; care was taken to assure that equivalent categories were used for both parties to the conflict, based on international human rights instruments and international humanitarian laws, as well the common principles contained in both.

The categories were defined as the following:

1. Human rights violations and acts of violence that resulted in death:
1.1   Arbitrary executions
1.2   Massacres[5]
1.3   Death by forced displacement
1.4   Civilian death during hostilities
1.5   Civilian death as a result of an indiscriminate attack
1.6   Civilian death as a result of land mines
1.7   Death resulting from being used as a human shield;

Human rights violations and acts of violence that resulted in serious wounds:
2.1   Wounded by an assassination attempt
2.2   Wounded during forced displacement
2.3   Civilian wounded during hostilities
2.4   Civilian wounded during an indiscriminate attack
2.5   Civilian wounded as a result of land mines
2.6   Wounded as a result of being used as a human shield;

Disappearance
3.1   Forced disappearance

3.2 Disappearance by unknown causes

Torture, and cruel, inhumane and degrading treatment

Rape

Kidnapping

Others
7.1   Death threats
7.2   Burning of crops or fields
7.3   Deprivation of liberty
7.4   Forced recruitment
7.5   Combatants' death[6]

The "other" category, while not compiled systematically, was created to register information provided in testimonies that had been used to open cases under one of the previous categories. Statistical results referring to this category were not significant, with the exception of deprivation of liberty. However, this information was useful to illustrate situations or concrete phenomena related to the armed confrontation.

The category of "Disappearance by unknown causes" was created to register cases in which a person disappeared, but where no signs of detention were discovered, making it impossible to prove that they were forced disappearances. Nonetheless, these cases were not excluded from the Data Base, because given the context (date, place), type of victims and the frequencies of this type of event it could be presumed that they were in some way connected to the armed confrontation, while recognizing the difficulties due to the scarcity of information on the circumstances of the events.

The following categories were applied in the Data Base and used for statistical purposes when referring to perpetrators of human rights violations and acts of violence:

Army: when members of the Guatemalan Army are responsible for acts referred to in a case.

National Police: when members of the National Police are responsible for acts in a case.

Treasury Police: when members of the Treasury Police are responsible for acts.

Security Forces: when the exact State security force cannot be determined, but it is known that the acts in the case were perpetrated by some apparatus of the State security system.

Military Commissioners: when Military Commissioners are responsible for acts.

Civil Defense Patrols: when a member or members of the Civil Defense Patrols is/are responsible for acts.

Death Squads: this category refers to an armed group identified by a specific name and when said group is pars-State in nature, carries out actions in a structured manner, with an established pattern of repeated criminal activity.

Guerrilla groups: when the URNG or one of its member organizations or fronts are responsible for acts.

Civilians: when an individual or individuals without position of public authority nor belonging to previously mentioned categories is/are responsible for acts.

Public Official: when an individual or individuals holding public office, whether by election or appointment, and not belong to previously mentioned categories is/ are responsible for acts.

Other Armed Groups: when no specific information can be discerned from case information or regional context, to identify the perpetrator(s) of the acts. However, sufficient information exists to know the acts were committed by a group of armed subjects.

Unidentified: when testimonies provide no indication of the participation of an armed group or when an unidentified individual committed the acts or when there is no reasonable indication regarding the identity of the perpetrator(s) or their belonging to any group or institution.

Qualitative information

The qualitative information available in the Data Bases comes from the narrative case summaries based on the information provided by those giving testimony and refers to descriptions of the acts, their circumstances and context.

In order to classify this information, a glossary of thematic key words was compiled to assist analysts. Cases were classified according to key words contained in the glossary. This facilitated rapid access to the cases.

Data Base results

208. The Data Base results are as follows:

1. Inputs for analysts
Qualitative: Case lists were generated that contained basic information arranged and selected according to criteria defined by the investigators: for example, specific phenomena, cases by year, place, type of victims, authors, type of violation, etc. These lists allowed investigators to consult the physical files of registered cases in the Data Base more easily and facilitated their use for formulating and testing hypotheses.

Quantitative: These included reports, charts, graphs and statistics obtained from the CEH Data Base. This information was useful to compare and contrast hypotheses on a range of topics.

Total number of victims

209. Given the need to establish a figure that reflects the total number of victims who were executed or disappeared during the armed confrontation, the CEH requested that the American Association for the Advancement of Science (AAAS) conduct a scientific study of the statistics produced by the CEH and other organizations, including the inter-diocesan project entitled "The Recuperation of Historical Memory" (REMHI), and information from the International Center for Human Rights Investigation (CI IDH).

210. The AAAS study, included in Appendix III of this Report, established that 132,000 people were executed between 1978-1996, with a 5% margin of error (between 119,300-145,000 people).

211. For scientific reasons, the study only included the period between 1978-1996. For similar reasons some regions were also excluded, and even though they represent relatively small areas, their exclusion artificially reduced the overall estimate.

212. Considering these limitations to the statistical study, given the scarcity of information for certain periods of the armed confrontation, the CEH also conducted a comparative study of the available, relevant literature

Summary of estimated victims of execution

Source	Total	1966-67	1967-68	1960-69	1970-74	1970-77	1966-77	1978-96
CEH (projection)[7]								132,000
CIIDH (newspaper sources)[8]				1,507		1,940		3,113
REMHI[9]	200,000							
JONAS1[10]	200,000		8,000			20,000		
Violence in Guatemalan[11]		4,000	2,000					
Melville & Melville[12]			2,800					
Aguilera Peralta[13]		6,000						
Amnesty International[14]							20,000	
Torres-Rivas[15]					7,200			

The different estimates regarding the total number of disappeared average approximately 40,000 victims.

Estimated disappearances

Source	Estimate
REMHI (press conference)	50,000
Central American Association of the Families of the Detained and Disappeared. The Practice of Forced Disappearance in Guatemala,	
Guatemala: ACAFADE. 1988.	38,000
Jonas (op.cit.)	40,000
GAM	40,000

Of the violations documented by the CEH, the ratio of executions to disappearances is approximately 4:1. The estimation of 40,000 disappearances is compatible with this ratio. The CEH estimates that approximately 160,000 executions were committed and 40,000 disappearances.

	Estimate
1960-67 (from sources)	5,000
1968-69 (from sources)	5,000
1970-77 (from sources)	12,000
1978-96 (CEH projection)	132,000
Regions excluded from the projection	7,500
Disappeared	40,000
Total	201,500

Notes

1.   This figure includes both collective and individual testimonies presented to the CEH.
2.   Equivalent to certainty level 1 in the Appendix of Presented Cases [in Spanish, convicciOn plena].
3.   Equivalent to certainty level 2 in the Appendix of Presented Cases [in Spanish, presunciOn fundada].
4.   Equivalent to certainty level 3 in the Appendix of Presented Cases [in Spanish, presunciOn simple].
5.   In the published statistics, these are included with arbitrary executions.
6.   Although death in combat is not precisely or necessarily a legal violation, the category was established in order to register the number of people killed in combat.
7.   The CEH estimation is presented in the next section [of the Final Report].
8.   Data compiled by the CIIDH includes assassinations and documented disappearances. It is not merely an estimation. See: Patrick Ball, Paul Kobrak and Herbert F. Spirer, *Institutional Violence in Guatemala, 1960-1996: a Quantitative Reflection,* Washington, D.C.: AAAS, 1999. For additional data, see Internet: http://hrdata. aaas.orgiciidh/data.html
9.   This figure was presented during a press conference prior to the presentation of the REMHI report in April 1998.
10.   Susan Jonas, The *Battle for Guatemala,* FLACSO, Editorial Nueva Sociedad, Guatemala, 1994.
11.   *The Violence in Guatemala, a* dramatic and documented denunciation of "the third revolutionary government," Mexico, D.F., Fondo de Cultural Popular, 1969.
12.   Thomas Melville and Marjorie Melville, *Guatemala: The Politics of Land Ownership,* New York, The Free Press, 1971.
13.   Gabriel Edgardo Aguilera Peralta, *Violence in Guatemala as a Political Phenomenon,* San Jose, Costa Rica, Centro Intercultural de Documentación, Cuaderno 61, 1971.
14.   Amnesty International, *Annual Report,* London, AI, 1977.
15.   Edelberto Torres-Rivas, *Introduction: Guatemalan Profile,* Tribunal Permanente de los Pueblos, Madrid, IEPALA, 1994.

Appendix II

Guatemala: Memory of Silence Recommendations

I. Introduction

The Accord of Oslo establishes as one of the three objectives of the CEH that it: "Formulate specific recommendations to encourage peace and national harmony in Guatemala. The Commission shall recommend, in particular, measures to preserve the memory of the victims, to foster a culture of mutual respect and observance of human rights and to strengthen the democratic process."

As expressly noted in other agreements, such as the Comprehensive Agreement on Human Rights, the Agreement on the Implementation, Compliance and Verification Timetable for the Peace Agreement and the Agreement on the Basis for the Legal Integration of the Guatemalan National Revolutionary Unity, the CEH should also outline recommendations for reparatory measures for the victims of the armed confrontation.

The CEH regarded it as imperative to formulate its recommendations taking into consideration the contents of the Peace Accords. The rigorous application of the Accords, and likewise their broad dissemination, are essential elements in establishing the foundations of a democratic rule of law. For this reason, the CEH believes it vital to emphasize and reiterate certain commitments already established in the Accords.

The methodology followed in preparing the recommendations was based on findings that arose from the investigation carried out by the CEH and from the extensive process of consultation of various sectors of civil society. The National Forum on Recommendations, convened by the CEH and held on 27 May 1998, was attended by 400 people, belonging to 139 organizations from civil society, and has been a useful source of reflection on those proposals of fundamental importance to the CEH. The needs and suggestions expressed in the personal testimonies given to the CEH and during the aforementioned process of consultation were a source of constant reference in the formulation of this chapter.

The CEH believes it necessary that its recommendations be implemented so that the mandate entrusted to it within the framework of the peace process achieves its objectives. To accomplish this, the joint participation of the State and civil society is necessary, as every Guatemalan without distinction should benefit from the recommendations.

On this basis, the CEH presents its recommendations laid out under the following sections:

1.   Measures for the preservation of the memory of the victims;
2.   Measures for the compensation of the victims;
3.   Measures to foster a culture of mutual respect and observance of human rights;
4.   Measures for strengthening the democratic process;
5.   Other recommendations to favor peace and national harmony; and,
6.   Body responsible for promoting and monitoring the fulfillment of the recommendations.

The effects of the armed confrontation and the violence connected with it were not limited solely to the two factions. Neither do the victims come only from certain sectors of the population. Almost all Guatemalans have been affected in one way or another by the violence that has been so widespread and lasted for such a long period of time. For this reason, the CEH's recommendations are fundamentally designed to facilitate unity in Guatemala and banish the centuries-old divisions suffered. Reconciliation is the responsibility of everyone.

The CEH is convinced that construction of peace, founded on the knowledge of the past, demands that those affected by the armed confrontation and the violence connected with it are listened to and no longer considered solely as victims, but as the protagonists of a future of national harmony.

The violence and horrors described in the Report should leave no room for despair. Subsequent generations in Guatemala have the right to a brighter, better future. Guatemalans can, and must, encourage a common project of nationhood. To bring about a reconstruction of Guatemala's social fabric, based on lasting peace and reconciliation, it is vital to foster an authentic sense of national unity among the diversity of peoples that make up the nation. By means of its recommendations, the CEH aims to help strengthen the hope of the people of Guatemala that its violent history will never be repeated.

II. Measures to preserve the memory of the victims

The Accord of Oslo emphasizes the need to remember and dignify the victims of the fratricidal confrontation that took place in Guatemala. The CEH believes that the historical memory, both individual and collective, forms the basis of national identity. Remembrance of the victims is a fundamental aspect of this historical memory and permits the recovery of the values of, and the validity of the struggle for, human dignity.

On the basis of these considerations, and considering the appeal for forgiveness made by the President of the Republic on 29 December 1998, and the partial appeal for forgiveness made by the Guatemalan National Revolutionary Unity on 19 February 1998, the CEH recommends:

Dignity for the Victims

1.   That, in the name of the State of Guatemala and with the primary aim of restoring dignity to the victims, the President of the Republic recognize, before the whole of Guatemalan society, before the victims, their relatives and their communities, those acts described in this Report, ask pardon for them and assume responsibility for the Human Rights violations connected with the internal armed confrontation, particularly for those committed by the Army and the state security forces.
2.   That the Congress of the Republic issue a solemn declaration reaffirming the dignity and honor of the victims and restoring their good name and that of their relatives.
3.   That the ex-Command of the Guatemalan National Revolutionary Unity, with the primary aim of restoring dignity to the victims, ask forgiveness, solemnly and publicly, before the whole of society, before the victims, their relatives and their communities, and assume responsibility for those acts of violence committed by the ex-guerrillas connected with the armed confrontation that have caused the Guatemalan population to suffer.

Remembrance of the victims

4.   That the Guatemalan State and society commemorate the victims by means of various activities carried out in co-ordination with organizations from civil society, among which it is essential that the following measures be included:

   a)   Designation of a day of commemoration of the victims (National Day of Dignity for the Victims of the Violence).
   b)   The construction of monuments and public parks in memory of the victims at national, regional and municipal levels.
   c)   The assigning of names of victims to educational centers, buildings and public highways.
5.   That the commemorations and ceremonies for the victims of the armed

confrontation take into consideration the multicultural nature of the Guatemalan nation, to which end the Government and local authorities should promote and authorize the raising of monuments and the creation of communal cemeteries in accordance with the forms of Mayan collective memory.

6.   That the sacred Mayan sites violated during the armed confrontation are reclaimed and their importance highlighted in accordance with the wishes of the communities affected.

III. Reparatory measures

The CEH considers that truth, justice, reparation and forgiveness are the bases of the process of consolidation of peace and national reconciliation. Therefore, it is the responsibility of the Guatemalan State to design and promote a policy of reparation for the victims and their relatives. The primary objectives should be to dignify the victims, to guarantee that the human rights violations and acts of violence connected with the armed confrontation will not be repeated and to ensure respect for national and international standards of human rights.

On this basis, the CEH recommends:

National Reparation Programme

7.   That the Guatemalan State, by means of appropriate measures taken by the Government and the Congress of the Republic, urgently create and put into effect a National Reparation Programme for the victims, and their relatives, of human rights violations and acts of violence connected with the armed confrontation.

8.   That, to this end, the Government present to the Congress of the Republic, with the utmost urgency, a legislative bill on reparation for the victims of the armed confrontation which activates the National Reparation Programme. The said bill should set out the general principles and the structure of the programme, the categories of the beneficiaries, the measures, the procedures for the identification of the beneficiaries, the manner and the financial mechanisms, to be set forth below.

Principles and measures

9.   That the National Reparation Programme include a series of measures inspired by the principles of equality, social participation and respect for cultural identity, among which at least the following should figure:

a)   Measures for the restoration of material possessions so that, as far as is possible, the situation existing before the violation be re-established, particularly in the case of land ownership.

b)   Measures for the indemnification or economic compensation of the most serious injuries and losses resulting as a direct consequence of the violations of human rights and of humanitarian law.

c) Measures for psychosocial rehabilitation and reparation, which should include, among others, medical attention and community mental health care, and likewise the provision of legal and social services.

d) Measures for the satisfaction and restoration of the dignity of the individual, which should include acts of moral and symbolic reparation.

10. That, depending on the type of violation, the reparatory measures be individual or collective. Collective reparatory measures should be implemented in such a way as to facilitate reconciliation between victims and perpetrators, without stigmatizing either. Therefore, collective reparatory measures for survivors of collective human rights violations and acts of violence, and their relatives, should be carried out within a framework of territorially based projects to promote reconciliation, so that in addition to addressing reparation, their other actions and benefits also favor the entire population, without distinction between victims and perpetrators.

11. That, for the process of reparation to become one of the principal bases for the process of national reconstruction and reconciliation, it is vital that Guatemalan society participate actively in the definition, execution and evaluation of the National Reparation Programme. This participation is especially important in the case of the Mayan population, which was affected with particular severity by the violence. In the specific case of measures for collective reparation it is essential that the beneficiaries themselves participate in defining the priorities of the reparation process.

Beneficiaries

12. That the beneficiaries of the moral and material reparatory measures must be the victims (or their relatives) of the human rights violations and of the acts of violence connected with the internal armed confrontation.

13. That for the purposes of the programme, victims are considered to be those persons who have personally suffered human rights violations and acts of violence connected with the internal armed confrontation.

14. That in those cases where individual economic indemnification is appropriate, prioritisation of the beneficiaries must be established, taking into consideration the severity of the violation, their economic situation and social vulnerability, and paying particular attention to the elderly, widows, minors or those who are found to be disadvantaged in any other way.

15. That the identification of Programme's beneficiaries should be guided by criteria of clarity, justice, equality, speed, accessibility and broad-based participation.

Structure of the programme

16. That the Board of Directors of the Programme be composed of nine members: i) two persons appointed by the President of the Republic; ii) two persons appointed by the Congress of the Republic; iii) one person designated by the Human Rights Ombudsman; iv) a representative from the victims' organisations; v) a representative from the human rights organisations; vi) a representative from the Mayan organisations; vii) a representative from the women's organisations.

17. That, with the aim of facilitating the appointment process for the representatives of the aforementioned organisations, the person designated by the Human Rights Ombudsman convene and facilitate appointment processes of the respective sectors.

18. That the Programme's Board of Directors should have the following functions:

   a) Receive individual or collective applications from potential beneficiaries.

   b) Assess, according to the circumstances of each case, whether the potential beneficiary has the status of victim or relative of a victim. Victims of cases contained in the case annexes of this
   Report should be automatically qualified as victims without the need for another case study.

   c) Assess the socio-economic status of potential beneficiaries previously identified as victims.

   d) On the basis of the former, decide who the beneficiaries are.

   e) Decide on the relevant reparatory measures.

Financing

19. That the State fund the National Reparation Programme by putting into effect the universally progressive tax reform established by the Peace Accords. To achieve this, a redistribution of social spending and a decrease in military spending would be appropriate. These measures should constitute the principal source of financing.

20. That, to the same end, the State solicit international co-operation from those countries which, during the internal armed confrontation, lent military and financial aid to the parties.

Period of operation

21. The National Reparation Programme should cover the time period necessary for it to achieve its objectives. This should not be less than ten years, considering the period determined for the presentation of the applications and the time necessary for allocating and delivering the benefits.

Forced disappearance

Given the extent of the crime of forced disappearance, developed as a repeated practise in Guatemala during the period of armed confrontation, and considering that forced disappearance not only causes those close to the detained person long-term distress due to the uncertainty of the fate of their loved one, but also generates a series of legal and administrative problems, it becomes vital to rectify these problems so that the suffering and complications occasioned by the disappearance are not prolonged. Therefore, so that it may be included in the National Reparation Programme, the CEH recommends:

Search for the disappeared

22. That the Government and the judiciary, in collaboration with civil society, initiate, as soon as possible, investigations regarding all known forced disappearances. All available legal and material resources should be utilised to clarify the whereabouts of the disappeared and, in the case of death, to deliver the remains to the relatives.
23. That the Guatemalan Army and the former Guatemalan National Revolutionary Unity provide whatever information they may have in relation to the disappearances of people that occurred during the period of internal armed confrontation.

Request: In relation to the search for the disappeared, the International Committee of the Red Cross (ICRC), an international body specialising in such matters, is requested to lend its advice and technical support to the various organs of the Guatemalan State responsible for these activities.

Specific recommendations concerning children who have been disappeared, illegally adopted or illegally separated from their families.

24. That the Government urgently activate the search for children who have been disappeared including, at the very least, the following measures:
  a) Establishment of a National Commission for the Search for Disappeared Children whose aim should be to look for children who have been disappeared, illegally adopted or illegally separated from their parents and of documenting their disappearance.

  Suggestion and request: That the said Commission be composed of the Human Rights Ombudsman and representatives from the national non-governmental organisations for human rights and children, with the advice and technical and financial support, as available, of UNICEF, the ICRC and international non-governmental organisations specialising in children's issues, from whom the CEH solicits co-operation.

b)   The promotion of legislative measures by which, at the request of interested parties, the courts and tribunals of the judiciary and the bodies charged with the protection of unaccompanied children, allow access to their files, facilitating the acquisition of information regarding the identity, ethnic origin, age, place of birth, current whereabouts and real name of the children given up for adoption or taken into care during the armed confrontation.

c)   The implementation of a wide-reaching general information campaign in Spanish and all the native languages, across every region of the country and in refugee sites located in other countries, concerning the activities and measures connected with the search for these children.

25.   That the media actively assist the initiatives in the search for disappeared children.

26.   That the Government promote extraordinary legislative measures that, on the request of the adopted person or his/her relatives, allow for the review of adoptions brought about without the knowledge, or against the will, of the natural parents. The said review should always take place taking into consideration the views of the person who was adopted and in such a way as to promote cordial relations between the adoptive and natural families so that subsequent trauma for the adopted person is avoided.

Recognition of the legal status of absence due to forced disappearance

27.   That the Government prepare and present a bill of law to the Congress of the Republic, by which the declaration of absence due to forced disappearance is recognised as a legal category with the purpose of validating for legal purposes filiation, succession, reparation, and other civil ends related to it.

Active policy of exhumation

The CEH believes that the exhumation of the remains of the victims of the armed confrontation and the location of clandestine and hidden cemeteries, wherever they are found to be, is in itself an act of justice and reparation and is an important step on the path to reconciliation. It is an act of justice because it constitutes part of the right to know the truth and it contributes to the knowledge of the whereabouts of the disappeared. It is an act of reparation because it dignifies the victims and because the right to bury the dead and to carry out ceremonies for them according to each culture is inherent in all human beings.

On this basis, and taking into consideration the high number of clandestine cemeteries referred to in this Report, as well as those still not publicly known, the CEH recommends:

28.   That the Government prepare and develop an active policy of exhumation and urgently present to the Congress of the Republic legislation for a Law of Exhumation which establishes rapid and effective procedures for this and which takes into account the three following recommendations.

29.   That the process of exhumation is carried out with full respect for the cultural values and dignity of the victims and their families, considering the process of exhumation not only as a judicial procedure, but above all as means for individual and collective reparation.

30.   That the bodies and remains of the victims be handed over to their relatives for a dignified burial according to their particular culture.

31.   That the work of the non-governmental organisations specialising in forensic anthropology and the investigation and identification of human remains be promoted and supported. The said specialist organisations should work in association with the Human Rights Ombudsman, whose office should serve as the depository for the relevant data.

Request: Given the economic cost entailed by such specialist activity, the financial support and technical advice of the international community is particularly requested.

IV. Measures to foster a culture of mutual respect and observance of human rights

IV.1. Culture of mutual respect

As reflected in the previous chapters of the Report, a culture of violence has developed in Guatemala, which has resulted in mistrust and a lack of respect among its people. This clearly needs to be transformed into a culture of tolerance and mutual respect.

The CEH believes that the Peace Accords are a basic foundation for the development of peaceful and tolerant relations between the various sectors of Guatemalan society. Consequently, the knowledge and assimilation of the past, the knowledge of the causes and the scope of the uncontrolled violence and, likewise, of the basic principles of respect for human rights, of the mechanisms for their defence and the peaceful solution of disputes are essential elements for the consolidation of a peaceful future.

The CEH believes that to achieve national harmony and reconciliation, a concerted effort at cultural change is required and that this can only be contemplated through an active policy of education for peace.

The relationship between the State and the indigenous population of Guatemala—particularly the Mayan people—has subsisted within an environment of racism, inequality and exclusion. As this can be considered to be one of the historical causes of the armed confrontation, measures guaranteeing the protection of the individual and collective rights of the indigenous population, the respect for cultural plurality and the promotion of intercultural relations become vital.

On this basis, the CEH recommends:

The dissemination and teaching of the contents of the Report

32.   That the State, as a moral imperative and as a duty, embrace the contents of this Report and support all initiatives put into effect for its dissemination and promotion among all Guatemalans.

33.   That, to this end, and in co-ordination with the organisations of civil society in Guatemala and particularly with indigenous and human rights organisations, the Government promote a campaign for the general dissemination of the Report, that takes into consideration the social, cultural and linguistic reality of Guatemala.

34.   That, respecting the multilingual character of Guatemala, the Guatemalan Academy of Mayan Languages carry out the translation of the Report, with public financing, into the following languages:

•   the entire Report should be translated into, and published in, at least five Mayan languages: k'iche, kaqchikel, mam, q'eqchi' and ixill; and,

•   the Report's conclusions and recommendations should be translated into the twenty-one Mayan languages and disseminated in both written and oral forms.

35.   That the Government provide for and finance the translation of the Report's conclusions and recommendations into garífuna and xinca.

36.   That the curricula of primary, secondary and university level education include instruction on the causes, development and consequences of the armed confrontation and likewise of the content of the Peace Accords with the depth and method relevant to the particular level.

Education for a culture of mutual respect and peace

37.   That the State, along with the national human rights non-governmental organisations, co-finance an educational campaign to promote a culture of mutual respect and peace, to be developed by the aforementioned non-governmental organisations and aimed at the country's diverse political and social sectors. The said campaign should be based on principles such as democracy, tolerance, respect for human rights and on the use of dialogue as an instrument for the peaceful solution of disputes. Likewise, it should include the promotion of the development and free circulation of information, with particular emphasis on the content of the Universal Declaration of Human Rights and on the fundamental principle of peace.

38.   That the Government, by means of the educational reform envisaged by the Peace Accords, foster an environment of tolerance and respect and promote self-awareness and awareness of the other, so that the dividing lines created by the ideological, political and cultural polarisation may be erased.

Request: considering the activities so far developed in this area in Guatemala, the CEH requests that the Organization of American States (OAS), through the Cultural Dialogue Programme: Development of Resources for the Construction of Peace (OAS/PROPAZ), lend its support and technical advice to the implementation of the recommendations regarding a culture of mutual respect. Likewise, considering its expertise and activity at the universal level, the Culture of Peace Programme of the Organisation of the United Nations for Education, Science and Culture (UNESCO) is requested to afford whatever assistance possible to this process.

IV.2. Observance of human rights

With the aim of strengthening a culture of mutual respect and observance of human rights and of effectively protecting those working for their defence, the CEH recommends:

Mechanisms for international protection

39.   That the executive and legislative branches take all necessary steps to allow the Guatemalan State to ratify those international human rights instruments still pending, as well as the corresponding implementation mechanisms. The CEH particularly recommends giving priority to the following:
   * International Convention on the Elimination of All Forms of Racial Discrimination, with recognition of the competence of the Committee for the Elimination of All Forms of Racial Discrimination to receive individual complaints.
   * First optional Protocol to the International Covenant on Civil and Political Rights.
   * Convention against Torture and Other Cruel, Inhuman or Degrading Treatment or Punishment, with recognition of the competence of the Committee against Torture to receive individual complaints.
   * Additional Protocol of the American Convention on Human Rights for the Question of Economic, Cultural and Social Rights ("Protocol of San Salvador").
   * Inter-American Convention on Forced Disappearances.
   * Statute of the International Criminal Tribunal.

International humanitarian law

40. That the Government take the necessary measures to fully incorporate into national legislation, the standards of international humanitarian law and that it regularly provide instruction regarding these norms to the personnel of state institutions, particularly the Army, who are responsible for respecting, and in turn engendering respect in others for said norms.

Human rights defenders

41. That the Government promote, with prior consultation the organisations for human rights, legislative measures specifically orientated towards the protection of human rights defenders.

Administrative measures related to public officials responsible for human rights violations

At the same time as reiterating the importance of the measures and commitments assumed by the signatories to the Comprehensive Agreement on Human Rights, and as a solely preventative rather than repressive or punitive measure, the CEH recommends:

42. That a commission should be established by the President of the Republic using his constitutional prerogative, to be under his immediate authority and supervision, and which will examine the conduct of the officers of the Army and of the various bodies of state security forces active during the period of the armed confrontation. Its purpose is to assess the adequacy of their conduct in the execution of their duties during the said period, in regard to the minimum standards established by the instruments of international human rights and humanitarian law.
43. That the said Commission be composed of three independent civilians of recognised honesty and irreproachable democratic trajectory.
44. That the aforementioned Commission should carry out its tasks by the procedure it deems most appropriate, but in any case should listen to the interested parties, bearing in mind the CEH's Report and the personal record of the officers.
45. That consequently, and in view of the magnitude and severity of human rights abuses, administrative measures be adopted that take into account the content of the draft document "Set of Principles for the Protection and Promotion of Human Rights through Action to Combat Impunity" 2 of the United Nations Commission on Human Rights.

V. Measures to strengthen the democratic process

V.1. Administration of justice and traditional forms of conflict resolution

V.1.a Administration of justice

In various sections of the Peace Accords express reference is made to Guatemala's system for the ad mi nistration of justice. Specific reference is made to it in the Agreement on the Strengthening of Civil Power and the Role of the Armed Forces in a Democratic Society, in which it is described as "one of the greatest structural weaknesses of the Guatemalan State." In fulfilling the said agreement, the Commission on the Strengthening of the Justice System produced a final report including various recommendations.

As a result of its own investigations, the CEH has also come to the conclusion that the weakness and dysfunction of the judicial system has contributed decisively to impunity and the misapplication of criminal law during the period covered by the CEH's mandate.

Also, as a result of the Peace Accords, the Congress of the Republic approved the National Reconciliation Law, which, according to Article 1, is considered to be a "basic instrument for the reconciliation of those people involved in the internal armed confrontation."

Considering the former, the CEH recommends:

Commitments pertaining to the Peace Accords

46.   That the powers of the Guatemalan State regard the fulfilment of their commitments on justice contained in the Agreement on the Strengthening of Civil Power and the Role of the Armed Forces in a Democratic Society, as of utmost importance. The recommendations contained in the final Report produced by the Commission on the Strengthening of the Justice System, and which the CEH assumes and reiterates as it own, should be carried out in full.

National Reconciliation Law

47.   That the powers of the State fulfil, and demand fulfilment of, the Law of National Reconciliation, in all of its terms and in relation to the rest of Guatemalan law. Those crimes for whose commission liability is not extinguished by the said law, should be prosecuted, tried and punished, particularly following Article 8 "crimes of genocide, torture and forced disappearance, as well as those crimes that are not subject to prescription or that do not allow the extinction of criminal liability,

in accordance with domestic law or international treaties ratified by Guatemala."

48.   That, in applying the National Law of Reconciliation, the relevant structures take into account the various degrees of authority and responsibility for the human rights violations and acts of violence, paying particular attention to those who instigated and promoted these crimes.

Right to habeas data

49.   That a bill of law be presented by the Government to the Congress of the Republic which quickly and effectively establishes the right of *habeas data* as a specific mechanism of protection and activates the constitutional right, recognised in Article 31 of the Constitution, of access to information contained in archives, files or any other form of state or private record. It should also penalise the gathering, storage or concealment of information about individuals, their religious or political affiliation, their trade union or social activism and any other data relating to their private lives.

V.1.b Traditional forms of conflict resolution

The Commission on the Strengthening of the Justice System included a series of recommendations in its final Report that uses as its starting point the fact that it is "necessary to proceed with the search for formulas that encompass traditional methods of conflict resolution and the state judicial system, capable of complementing both components."

As outlined in its Report, the CEH has noted that disrespect for the traditional methods of conflict resolution, and for the authorities charged with applying them, to the point of the perpetration of acts aimed at eliminating them, has been an almost constant characteristic from 1980 until the end of the armed confrontation.

Considering all the former, and reiterating the need to fulfil the recommendations made by the Commission on the Strengthening of the Justice System, the CEH especially recommends:

Legal integration

50.   That what is known as customary law is recognised and integrated into the Guatemalan legal framework, formalising and ordering a respectful and harmonious relationship between the jud icial system and the traditional forms of conflict resolution, with their principles, criteria, autho-rities and procedures, as long as the rights recognised in the Guatemalan Constitution and in international treaties on human rights are not violated.

Instruction

51. That the universities and other state educational bodies which teach the law include knowledge of the norms of the traditional forms of conflict resolution as a distinct subject in their study programme.
52. That the Ministry of Education support the publication of materials which contain the latest advances in the research into the practices that constitute what is known as customary law.

V.2. Primacy of civilian power and the role of the Armed Forces

V.2.a Legal reform

Considering the grave human rights violations committed by Army agents during the armed confrontation and the marked weakening of the social fabric as a direct consequence of the militarization, the CEH believes it vital to promote legislative measures which establish the fundamental bases for the correct relationship between the Army and civil society within a democratic system, and the necessary subordination of the Army to civilian rule. These measures should include the adaptation of the military norms and fulfilment of its constitutional mandate to promote respect for human rights, the exercise of discipline only according to the law, the apolitical role of the military and restricting its role to external defence.

The CEH also recognises the pernicious effect of the activities of military intelligence on the human rights situation and on civilian-military relations. Equally, it recognises the severe abuse of authority committed in the past through anti-democratic behaviour and the serious violation of human rights by forces directly linked to such intelligence services and often carried out by means of covert actions.

The CEH believes that unquestioning obedience to any kind of order is one of the most significant and most dangerous factors generating human rights violations.

On the basis of the former, the CEH recommends:

53. That the Government present to the Congress of the Republic the necessary legislative reform bills that include measures to implement the Recommendations number 54 to 59 below. These bills should be based on, and complement, what was established in the Agreement on the Strengthening of Civilian Power and the Role of the Armed Forces in a Democratic Society.

Reform of the Constitutive Law of the Army

54. That the Presidential and Vice-presidential General Staff (*Estado Mayor Presidencial y Vicepresidencial*) structures be abolished, being unnecessary in a democratic State.

Reform of military legislation

55. That a new Military Code be drafted and put into effect based on legal, moral and doctrinal criteria in accordance with the Constitution of the Republic and the reforms to the same derived from the Peace Accords.
56. That the Military Code include the correct concept, already contained in the Constitution of the Republic, of discipline and obedience solely within the law and never outside it, and that reference be removed in the Military Code to obedience being owed to whatever kind of order.
57. That the death penalty for the military offence of disobedience be abolished.

New legislation regarding the state intelligence apparatus

58. That the Government present to Congress of the Republic the corresponding legislation that:
   a) Precisely define the structures, tasks and limits of civil and military intelligence, restricting the latter to exclusively military affairs; and
   b) Establish clear mechanisms of effective control in Congress regarding all aspects of the apparatus of state intelligence.
59. That the commitments regarding intelligence contained in the Agreement on the Strengthening of Civilian Power and the Role of the Armed Forces in a Democratic Society be fulfilled as soon as possible, particularly those relating to the approval of the following: the Law on Methods of Supervision of the Organs of State Intelligence; the Law Regulating Access to Information on Military or Diplomatic Affairs relating to National Security; the delimitation of the jurisdiction of the Intelligence Office of the Army General Staff, reconciling these to the new role of the Army; the configuration of the Department of Civil Intelligence and Information Analysis and of the Secretary for Strategic Analysis.

V.2.b New military doctrine

60. That the Government promote a new military doctrine for the Guatemalan Army, that should result from a process of internal reflection and consultation with the organisations of civil society. This doctrine should establish the basic principles for the appropriate relationship between the Army and society within a democratic and pluralist framework. Among

these fundamental principles, at least the following should figure:

a) The function of the Army is the defence of the sovereignty and independence of the State and the integrity of its territory. Its organisation is hierarchical and based on the principles of discipline and obedience within the law.

b) The Army should accept that sovereignty resides in the Guatemalan people. As a consequence, the Army should respect whatever social reforms and changes which result from the exercise of this sovereignty, reconciling itself to the mechanisms established in the Constitution.

c) The Army will base its legal standards, as well as its conduct, on systematic respect for human rights.

d) The Army will be subordinate to political power, which emanates from the ballot box through the procedures established by the Constitution.

e) The Army will show respect for the Constitution in all its aspects.

f) The Army is apolitical. It should remain at the margins of party politics and respect all those political forces legally constituted. None of these may be persecuted or submitted to surveillance or control of any of their activities that are carried out within the law.

g) Members of the military accept the limitation inherent in their career, specifically intended to preserve the apolitical nature of the institution, that, whilst they are in military service, they may not affiliate to, nor become a member of, any party or trade union.

h) Members of the military may exercise their right to vote freely and secretly in national and local elections. Nevertheless, whilst they remain in active service they may not reveal their political preferences in any public act or through any medium of social communication.

61. That the basic values of members of the military must conform to the following concepts and fundamental principles:

a) that members of the military are citizens in the public service of national defence;

b) that military discipline has to be based on the concept of strict obedience within the law, and never outside it;

c) that the concept of military honour must be inseparable from respect for human rights; and,

d) that the esprit de corps must conform to a high standard of ethics and be based on principles of justice and public service.

V.2.c Reform of military education

62. That the Government take measures for the revision of the curricula of the Guatemalan Army's various training centres, in such a way as to include, as basic subject material, the points numbered previously.

63. That the CEH's Report be studied as part of the Guatemalan Army's educational curriculum.

64. That the Guatemalan Army's various educational centres promote a review of the teaching staff and remove military personnel involved in present or past human rights violations from educational functions. Maximum professional and ethical rigor from the teaching staff is required.

65.   That the civilian Faculty of the Guatemalan Army's training centres be made up of persons of recognised democratic trajectory.

V.2.d Other recommendations pertaining to the Army

Civil service: military and social

Considering that forced and discriminatory recruitment has been a continuous and abusive practice throughout the armed confrontation, having affected almost every Mayan community, and considering the future approval of the Civil Service Law contemplated in the Agreement on the Strengthening of Civilian Power and the Role of the Armed Forces in a Democratic Society, which will regulate military and social service, the CEH particularly recommends with regard to this law:

66.   That the regulations of military service maintain strict respect for the principle of equality before the law in the mechanisms and process of recruitment.
67.   That the option of conscientious objection be established and registered for those whose religious, ethical or philosophical convictions do not permit them to carry arms, so that they are not obliged to do so, but instead allowed to perform other types of civic service to the community.
68.   That young men of military service age who themselves, or whose family members within first degree consanguinity, were victims of human rights violations and acts of violence connected with the armed confrontation, remain exempt from military service and be directly assigned to civil service.

Special forces

69.   That, in conformity with the principles of military doctrine and education stated previously, the training programmes of the armed forces be subject to drastic and profound revision, especially those conceived specifically for counter-insurgency, such as that known as the *Kaibil* School.

Respect for Mayan cultural names and symbols

70.   That, with the aim of respecting the Mayan people's cultural identity, which was severely violated during the armed confrontation, the Army no longer the use of names of particular Mayan significance and symbolism for its military structures and units.

Civic defence of the peace

In a world in which national and international peace is the responsibility of all and in which the fundamental duty of the armed forces should be the defence of peace, the CEH recommends:

71. That, as one of its priorities, the Army promote participation in peace initiatives and international security under the authority of the United Nations Organisation or the Organization of American States.
72. That the military professionals make every effort to achieve a Guatemalan Army dedicated to the service of peace and to the citizens of Guatemala, of which every Guatemalan may feel proud.

Request: The governments of those countries whose armies have undergone similar transitions to that required of the Guatemalan Army, are asked to lend their technical and financial co-operation to facilitate the implementation of the recommendations listed above in part V.2.

V.3. Public security

The principal aim of the restructuring of the security forces, their professionalisation and their instruction regarding the law, democracy, human rights and a culture of peace, as stipulated in the Agreement on the Strengthening of Civilian Power and the Role of the Armed Forces in a Democratic Society, is to convert the role of the police into one of genuine public service. This implies the exclusively civilian character of the police force and respect for the multiethnic nature of the Guatemalan nation in the recruitment, selection, training and deployment of the police.

Given the discrediting of former police institutions for grave human rights violations and the general deficiency of service to public security afforded to the community, the new National Civilian Police (PNC) must implement, in their doctrine, professional conduct and in the development of a professional and modern police force, the minimum principles contained in the relevant international instruments regarding respect for human rights, public liberties, rule of law and democracy.

On this basis and with a view to guaranteeing suitable future development of the duties of the police, the CEH particularly recommends:

Security forces doctrine

73. That under the guidance of the Ministry of the Interior, the PNC begin a process of internal reflection in consultation with organisations from

civil society, with the aim of producing and defining the doctrine of the civilian security forces, whose bases should be:

a) service to the community, without discrimination of any type and with respect for the multiethnic character of the Guatemalan nation;

b) development of the civilian nature of the police force and the demilitarization of its organisation, hierarchy and disciplinary procedures;

c) complete respect for human rights and the consequent investigation, prosecution and conviction of any members who have committed human rights violations;

d) respect for democracy and the rule of law; and

e) the continuous professional training and instruction of the police at every rank.

Internal control

74. That under the supervision of the Ministry of the Interior, the Directorate of the PNC take the relevant measures to ensure the removal from the police of those elements who have acted, or act, against its doctrine of public service and create a new unit for internal control or inspection, which is accessible both to the public and the Human Rights Ombudsman, and which has autonomy to investigate and sanction both individual and institutional professional misconduct.

Indigenous participation

75. That the directorate of the PNC promote measures which genuinely open the way for participation by indigenous peoples in public security service, such as:

a) taking into consideration bilingualism in the academic evaluation, as well as eventual deployment of a police candidate;

b) the elimination of discrimination in the summoning and selection processes and their adaptation to the realities of a multiethnic country;

c) the education in the PNC Academy on the multicultural nature of Guatemala and intercultural harmony; and

d) the organisation of the police service in such a way that indigenous members are able to use their native language skills in contact with the public, promote positive relations with indigenous institutions and authorities and respect forms of conflict resolution characteristic of their cultures.

Resources

76. That, when determining the national budget, the Government and the Congress of the Republic increase the financing of the National Civilian Police, guaranteeing adequate training and equipment with modern means and installations and dignified working conditions.

Civilian nature of the PNC

77. That the new Public Order Law, referred to by the Agreement on the Strengthening of Civilian Power and the Role of the Armed Forces in a Democratic Society, considers the civilian nature of the Police during emergency situations of whatever type, and does not oblige it to participate in duties which appertain to the Army.

78. That, in case the reforms proposed in the Peace Accords are unsuccessful, Congress take the necessary legislative action to separate the functions of the Army and of the Police, limiting the participation of the Army in the field of public security to an absolute minimum.

VI. Other recommendations to promote peace and national harmony

The CEH believes that for the promotion of peace and national harmony it is necessary to know and face the causes of the armed confrontation and its consequences, in such a way as to put an end to the social, ethnic and cultural divisions in Guatemala.

Equally necessary, are social participation and the contribution of all Guatemalans without discrimination in the fulfilment of public duties.

Although the CEH's Report should serve as a fundamental reference point in the investigation of Guatemala's past, it does not in itself bring to a close the investigation and analysis that must be carried out regarding the armed confrontation, its causes, the extent of the violence and its effects. The Report of the CEH should serve as a platform for continuing investigation within Guatemala. On this basis, the CEH recommends:

Investigation and analysis of the past

79. That the Guatemalan people continue the investigation and analysis of the events of the past, so as to construct firm foundations for the future based on their knowledge of the past, and thereby avert a repetition of the mistakes that provoked the confrontation.

Political participation of indigenous peoples

The CEH, without prejudice to the commitments already established in the Agreement on Identity and Rights of Indigenous Peoples, would like to reiterate the importance of the obligations assumed by the Government to promote social and political participation by the indigenous population and to bring about regional administration coherent with ethnic identity. For this reason the CEH particularly recommends:

80. That among the public officials and other personnel employed by the State, room is given, in sufficient number, to indigenous professionals with the qualifications and experience relevant to the demands of the various posts.
81. That, to the end expressed in the previous paragraph, the State establish and finance a system of grants for the training and specialisation of the aforementioned indigenous professionals.

Elimination of racism and of the subordination of indigenous peoples

Given that the relationship between the State and the indigenous population of Guatemala —particularly the Mayan people—has subsisted within an environment of racism, inequality and exclusion, and that this is one of the historical causes of the armed confrontation, measures guaranteeing the protection of the individual and collective rights of the indigenous population, respect for cultural plurality and promotion of intercultural relations, become vital.

On this basis, the CEH reiterates:

82. That the Agreement on Identity and Rights of Indigenous Peoples be implemented, in its entirety.

Fiscal Reform

Considering the Agreement on Social and Economic Aspects and the Agrarian Situation and the need for all Guatemalans to contribute to social development and the improvement of public services, the CEH reiterates:

83. That the Government promote measures designed to encourage the mobilisation of national resources, carrying out urgent fiscal reform that is just, equitable and progressive, as established in the Agreement on Social and Economic Aspects and the Agrarian Situation.

VII. Body responsible for promoting and monitoring the implementation of the recommendations

The CEH believes it vital that these recommendations be fulfilled so that the mandate entrusted to the CEH within the framework of the peace process achieves its objectives. To accomplish this, the joint participation of the State and civil society is needed, as every Guatemalan without distinction should benefit from the recommendations.

Therefore, the CEH recommends the establishment of a follow-up body in which both State and civil society are represented, to aid, promote and monitor the implementation of the recommendations. Consolidation of the peace and reconciliation process in Guatemala requires that the State and civil society work together to achieve their common objectives.

Although the monitoring and implementation of the recommendations regarding the consolidation of peace and reconciliation falls to Guatemala, continuing support from the international community will be necessary.

On this basis, the CEH considers it necessary and, therefore, recommends:

84.   That the Congress of the Republic, through the initiative of its Commission on Human Rights, approve, no more than 60 days from the publication of the CEH's Report and through the corresponding legislative measure, the establishment of a body responsible for implementing and monitoring the recommendations of the CEH under the name of "Foundation for Peace and Harmony" (hereinafter, "the Foundation"), whose mandate, composition, appointment procedure, constitution, installation, period of operation, human and material resources and financing are outlined below.

Mandate

The Foundation's principal objective will be to facilitate the implementation of the recommendations made by the CEH, regarding the five principal areas of activity covered by the mandate:

a)   Direct implementation of specific recommendations;
b)   Backing and assistance in the implementation of the recommendations;
c)   Monitoring the adequate implementation of the recommendations;
d)   Promotion of and support for historical research;
e)   Assistance in seeking funds to finance projects for the implementation of the recommendations.

Composition

The Foundation shall be composed of seven members who will be appointed for a period to be determined by the corresponding legal resolution. Their distribution shall be as follows:

- Two persons appointed by the Congress of the Republic, who shall be of different political affiliations.
- One person appointed by the Government.
- An independent person, of recognised democratic trajectory and commitment to the peace process.

- Two representatives from Guatemalan non-governmental organisations for human rights and victims.
- One representative from the Guatemalan Mayan organisations.

The appointment by the relevant institutions shall be made no later than two months from the date of the congressional resolution.

Appointment procedure

The Congress of the Republic and the Government respectively shall appoint the relevant persons. It is suggested that the person appointed by the Government should be the Secretary of the Peace.

The independent person of recognised democratic trajectory and commitment to the peace process shall be appointed by the Secretary-General of the United Nations, by the procedure he deems most appropriate.

The representatives of the non-governmental organisations for human rights and the Mayan organisations shall be chosen by the organisations of each sector through an election process, to be convened and facilitated by the independent person appointed by the Secretary-General of the United Nations.

Constitution

The Foundation shall hold its constitutive meeting as soon as the members have been appointed.

Installation

The Foundation shall be fully installed and operational, at the latest, five months after having been initially integrated and constituted.

Period of operation

The Foundation shall have an initial operational period of three years from the date of its installation, which can be extended by Congress in view of advances made in the implementation of the recommendations.

Human resources:

The personnel shall be essentially Guatemalan, looking for qualified persons who have experience in the field of the investigation and defence of human rights.

Material resources:

The CEH has left instructions with UNOPS enabling the latter, in consultation with the donors to the CEH and on viewing the Foundation's draft budget and plan of operation, to determine the material resources and the computing and communications assets of the CEH to be transferred by UNOPS to the Foundation, by the way of a CEH donation.

National and international support

It is suggested that the Foundation seek both the national and international support necessary to achieve the aforementioned objectives.

VIII. Request to the United Nations

The CEH requests that the Secretary-General of the United Nations lend his support, through the United Nations Verification Mission in Guatemala (MINUGUA) and within the framework of the Mission's mandate, so that the recommendations laid out previously may be implemented and may achieve their objectives.

The CEH also requests that the Secretary-General appoint the Foundation's independent member and that, through the UN body deemed to be most appropriate, he establish an international mechanism to provide the Foundation with technical support and to channel donations from the international community.

Works Cited

Association for the Advancement of the Social Sciences. *Edición íntegra del informe de la Comisión para el Esclarecimiento Histórico de las Violaciones a los Derechos Humanos y los Hechos de Violencia que han Causado Sufrimientos a la Población Guatemalteca*. Guatemala: Comisión para el Esclarecimiento Histórico/AAAS, 2000. (CD-ROM) [Complete Edition of the Report by the Comission on Historical Clarification of the Violations of Human Rights and the Acts of Violence that Have Caused the Suffering of the Guatemalan People.]

Association for the Advancement of the Social Sciences. *Guatemala, Assistance and Control: Policies toward Internally Displaced Populations in Guatemala*. Washington, D.C.: Center for Immigration Policy and Refugee Assistance, Georgetown University, 1990.

Americas Watch. *Guatemala: A Nation of Prisoners*. New York: Americas Watch, 1984.

Cabarruz, Carlos. *Q'eqchi' Cosmovision*, San Salvador: UCA, 1979.

Casaús Arzú, Marta. *Guatemala: linaje y racismo*. 2d ed. San José, Costa Rica: FLACSO, 1995.

Castañeda. Salguero, César. *Lucha por la tierra, retornados y medio ambiente en Huehuetenango*. Guatemala: FLACSO, 1998.

CEH—see Comisión para el Esclarecimiento Histórico

CEIDEC. *Guatemala, polos de desarrollo: el caso de la desestructuración de las comunidades indígenas*. [Mexico]: CEIDEC, [1998]-1990.

Centro de Estudios Militares del Ejército de Guatemala. *Manual de Inteligencia*. G-2, 1972. [Center for Military Studies. Intelligence Manual.]

Centro de Estudios Militares del Ejército de Guatemala. *Manual de contraguerrilla*, 1982. [Counter-guerilla Manual.]

Centro de Estudios Militares del Ejército de Guatemala. *Manual de guerra contrasubversiva*, Edición 1983 [Manual of Counter-subversive War.]

Central American Development Foundation, *Diagnóstico y Plan de Desarrollo del Municipio de Zacualpa, Departamento de Quiché*, Guatemala, 1995. [Analysis and Development Plan for the Municipality of Zacualpa, Department of Quiché.]

Chang, Myrna Mack. "Notas del Campo." April, 1988. [Field Notes.]

CIA Declassified USA document, CIA; G5-41, pg. 41, released 002/98, February 1982,

Ciencia y Tecnología para Guatemala (CITGUA), *Counterinsurgency and environmental deterioration in Guatemala*, Mexico, 1992.

Cojti Cuxil, Demetrio. *Configuracion del pensamiento politico del pueblo maya.* Quezaltenango, Guatemala: Asociacion de Escritores Mayances de Guatemala, 1991.

Cojtí Macario, Narciso. *El Idioma Ixil,* collection in "Conozcamos Guatemala," *Prensa Libre,* September, 1995. [The Ixil Language, in "Let Us Know Guatemala."]

Cojtí [Macario], Narciso. "Estimación de cifras poblacionales por área lingüística" [Estimates of Population Figures by Linguistic Area]. Proyecto: Aprendamos con Prensa Libre, 1995 [Project Let's Learn with Prensa Libre.]

Comisión Interamericana de Derechos Humanos, *Compilación de Informes publicados sobre la situación de los derechos humanos en Guatemala, 1980-1995, Tomo I (1980-1985),* Washington, D.C., 1995.

Comisión para el Esclarecimiento Histórico *Guatemala, memoria del silencio.* Cited as CEH. [Commission on Historical Clarification in Guatemala. Guatemala, Memory of Silence.] http://shr.aaas.org/guatemala/ceh/mds/spanish/toc.html

Comisión para el Esclarecimiento Histórico (CEH). Document, *La Estrategia politico-militar del Ejército Guerrillero de los Pobres* [Military-Political Strategy for the Guerrilla Army of the Poor], EGP.

Comisión para el Esclarecimiento Histórico (CEH). Database, *Muestra de 7,109 casos registrados,* September 4, 1998. [Exhibit of 7,109 registered cases]

Diario El Imparcial. 1982. [Impartial (Guatemalan newspaper).]

Equipo de Antropología Forense de Guatemala (EAFG). *Las Masacres en Rabinal: Estudio histórico-antropológico de la masacres de Plan de Sánchez, Chichupac y Río Negro.* Guatemala City: EAFG, 1995. [Guatemalan Forensic Anthropology Team, The Massacres in Rabinal: A Historical-Anthropological Study of the Massacres at Plan de Sánchez, Chichupac, and Río Negro.]

Fundación de Antropología Forense de Guatemala. Informe. for the CEH, Guatemala, 1998

Ejército de Guatemala. "Apreciación de asuntos civiles (G-5) para el área ixil," *Revista Militar,* September - December 1982, p. 31?? also 36-37. [Guatemala Army. Appraisal of Civil Affairs in the Ixil Region (G5), in Military Review.]

This document was published with "A Solution to the Ixil Operation. Plan de AACC operación Ixil," *Revista Militar* pp. 25-54. ["A solution to Operation Ixil. AACC Plan Operation Ixil" in Military Review.]

[= in note 64 to paragraph 3240 Also cited note to section 3251]

Ejército de Guatemala [Guatemala Army]. Summary of Intelligence on the Operations Plan, Great Offensive in the military area of Huehuetenango, Annex B. [note to #3502] [see also note to #3521]

Ejército de Guatemala. Plan de Campaña *Victoria* 82. Guatemala 1982. [Guatemala Army. Campaign Plan *Victory* 82.]

Ejército de Guatemala, campaña *Victoria 82,* Anexo H, *«Ordenes permanentes para el desarrollo de las operaciones contrasubversivas.»*

Ejército de Guatemala. Plan de Campaña *Firmeza 83-1* [Guatemala Army. Campaign Plan *Firmness* 83-1.]

Ejército de Guatemala. *Plan Nacional de Seguridad y Desarrollo*, CEM, Guatemala, 1982. [Guatemala Army National Plan for Security and Development]

Ejército Guerrillero de los Pobres (EGP). *El Informador Guerrillero*, Publicación quincenal, No. 4, del 16 de Febrero de 1982 al 15 de Marzo de 1982, pg. 1, y No. 5, del 16 de Marzo de 1982 al 15 de Abril de 1982.

Falla, Ricardo, SJ. *Massacres in the Jungle: Ixcan, Guatemala, 1975-1982.* Boulder: Westview, 1994.

Foreign Broadcast Information Service, Central America, Ríos Montt Views on Peasant Killings, Communism, June 2, 1982.

Fundación de Antropología Forense de Guatemala. *Informe Especial de la Fundación de Antropología Forense de Guatemala, 1996-1999*, Guatemala City: Fundación de Antropología Forense de Guatemala, 2001. [Guatemala Forensic Anthropology Foundation, Special Report of the Guatemala Forensic Anthropology Foundation, 1996-1999.]

Giddens, Anthony. *Sociologia*, Alianza Editorial S.A. [*Sociology*.]

Gramajo Morales, Héctor Alejandro. *De la guerra... a la guerra: La difícil transición política en Guatemala*. Guatemala. Fondo de Cultura Editorial, 1995. [From War ... to War. The Difficult Political Transition in Guatemala.]

Gramajo Morales, Héctor Alejandro. "La Tesis de la Estabilidad Nacional Doce Años Después," *Visión Nacional*, Fundación para el Desarrollo Institucional de Guatemala, #1. October, 1994. [The Thesis of Nacional Stability Twelve Years Later.]

Grandin, Greg. *The Last Colonial Massacre: Latin America in the Cold War*, Chicago: University of Chicago Press. 2004.

Gutiérrez, Edgar. Un Nuevo Tejido Social para Guatemala: dinámica maya en los años noventa.

ICTY (International Criminal Tribunal Yugoslavia). *Prosecutor v Radislav Krstic* (IT-98-33), Appellate judgment of 19 April 2004.

ICTY *Prosecutor's Pre-Trial Brief,* Milan Kovacevic (IT-97-24-PT), para. 3 and 22. 20 April 1998.

ICTR (International Criminal Tribunal Rwanda). *Prosecutor v Jean-Paul Akayesu* (ICTR-96-4-T), judgment of 2 September 1998.

International Court of Justice, *Reservations to the Convention on the Prevention and Punishment of the Crime of Genocide*, Advisory Opinion, 28 May 1951.

Lovell, George. "Maya Survival in Ixil Country, Guatemala" *Cultural Survival Quarterly*, Volume 14, 1990, Number 4.

Macias, Julio César. *La Guerrilla fue mi camino*. Guatemala: Ed. Piedra Santa, 1997. [The Guerillas Were My Path.]

Manz, Beatriz. *Guatemala: cambios en la comunidad, desplazamientos y repatriación*. México, Iglesia Guatemalteca en el Exilio. México, D.F.: Editorial Praxis 1986. [Translated as: Manz, Beatriz. *Repatriation and reintegration: an arduous process in Guatemala*. Washington, D.C.: Hemispheric

Migration Project, Center for Immigration Policy and Refugee Assistance, Georgetown University, c1988.]

McCreery, David. "Land, Labor, and Violence in Highland Guatemala: San Juan Ixcoy (Huehuetenango), 1890-1940," *The Americas*, (October, 1988), 237-249. Spanish translation in *Revista de Historia* (Costa Rica) 19 (Enero-Junio, 1989), 19-35 and *Anales de la Academia de Geografía de Guatemala* LXV: LXVIII (Enero-Diciembre de 1989), pg. 101-112.

McCreery, David. *Rural Guatemala, 1760-1940*, Stanford: Stanford University Press, 1994.

National Academy of Sciences. *Scientists and Human Rights in Guatemala: Report of a Delegation*, 1992.

National Institute of Human Rights. "Declaration on the Norms of International Humanitarian Law Relative to the Carrying out of Hostilities in Non-International Armed Conflicts." *International Review of the Red Cross*, September 1990, No. 101, p. 434.

Power, Samantha. *"A Problem from Hell": America and The Age Of Genocide*, New York: Perennial, 2002.

PRODERE-UNOPS (Program for Displaced People, Refugees and Returnees in Central America), *Executive Summary of the PRODERE Guatemala sub-program final report*, 1995.

Proyecto Interdiocesano Recuperación de la Memoria Histórica. *Guatemala: Nunca Más*. Guatemala: Proyecto Interdiocesano, 1999. Cited as REMHI. [Excerpted and translated as *Guatemala: Never Again!* Maryknoll, N.Y.: Orbis Books, 1999.]

REMHI. *Report on the Massacres in Huehuetenango.*

Salguero, César Castañeda. *Struggle for land, returnees, and the environment.* Guatemala City: FLACSO, 1988.

Schirmer, Jennifer. *The Guatemalan Military Project: A Violence Called Democracy*, Philadelphia: University of Pennsylvania Press, 1998.

Stanton, Gregory, *The Eight Stages of Genocide*, Washington: Genocide Watch, 1998.

Stoll, David. "'The Land No Longer Gives': Land Reform in Nebaj, Guatemala." *Cultural Survival Quarterly* 14.4 (1990): 4-9.

United Nations. "Convention for the Prevention, and Sanction of the Crime of Genocide." General Assembly, December 22, 1995, resolution 50.192

United Nations. *Report of the Independent Inquiry into UN actions during the 1994 Rwanda Genocide* ("Carlsson report"), 15 December 1999. www.un.org/News/ossg/rwanda_report

United Nations. *Report to the Secretary-General of the International Commission of Inquiry on Darfur,* February 2005. www.un.org/News/DH/Sudan/com_inq_darfur

United Nations. *Report to the Secretary-General of the Group of Experts for Cambodia,* February 1999. http://www1.umn.edu/humanrts/cambodia-1999.html

United Nations. II. Additional Protocol of 1977 to the Geneva Conventions of August 12, 1949 relative to victims of armed conflicts of a non-international character, June 8, 1977 Article 14.

"Displacement, survival and life in the model villages," *Study of a typical community* = note to #3393

Books

There are quite a number of English-language books written about the civil war in Guatemala. These books address the subject from a number of different perspectives—biography, history, ethnology, sociology, political science, anthropology, literature, and so on.

- Archdiocese of Guatemala. *Guatemala: Never Again!* Orbis Book. 1999.
- Arturo Arias. *The Riboberta Menchú Controversy*. University of Minnesota Press: Minneapolis, MN. 2001.
- Stephen Connely Benz. *Guatemalan Journey*. University of Texas Press: Austin, TX. 1996.
- Robert S. Carlsen. *The War for the Heart & Soul of a Highland Maya Town*. University of Texas Press: Austin, TX. 1997.
- Robert M. Carmack. *Rebels of Highland Guatemala: The Quiche-Mayas of Momostenango*. University of Oklahoma Press: Norman, OK. 1995.
- Central Intelligence Agency. *Secret History: The CIA's Classified Account of Its Operations in Guatemala, 1952-1954*. Stanford University Press: Stanford, CA. 1999.
- Greg Grandin. *The Blood of Guatemala: A History of Race and Nation*. Duke University Press: Durham, NC. 2000.
- Linda Green. *Fear as a Way of Live: Mayan Widows in Rural Guatemala*. Columbia University Press: New York, NY. 1999.
- Jennifer Harbury. *Bridge of Courage: Life Stories of the Guatemalan Compañeros and Compañeras*. Common Courage Press. 1995.
- Jennifer Harbury. *Search for Everardo: A Story of Love, War, and the CIA in Guatemala*. Warner Books. 2000.
- Paul Jeffrey. *Recovering Memory: Guatemalan Churches and the Challenge of Peacemaking*. Life & Peace Institute: Uppsala, Sweden. 1998.
- Susanne Jonas. *The Battle for Guatemala: Rebels, Death Squads, and U.S. Power*. Westview Press. 1991.
- Susanne Jonas and Marrack Goulding. *Of Centaurs and Doves: Guatemala's Peace Process*. Westview Press. 2000.
- Deborah Levenson-Estrada. *Trade Unionists against Terror: Guatemala City, 1954-1985*. University of North Carolina Press: Chapel Hill, NC. 1994.
- Beatriz Manz. *Refugees of a Hidden War: The Aftermath of Counterinsurgency in Guatemala*. State University of New York Press. 1998.
- Rachel M. McCleary. *Dictating Democracy: Guatemala and the End of Violent Revolution*. University Press of Florida. 1999.
- Marcos McPeek Villatoro. *Walking to La Milpa: Living in Guatemala with Armies, Demons, Abrazos, and Death*. Moyer Bell Inc. 1996.

- Rigoberta Menchú. *I, Rigoberta Menchú: An Indian Woman in Guatemala*. Verso Books. 1987.
- Rigoberta Menchú. *Crossing Borders*. Verso Books. 1998.
- Ben Mikaelsen *Red Midnight*. HarperCollins Children's Books. 2002.
- Victor Montejo. *Testimony: Death of a Guatemalan Village*. Curbstone Press. 1987.
- Victor Montejo. *Voices from Exile: Violence and Survival in Modern Mayan History*. University of Oklahoma Press. 1999.
- Diane M. Nelson. *A Finger in the Wound: Body Politics in Quincentennial Guatemala*. University of California Press: Berkeley, CA. 1999.
- Lisa L. North. *Journeys of Fear: Refugee Return and National Transformation in Guatemala*. McGill Queens University Press. 2000.
- Dianna Ortiz. *The Blindfold's Eyes: My Journey from Torture to Truth*. Orbis Books. 2002.
- Victor Perera. *Unfinished Conquest: The Guatemalan Tragedy*. University of California Press: Berkeley, CA. 1995.
- Victoria Sanford. *Buried Secrets: Truth and Human Rights in Guatemala*. Palgrave Macmillan. 2004.
- Jennifer Schirmer. *The Guatemalan Military Project: A Violence Called Democracy*. University of Pennsylvania: Philadelphia, PA. 2000.
- Steven C. Schlesinger. *Bitter Fruit: The Story of the American Coup in Guatemala*. Harvard University Press: Boston, MA. 1999.
- Rachel Sieder. *Guatemala after the Peace Accord*. Institute of Latin American Studies. 1999.
- Michael Silverstone and Charlotte Bunch. *Rigoberta Menchú: Defending Human Rights in Guatemala*. Feminist Press. 1999.
- Jean-Marie Simon. *Guatemala: Eternal Spring, Eternal Tyranny*. W.W. Norton & Company: New York, NY. 1988.
- David Stoll. *Between Two Armies in the Ixil Towns of Guatemala*. Columbia University Press: New York, NY. 1993.
- David Stoll. Rigoberta *Menchú and the Story of All Poor Guatemalans*. Westview Press. 2000.
- Michelle Tooley. *Voices of the Voiceless: Women, Justice, and Human Rights in Guatemala*. Herald Press. 1997.
- Robert H. Trudeau. *Guatemalan Politics: The Popular Struggle for Democracy*. Lynne Rieder Publishers. 1993.
- Daniel Wilkinson. *Silence on the Mountain: Stories of Terror, Betrayal, and Forgetting in Guatemala*. Houghton-Mifflin. 2002.
- Marc Zimmerman, Raul Rojas and Patricio Navia (eds). *Voices from the Silence: Guatemalan Literature of Resistance*. Ohio Univ Ctr for Intl Studies. 1998.
- Judith N. Zur. *Violent Memories: Mayan War Widows in Guatemala*. Westview Press. 1998.

Films

- *Against Forgetting: Digging Up and Confronting the Past in Guatemala* (1996)
- *An American Genocide—Guatemala*
- *Approach of Dawn*
- *The Devil's Dream* (1992)
- *Dirty Secrets: Jennifer, Everardo and the CIA in Guatemala* (1998)
- *Discovering Dominga: A Survivor's Story* (2003)
- *El Norte*
- *Guatemala: Roads of Silence* (1988)
- *Haunted Land* (2001)
- *Hidden Holocaust* (198?)
- *Rigoberta Menchu: Broken Silence* (1992)
- *Rub' el kurus* (Bajo la cruz)
- *Todos Santos: The Survivors* (1989)
- *Under the Gun: Democracy in Guatemala* (1987)
- *When the Mountains Tremble* (1983)

Contributors

GREG GRANDIN

Greg Grandin is a Professor of History at New York University and author of *The Blood of Guatemala: A History of Race and Nation, The Last Colonial Massacre: Latin America in the Cold War*, most recently, of *Empire's Workshop: Latin America, the United States, and the Rise of the New Imperialism*. His essays have appeared in *The Nation, Harper's, The Boston Review*, as well as in *The American Historical Review* and *The Hispanic American Historical Review*. He has recently been awarded fellowships from the John Simon Guggenheim Memorial Foundation and the American Council on Learned Societies Charles Ryskamp Foundation.

BLAZ GUTIERREZ

Blaz Gutierrez is the Development Officer for Umam Documentation and Research, a Lebanese cultural and human rights archive. Prior to this he worked at the International Center for Transitional Justice (ICTJ) where he provided support to the Americas, Truth Seeking, Prosecutions and Gender programs and helped to establish the ICTJ's field office in Colombia. He holds a B.M. in Cello Performance from the University of Redlands and is a Master's candidate in Latin American Studies at Tulane University. He has traveled extensively throughout Latin America and has interned with Creative Associates International Inc. in San Salvador, the Fundación Rigoberta Menchú Tum in Mexico City, and the ICTJ.

ETELLE HIGONNET

Etelle Higonnet is working in Iraq as Analysis Director with the Iraq History Project, a human rights documentation initiative that has gathered close to 10,000 testimonies from victims around Iraq. Prior to moving to Iraq, Etelle served as a consultant to UNICEF in New York and produced a documentary film on sexual violence in Cote d'Ivoire. From 2006 to 2007, Etelle worked in Human Rights Watch investigating crimes against humanity in Côte d'Ivoire. Before this, she was Senior Research Fellow for the International Human Rights Law Institute. A graduate of Yale Law School and Yale University, she also worked for the Royal Cambodian Government Task Force for the creation of a war crimes tribunal for the Khmer Rouge, the Special Court for Sierra Leone, and Sullivan & Cromwell, LLP.

BEN KIERNAN (Sponsor)

Ben Kiernan is the A. Whitney Griswold Professor of History at Yale University, and founding Director of Yale's Cambodian Genocide Program and Genocide Studies Program. Kiernan is one of the world's foremost experts on the Cambodian genocide and the prizewinning author of many works on Southeast Asia and the history of genocide. He is a member of the Editorial Boards of numerous journals. His edited collection Conflict and Change in Cambodia won the Critical Asian Studies Prize for 2002. He is co-editor of *The Specter of Genocide: Mass Murder in Historical Perspective* and is the author of *Blood and Soil*, a global history of genocide.

JUAN MÉNDEZ

A native of Lomas de Zamora, Argentina, Mr. Méndez has dedicated his legal career to the defense of human rights and has a long and distinguished record of advocacy throughout the Americas. As a result of his involvement in representing political prisoners, the Argentinean military dictatorship arrested him and subjected him to torture and administrative detention for more than a year. During this time, Amnesty International adopted him as a "Prisoner of Conscience." In 1977 he was expelled from his country and he moved to the United States. For 15 years, he worked with Human Rights Watch, and from 1996 to 1999, Mr. Méndez was the executive director of the Inter-American Institute of Human Rights in Costa Rica. Between October 1999 and May 2004 he was professor of Law and director of the Center for Civil and Human Rights at the University of Notre Dame, Indiana. Between 2000 and 2003 he was a member of the Inter-American Commission on Human Rights of the Organization of American States, and served as president in 2002. From July 2004 to April 2007, Mr. Méndez was the United Nations special adviser on the prevention of genocide, which he discharged concurrently with his current full-time position as the president of the International Center for Transitional Justice.

MARCIE MERSKY

Marcie Mersky is the Director of the Access to Justice Program funded by the Soros Foundation-Guatemala and the Swedish International Development Cooperation Agency. She has lived and worked in Guatemala for the past 25 years, and played a vital role in the two reports that exposed the massive violations of human rights of Guatemala's 36 year war. She was the field coordinator for the Catholic Church Project Report on Guatemalan Historical Memory (REMHI) and the coordinator of the Final Report for the U.N.-sponsored Guatemalan Historical Clarification Commission (Comisión para el Esclarecimiento Histórico, CEH). She was also the Chief of the Transition Unit at MINUGUA.

NAOMI ROHT-ARRIAZA
Naomi Roht-Arriaza is Professor of Law at the University of California, Hastings College of the Law. She is the author of *Impunity and Human Rights in International Law and Practice* (1995), *The Pinochet Effect: Transnational Justice in the Age of Human Rights* (2005), and *Transitional Justice in the Twenty-First Century: Beyond Truth vs. Justice* (2006). She has lived and worked in Latin America for many years.

DANIEL ROTHENBERG
Daniel Rothenberg is Deputy Executive Director at the International Human Rights Law Institute. Previously, he was a Senior Fellow at the Orville H. Schell, Jr. Center for International Human Rights at Yale Law School, an Assistant Professor in the Department of Anthropology at the University of Michigan, a Visiting Professor at the University of Michigan Law School and a Fellow in the Michigan Society of Fellows. He works on transitional justice issues, particularly truth commissions, amnesty laws, and tribunals and is editor of the forthcoming Guatemala: Memory of Silence, a one-volume critical version of the Guatemalan Truth Commission report.

Printed in the United States
219941BV00001B/4/P